Dick Gregory's Political Primer

By the same author

No More Lies:
The Myth and the Reality
of American History

Write Me In!

The Shadow That Scares Me

What's Happening

Nigger

From the Back of the Bus

Dick Gregory's Political Primer

by Dick Gregory

Edited by
James R. McGraw

Harper & Row,
Publishers
New York, Evanston,
San Francisco, London

Quotations from the following sources are used by permission of the publisher:

Boss: Richard J. Daley of Chicago, by Mike Royko. Copyright © 1971 by Mike Royko. Published by E. P. Dutton & Co., Inc.

America, Inc., by Jerry S. Cohen and Morton Mintz. Copyright © 1971 by Jerry S. Cohen and Morton Mintz. Published by The Dial Press.

The table on page 232 © 1971 by The New York Times Company.

The Poisons in Your Food, by William Longgood. Copyright © 1960 by William Longgood. Published by Simon and Schuster, Inc.

DICK GREGORY'S POLITICAL PRIMER. Copyright © 1972 by Richard Claxton Gregory. All rights reserved. Printed in the United States of America. No part of this book may be used or reproduced in any manner whatsoever without written permission except in the case of brief quotations embodied in critical articles and reviews. For information address Harper & Row, Publishers, Inc., 49 East 33rd Street, New York, N.Y. 10016. Published simultaneously in Canada by Fitzhenry & Whiteside Limited, Toronto.

FIRST EDITION

STANDARD BOOK NUMBER: 06–011601–3

LIBRARY OF CONGRESS CATALOG CARD NUMBER: 71–160648

To Dr. Alvenia Fulton,
Dr. Roland Sidney,
America's health-food stores,
chiropractors,
and naturopaths,
and all others concerned
with purifying the system

LIBRARY
ALLEGANY COMMUNITY COLLEGE
Cumberland, Maryla d

Contents

Acknowledgments

While preparing this manuscript, I have been on an extended fast, having vowed April 24, 1971, not to consume anything but liquids until the war is over in Vietnam. Therefore, my first expression of gratitude is reserved for Dr. Alvenia Fulton, of Chicago, Illinois, who is my adviser, my counselor, the guardian of my body, and an inspiration to my mind. I could never put into words what she has meant to me during my many fasts.

Once again my repeated thanks to Jeannette Hopkins of Harper & Row for her insights, her encouragement, and her patience, all necessary to seeing this manuscript completed.

For research assistance I am indebted to Susan Stallings, Mike Duberstein, Samuel F. Yette, Bob Johnson, editor of *Jet* magazine, A. Donald Bourgeois, Jean Williams, and Elaine Shepherd.

Ebony magazine was also very generous in providing research materials.

For the wisdom and assistance of Ralph Mann, Bob Chuck, Bernie Kleinman, and Dick Shelton, I shall always be grateful.

Thanks also to James Sanders and James R. McGraw for providing the help only they can give.

Finally, my love and gratitude to my wife, Lillian, and the kids—Michelle, Lynne, Pamela, Paula, Stephanie, Gregory, Miss, and Christian—who are a constant inspiration to me in my writing and in my living.

To the Student: Bicentennial Breakthrough

At the outset of the long Fourth of July weekend in 1971, President Nixon and others appeared on national television in what was the beginning of a five-year birthday celebration for the United States of America. In 1976 our nation will be two hundred years old, if one takes the Declaration of Independence rather than the Constitution as the official United States birth certificate.

The way things are going in America today, it is probably wise to get a five-year headstart in celebrating. It's hard to say for certain at this point if there will be elections in '76, much less a nation.

Nevertheless, we Americans are supposed to be reaching back into our rich national heritage, dwelling upon the words, wisdom, insight, and vision of our Founding Fathers, contemplating the struggles and the urge for freedom which marked the birth pangs of the United States. This is a dangerous idea. But that's what our President tells us to do.

The Good Old Days

There's no doubt things have gotten bad in this country. I used to hear older folks always talking about "the good old days." I once heard two old men, they must have been ninety years old apiece, standing on the street corner talking about "the good old days" and bad-mouthing today's youth. One of the oldsters said to his partner, "I don't know what's wrong with these kids today. We didn't steal automobiles when we were kids." Hell, they didn't *have* automobiles. And a person would have to be out of his mind to steal a *horse*. Any time you steal something that eats more food than you do, you're crazy!

Now it looks like President Nixon and his administration are bringing back "the good old days" and nobody wants them. Of course, I knew what would happen even back during the 1968 Presidential campaign. I could see by the look in Candidate Nixon's eye that if he ever got elected, he would "put a hurtin' " on white folks. And he has. I hear white folks crying and complaining now that never cried before. Each time another group of folks gets laid off from work, it looks more like Nixon's campaign pledge really meant, "Bring us together—*on the unemployment line!*"

Just the other day, during my daily travels across the country, I climbed aboard a plane and an old white cat gestured to me to come over, saying, "Can I speak to you, my *brother?*" I thought, "Your what????? Back when everything was going well for white folks, I was the 'nigger' and the 'coon.' But things have gotten so bad that I'm the 'brother' now."

So I walked over to the white cat, and in my best white folks' voice I said, "Yes, what's happening, my man?"

Right away he started complaining. "They're really messing things up for us, aren't they?"

I said, "Who? The Black Panthers?"

He said, "No. I mean Nixon and them."

And I told him, "I don't even want to talk about that. That's white folks' business."

But he was persistent. "It's black folks' business too. Nobody's got any money."

So I informed him, "That's where you're wrong, my man. Whatever money we black folks ain't got, you white folks can't get."

Finally, in desperation, he said, "But I was just reading

here in the *Wall Street Journal* that the country might be headed into another Depression."

So I calmly told him the truth. "You white folks might be. Us black folks never came out of the last one."

Of course, when the money goes bad in the United States, things are messed up financially all over the world. Even the Rolls-Royce company went bankrupt in England. I never thought I would see a time when Rolls-Royce stock was down to three cents a share and the same day even a bad roll of toilet paper was selling for sixteen cents in the ghetto.

Back at home the Nixon administration gave the Lockheed Aircraft Corporation a $250-million government "loan." Any way you look at it, that is nothing other than a big welfare check for Lockheed.

It is really ironic that two of President Nixon's own cousins are on welfare. The President doesn't seem to want to help his relatives out, but is willing to give Lockheed $250 million. And the same legislators who readily vote help for Lockheed quibble when it comes to providing welfare money for a poor black mother and her children, especially if those innocent children were born "out of wedlock." When it comes to giving welfare layouts to black folks and other poor folks, so many legislators say, "They ought to learn to pull themselves up by their own bootstraps."

So I sent the president of Lockheed Aircraft a telegram when I found out he was asking for $250 million. It read: "Why don't you learn to pick yourself up by your own landing gears?" I just can't understand Lockheed asking for all that welfare money and they don't even have any illegitimate planes!

But America's current problems cut much deeper into the national psyche than merely financial difficulties. More critical than the *recession* in U.S. economy is the *depression* in U.S. morality. Perhaps the supreme symbol of the United States moral depression and confusion during 1971 was the national reaction to the conviction of Lieutenant William Calley, as well as the action of President Nixon in the matter.

Beyond any shadow of reasonable doubt, Lieutenant Calley was found guilty of the premeditated murder of no fewer than twenty-two Vietnamese villagers. The lieutenant said he was guilty. A military tribunal affirmed that guilt. And then President Nixon promptly ordered Lieutenant Calley released from the stockade.

Lieutenant Calley immediately became a national symbol, and in many circles a national hero. A phonograph record, "The Ballad of Lieutenant Calley," became a hit in some quarters of the country. Protest demonstrations on his behalf mounted. Some folks advocated his candidacy for President!

I was passing through South Carolina just after the Calley trial. A white cat came up to me in the airport terminal wearing a "Lt. Calley for President" button. He pointed to the button and said, "What do you think of that, Dick Gregory?"

And I told him I didn't think much of a confessed murderer of women and children as a Presidential candidate, but I said, "You've got a right to go crazy if you want to."

Now that really surprised him. He said, "Whatta you mean?"

So I told him, "As long as you're going to go crazy, you might just as well go crazy all the way. Make Charles Manson your Vice President, Sirhan Sirhan your Attorney General, and James Earl Ray the head of your Civil Rights Commission!"

The strange thing about Lieutenant Calley is that he became a rallying symbol for both the Right and the Left. The "superpatriots" saw him as an officer doing his duty and obeying military orders as he understood them; and thought, therefore, he should not be punished. The radical Left saw him as just one of many Vietnam murderers and thought, therefore, he should not be punished.

So the Calley case was one more illustration of the terrible burden this nation has placed upon its young: the awesome problems we have left for young people to solve. Any time a nation turns a confessed murderer of defenseless women and children into a national hero, that nation is in deep, deep trouble. And that nation is gripped seriously by a moral depression.

Of course, it is true that Lieutenant Calley isn't the *only* murderer who should be brought to justice, nor was he the *only* American guilty of war crimes. I personally believe that Generals Westmoreland and Abrams should appear before the tribunal. And Lyndon Baines Johnson should face the full force of war-crimes charges.

I can remember when the *New York Times* reported an LBJ visit to Vietnam. LBJ, according to the *Times* account, walked into a mess hall, looked up, and saw some Vietcong ears nailed to the door, and said, "Thatta boy. Nail the coons to the wall." That was the President of the United States saying symbolically for all Americans that we can nail the ears of a dead Vietcong to the door of the mess hall and it doesn't even spoil our appetites.

President Nixon campaigned in 1968 on a heavily leaded law-and-order platform. How, then, does he justify having so little respect for due process of law and order that he orders a confessed murderer released from the stockade? Whose law and what order is it that the law-and-order boys, including the President, so gleefully embrace?

It really doesn't take much searching to answer those questions. We all know what the President's attitude would have been—indeed, the attitude of the Americans who supported Lieutenant Calley—if, instead of gunning down women and children in Vietnam, the lieutenant had taken a bazooka and blown up Fort Knox, or shot a flamethrower into the Bank of America and burned up the money. He could have kissed goodbye to any chance of a Presidential pardon.

As it was, that old American love of money and property over human life was illustrated further in the Calley case. Lieutenant Calley shared a place in the stockade with a man whose crime was forging checks. That man remained in the stockade even as President Nixon ordered Calley's release. The check forger stayed locked up while the murderer was set free—by Presidential decree. Indian folklore refers to money as "the metal that makes white men crazy." How well the Indian knew the truth about his invaders.

As a consequence of the Calley case, the world saw once and for all that America's leaders were not even sincere about their commitment to law and order. International reaction to President Nixon's release of Lieutenant Calley was quite different from the reaction at home. A world that knows America's war-crime guilt could only see the President's act as one more refusal to admit it.

Such is the nature of the moral depression in the United States. The United States never seems to be able to learn and admit the truth about itself. If, for example, violence was the answer to human problems, the United States would have straightened them all out long ago. Yet, with all its expertise in violence, some Vietcong in sneakers can send mighty America running for cover.

Miss Liberty Abroad

The bicentennial birthday celebration would be a perfect time for Americans to take a really good look at ourselves as others see us. Not long ago an Associated Press dispatch spoke of a stepped-up "Hate America" campaign in Russia. The dispatch reported that visitors to Moscow were greeted in Sheremetyevo International Airport with a huge billboard showing the Statue of Liberty through Russian eyes.

Miss Liberty was wearing sunglasses. The shades were covered with iron prison mesh. Miss Liberty's crown was an assortment of missiles and machine guns. Peeping out from behind the crown weaponry were a cowboy, an American soldier, and a Ku Klux Klanner. The Klansman's machine gun had a noose hanging from it. And to top it all off, Miss Liberty's torch was missing. The billboard was captioned "Freedom—American Style."

As the visitor drove into Moscow from the airport, he found nine more anti-American billboards along the route, as well as one anti-Israeli and one anti-South African. The AP dispatch reported an escalation of anti-American editorials in *Pravda,* especially emphasizing President Nixon's "hypocrisy and falsification" with regard to American actions in Vietnam.

Americans should give serious reflection to the Russian revision of Miss Liberty. For a long time Americans have been fond of saying, "You can trust the Communists to be Communists." What the Russian Statue of Liberty billboard is saying, by implication, is, "You can trust the Americans to be Americans." And the real tragedy is that America continues to project expressions of hate and violence which the Russians can magnify for their own propaganda interests. The Russians don't even need to lie about us.

As a matter of fact, the people of the United States and the American press are the best public-relations representatives the Communists have. Americans are always blaming everything good on the Communists. If a group of marchers are demonstrating carrying signs saying "FREE THE INDIAN," invariably folks will say, "That's Communist-inspired." Welfare mothers demonstrating for a little human dignity, Women's Liberation activists demanding that women be freed, folks demonstrating to insist that hungry people be fed—all end up branded by the favorite American label, "That's Communist-inspired."

I've never understood why the Communists never get blamed for anything bad. Communists never get the blame for pimping, prostitution, dope pushing, or any of the real social ills. You would think, if folks wanted to bad-mouth the Communists, they would point at a whorehouse and say, "See that place over there? It's a Communist house."

"How do you know?"

"It's got a red light in the front. And see all those comrades going in and out all day."

Whenever the Communists want to take over a new country, they should first go in with a whole bunch of American newspapers. The Communist advance men should say, "Look. I know you don't know much about our program. But just read what the Americans are saying about us. We're for feeding hungry folks, women's liberation, freedom and dignity and power for black folks and poor folks, Indian rights, and a whole lot of other things."

The cowboy on the Russian Statue of Liberty billboard, for example, is not a lie about America. It is a very realistic portrayal of America's image abroad. Most Americans do not realize what a violent image of America the cowboy legend portrays. America sends cowboy movies all over the world, extolling the violence of the Wild West, without realizing that those movies say more about America's infatuation with violence than any of the recent bombings attributed to radical left-wing militants. In the eyes of the world, America's actions at home are merely an extension of those cowboy movies. The man who will shoot up the streets of a frontier town, endangering the lives of innocent bystanders and forcing them to dive for cover, will think nothing of riding onto the university campus to continue his gunplay.

The Klansman in Miss Liberty's crown symbolizes, of course, America's hatred of color. Even if it is argued that the influence and power of the Klan as an official organization are diminished, America continues to project an image which says, "Whatever white folks do is OK."

For years America steadfastly refused to consider the inclusion of the People's Republic of China in the family of the United Nations. Yet even as AP was reporting Russia's "Hate America" campaign, American businessmen were in Moscow making deals and Sol Hurok was in town to sign the Bolshoi opera and ballet for another U.S. tour. It seems odd that Communist China was so long the villain to be ignored and Communist Russia the friend to be negotiated with. Every American soldier who is killed in Vietnam is shot down by a Russian-supplied bullet, and every American pilot who is shot down is the victim of a Russian-supplied missile. In the eyes of a rational watching world, can America's rejection of Communist China and acceptance of Communist Russia be based on any other consideration than that of color? The Russians are white, you will remember.

All of a sudden, word began to filter down from President Nixon that we were going to start liking the folks who live in what America has always called "Red China" or "Communist China." We even began to see the correct name—the People's Republic of China—printed in American newspapers. America sent its championship table-tennis team to play some exhibitions with the Chinese. And at the time of this writing President Nixon has announced that he too will visit China. Why? Because America's respect for power began to displace a disrespect for color. The People's Republic of China has the big bomb.

America isn't interested in having any weak friends. Black folks recognized this when we raised the cry "Black Power." You will notice that so far word has not filtered down from the White House that we should start liking Cuba. We're only interested in establishing friendly relationships with those we recognize as powerful. And when "power to the people" becomes a reality in this country, a whole lot of folks in high places will want to be friendly with the masses.

Otherwise, if a word from the White House is all that it takes to get Americans to start liking folks, why can't we have a situation here at home where the President issues a decree that all Americans will now start liking their Indian brothers? Or start actively liking Puerto Ricans, Mexican Americans, Jews, blacks, and Orientals right here at home? If the Russian accusations concerning America's color bias were really untrue, such a Presidential decree could easily and certainly expose that lie.

Speaking of color, it is very significant that Russia also displays anti-South African posters. It is one more reminder of two very crucial considerations: the importance of Africa on the world scene and the global population distribution, which is some ninety percent nonwhite. Africa is the most important continent in the world today because of her rich natural resources. Any country that wants to remain a major world power must establish a rapport with Africa. That means, of course, that America and Russia are in competition for African sympathies.

America continues to seem to be consciously calculating a loss in that competition. America's treatment of black Americans at home cannot inspire confidence or respect in Black Africa. America's refusal to take a stand against the racist South African regime is one more slap in the face of blackness. America could assume a role of moral leadership on a worldwide scale, but she continues to give color considerations a higher priority than a true concern for justice and morality.

200 Years Later

During the bicentennial celebration Americans should take a good look at our nation's political life and processes and consider what the Founding Fathers would think if they could suddenly reappear at the birthday party. For one thing, looking at the conduct of political life on Capitol Hill in Washington, D.C., the seat of our federal government, many of the Founding Fathers would find a situation very close to the English government they rebelled against. The Founding Fathers would probably be less concerned about "crime in the streets" of Washington, D.C., than about "crime on the Hill."

Consider, for example, what James Otis might say about the conduct of individual members of Congress were he to appear on national television on "Meet the Press" some Sunday afternoon. Brother Otis was a Boston lawyer and the man John Adams credited as being the real Founding Father of American Independence. James Otis, though his words might be "bleeped out" on national television, would probably give a description of Congress similar to the one he gave concerning the government in England during the 1750s. Otis said that the House of Lords (or Senate) was filled with members who had not risen above what they learned at Oxford and Cambridge Universities:

New York Times: "And what is that, Mr. Otis?"

Otis: "Nothing but whoring, smoking, and drinking."

Washington Post: "Well, then, Mr. Otis, what would you say about the members of Commons (or House of Representatives)?"

Otis: "They are a parcel of button makers, pin makers,

horse jockeys, gamesters, pensioners, pimps, and whore-masters."

And if Benjamin Franklin appeared on "Meet the Press" that afternoon, he would probably be saying the same things about life in America today that he was saying of life in England just before the American Revolution. Franklin spoke of the increasing "corruption and degeneracy of the people" of England. He said he could only see "numberless groundless quarrels, foolish expeditions, false accounts or no accounts, contracts and jobs" which "devour all revenue and produce continual necessity in the midst of natural plenty." If Franklin looked through the records of Senate committee hearings on hunger in America, he would certainly echo his earlier sentiments.

John Adams would undoubtedly join the chorus. He felt England was done for, and there is no reason to believe he wouldn't feel the same about America: "Corruption, like a cancer . . . eats faster and faster every hour. The revenue creates pensioners, and the pensioners urge for more revenue. The people grow less steady, spirited, and virtuous, the seekers more numerous and corrupt, and every day increases the circles of their dependents and expectants, until virtue, integrity, public spirit, simplicity, and frugality, become the objects of ridicule and scorn, and vanity, foppery, selfish-ness, meanness, and downright venality swallowing up the whole society."

And if Thomas Jefferson was a guest on the "David Frost Show" for one of David's famous hour-and-a-half depth in-terviews, I can well imagine Brother Tom getting around to offering the same evaluation of the United States today that he gave of England in his *Notes on Virginia:* "The sun of her

[England's] glory is fast descending on the horizon. Her philosophy has crossed the Channel, her freedom the Atlantic, and herself seems to be passing to that awful dissolution whose issue is not given human foresight to scan."

Of the United States today Jefferson would probably be saying, in a paraphrase: "The sun is fast setting on her greatness. Her initial love of freedom has been taken up by the spirited nations and peoples of the Third World. She has spanned the oceans to enforce her philosophy upon weaker nations at gunpoint, while she herself seems to be passing into a state of internal disintegration the final outcome of which is frightful to contemplate and difficult to predict."

Since American politics have become solidified in a two-party political system, a system increasingly under criticism as providing little real choice for the American electorate, our bicentennial reflections should include considering what the Founding Fathers, and the writers who influenced their thinking, thought of party politics. For the Founding Fathers, the terms "party" and "faction" were synonymous. Parties were viewed with the same scorn reserved today for such groups as the Black Panthers and the Weathermen. In Lesson Three we'll talk about how party politics came into being. For the moment, the initial disrepute of parties in general is our concern.

Early in life Founding Father John Adams, second President of the United States, said that the spirit of party "wrought an entire metamorphosis of the human character. It destroyed all sense and understanding, all equity and humanity, all memory and regard to truth, all virtue, honor, decorum, and veracity." In 1780 Brother John was saying:

"There is nothing which I dread so much as a division of the republic into two great parties, each arranged under its leader, and concerting measures in opposition to each other. This, in my humble apprehension, is to be dreaded as the greatest political evil under our Constitution."

And even late in life John Adams was writing to his old cohort and successor to the Presidency, Thomas Jefferson, blaming parties for the failure of the "science" of government to advance: "What is the reason? I say, parties and factions will not suffer improvements to be made. As soon as one man hints at an improvement, his rival opposes it. No sooner has one party discovered or invented any amelioration of the condition of man, or the order of society, than the opposite party belies it, misconstrues it, misrepresents it, ridicules it, insults it, and persecutes it."

Franklin, during the debate at the Constitutional Convention, gave warning against "the infinite mutual abuse of parties, tearing to pieces the best of characters." As a matter of fact, those arguing for and those arguing against the adoption of the United States Constitution were united in bad-mouthing parties. So "party" was a dirty word, and "faction" was even worse. In the 1790s, when the Republican Party (the party of Thomas Jefferson and the forerunner of the Democratic Party today) was beginning to take shape under Jefferson's leadership, the word "party" was usually avoided and members spoke rather of "the republican interest." Jefferson really laid into Alexander Hamilton in 1792 for "daring to call the Republican party *a faction.*"

Writers in England who influenced the thinking of the Founding Fathers also spoke strongly against parties. Jonathan Swift, in his *Thoughts on Various Subjects,* said in a line that could be straight out of an underground newspaper today, "Party is the madness of the many, for the gain of the few." English statesman Lord Bolingbroke offered the following formula in his *The Idea of a Patriot King:* "Faction is to party what the superlative is to the positive: party is a political evil, and faction is the worst of all parties." Elsewhere in the same work Bolingbroke wrote: "A man who has not seen the inside of parties, nor had opportunities to examine nearly their secret motives, can hardly conceive how little a share principle of any sort, tho principle of some sort or other be always pretended, has in the determination of their conduct."

George Washington, who was thought of (both by himself and by his admirers) as the embodiment of the Patriot King, or at least Patriot President, left a stern warning against parties in his Farewell Address. Since Brother George was not much of a speaker, his final address was written to be published (originally appearing in the Philadelphia *Daily American Advertiser,* September 19, 1796) and he had the help of both James Madison and Alexander Hamilton in preparing the text. Madison got first crack at it way back in 1792 and Hamilton took over closer to publication date.

But the final wording was George's own, and since he was the "Father of Our Country," we'll take an extended look at what he had to say about parties:

. . . The very idea of the power and the right of the people to establish government presupposes the duty of every individual to obey the established government.

All obstructions to the execution of the laws, all combinations and associations, under whatever plausible character, with the real design to direct, control, counteract, or awe the regular deliberation and action of the constituted authorities, are destructive of this fundamental principle and of fatal tendency. They serve to organize faction; to give it an artificial and extraordinary force; to put in the place of the delegated will of the nation the will of a party, often a small but artful and enterprising minority of the community, and, according to the alternate triumphs of different parties, to make the public administration the mirror of the ill-concerted and incongruous projects of faction rather than the organ of consistent and wholesome plans, digested by common counsels and modified by mutual interests.

However combinations or associations of the above description may now and then answer popular ends, they are likely in the course of time and things to become potent engines by which cunning, ambitious, and unprincipled men will be enabled to subvert the power of the people, and to usurp for themselves the reins of government, destroying afterwards the very engines which had lifted them to unjust dominion.

. . . Let me now take a more comprehensive view, and warn you in the most solemn manner against the baneful effects of the spirit of party generally.

This spirit, unfortunately, is inseparable from our nature, having its root in the strongest passions of the human mind. It exists under different shapes in all governments, more or less stifled, controlled, or repressed; but in those of the popular form it is seen in its greatest rankness and is truly their worst enemy.

The alternate dominion of one faction over another, sharpened by the spirit of revenge natural to party dissension, which in different ages and countries has perpetrated the most horrid enormities, is itself a frightful despotism. But this leads at length to a more formal and permanent despotism. *The disorders and miseries which result gradually incline the minds of men to seek security and repose in the absolute power of an individual, and*

The Logan Act, forbidding a private citizen to undertake diplomatic negotiations with a foreign nation on a subject of dispute between it and the United States.

As long as George Washington was in office, strong formal opposition was pretty difficult. After all, General Washington was the military hero of the American Revolution, and the whole concept of the Presidency was written into the Constitution on the assumption that he would be the first man to occupy the office.

When opposition and dissent did develop, a strong rebuke from President Washington was almost all that was needed to do it in. In 1793 a group of Democratic Societies (prefix "Students For" to the name and you will have a modern reminder of where the societies were in the eyes of the federal government) began to form in Philadelphia and elsewhere. The "left wing" of the time, the Democratic Societies were speaking most favorably of the French Revolution and most unfavorably of the Federalists in Congress and even George Washington himself. The societies were modeled after the Jacobin Club in Paris, and the old-guard Federalists, such as Alexander Hamilton, felt they were stirring up the masses.

In 1794 some frontier farmers in western Pennsylvania rose up in anger over Alexander Hamilton's Excise Act, passed in 1791, which placed a tax on whiskey. Known as the Whiskey Rebellion, the insurrection required President Washington's calling out fifteen thousand militia (National Guard) from Virginia, Maryland, New Jersey, and Pennsylvania to put it down.

When it was all over, Washington took a sympathetic view of the "insurgents," pardoning the two ringleaders who were convicted of treason, but he stayed mad at the Democratic Societies. Washington felt they were responsible for the uprising. In his November 1794 annual message to Congress, President Washington suggested that the Whiskey Rebellion had been "fomented by combinations of men who, careless of consequences and disregarding the unerring truth that those who arouse cannot always appease a civil convulsion, have disseminated, from an ignorance or perversion of facts, suspicions, jealousies, and accusations of the whole Government." He called the Democratic Societies "self-created societies" that were trying to destroy the government. In the contemporary rhetoric of the present administration, they would be the "bums, thugs, hoodlums, and outside agitators who are trying to overthrow the government."

After Washington's strong rebuke, the Democratic Societies disappeared rapidly between 1795 and 1796. But Thomas Jefferson and James Madison saw Washington's attack as really a slap in the face of efforts like their own to establish an organized version of "power to the people." "The game," said Madison, "was to connect the democratic societies with the odium of the insurrection, to connect the Republicans in Congress with these societies, [and] to put the President ostensibly at the head of the other party in opposition to both. . . ." Jefferson thought Washington's message was "an attack on the freedom of discussion." Even John Adams, who succeeded George Washington in the Presidency and who was certainly not one of the Jefferson-Madison "left-wingers," wrote that "political clubs must and ought to be lawful in every free country."

So when George Washington spoke of the dangers of

"despotism" in his Farewell Address, he knew what he was talking about. He had tried his hand at dictatorship two years before.

The Alien and Sedition Acts in 1798 pushed the suppression of dissent much further. John Adams was the President and he did not enjoy the mantle of near-infallibility draped upon George Washington. The old-guard Federalists in Congress were upset by the course of the French Revolution, feeling that the folks in France were "cutting up" a little too much with all their head-chopping activity, and a strong "hawk" sentiment was itching for a war with France.

So the Alien and Sedition Acts were enacted to crack down on the "doves" and the pro-French at home. Though President Adams never used the power given to him in the Naturalization Act to send folks back where they came from, two shiploads of Frenchmen split the country in anticipation that he would. The Logan Act came about when a Philadelphia Quaker, Dr. George Logan, went to Paris on a mission to preserve the peace. Newspaper editors and printers found themselves in hot water under the Sedition Act. It was politically enforced to wipe out pro-Republican sentiment in print. Twenty-five persons, most of them editors and printers, were prosecuted under the Sedition Act, and ten received convictions.

A distinguished philosopher, Dr. Thomas Cooper, got six months and a $400 fine from Judge Samuel Chase. Cooper had dared to criticize President Adams in what First Lady Abigail called "a mad democratic stile." Abigail sounds like the Martha Mitchell of her day. And Judge Chase would do well today presiding over a Black Panther or Conspiracy trial. In his instructions to the jury, Judge Chase called Cooper's publication "the boldest attempt I have known to poison the minds of the people." He further stated that it was meant "to mislead the ignorant, and inflame their minds against the President, and to influence their votes on the next election." Then the jury was released to render their unbiased verdict.

There were also less notable convictions under the Sedition Act. One poor boozer hanging out in a tavern in Newark, New Jersey, was busted and jailed for saying that he would like to see the wadding of a cannon fired in the President's honor land in Adams' butt. Another wandering "apostle of sedition" (the Federalist term for outside agitator) got four years for persuading the local "Jacobins" in Dedham, Massachusetts, to put up a liberty pole with a provocative inscription in front of Congressman Fisher Ames' house. Ames was a Federalist who was always bad-mouthing Jefferson and his crowd of Republicans, calling them "anarchists" and accusing them of pushing the country into chaos.

It is perhaps encouraging to remember, for all those suffering under political repression today, that Jefferson became President in 1801 and pardoned everyone convicted under the Sedition Act. Congress paid back all the fines with interest. And all the acts were done away with except the Logan Act, which is still on the books. So watch those overseas letters!

But the Sedition Act is still a healthy bicentennial reminder. About the same time President Nixon was inaugurating the bicentennial celebration, the *New York Times,* the *Washington Post,* and the *Boston Globe* were being hauled into court by the federal government for publishing a supposedly top-secret Pentagon document that detailed the steps and deceptions used by various Presidents in deepening the United States involvement in the war in Vietnam. For a while it looked like newspaper editors and publishers might again be rounded up and shipped off to jail. But the Supreme Court stepped in and upheld the right of the newspapers to publish.

While the legal battle was in process, I kept trying to understand America's thinking. The *New York Times* published a document that told the truth about the Vietnam war, and for a while it looked like the *Times* people would go to jail. And the Pentagon Papers showed that President Johnson didn't tell the truth to the American public, and LBJ got a new library dedicated in his honor! Now that just doesn't make sense to me. It's like a man coming home after work and when he walks in the door, his six-year-old boy tells him, "Mom's upstairs making love to the mailman." So the man runs and gets his pistol and comes back and beats his boy with it. Then he walks upstairs to the bedroom, ignores his wife, and says to the mailman, "How's the family, Ed?"

Of course, I knew the *New York Times* people were not going to go to jail. If they got in real trouble, they'd just say they got the Pentagon study from a black publication like *Jet* magazine.

The size of the Pentagon study is probably what worried the government most. It was forty-seven volumes and 2.5 million words. That's a whole lot of print, and it could cover more wars than just the war in Vietnam. We know that it reached at least as far back as May 1, 1950, where Presi-

26

dent Truman's approval of an initial $10 million in military aid to French forces in Indochina is described as the first "crucial decision regarding U.S. military involvement in Indochina." Wouldn't it be wild if we found out the Pentagon study revealed that on the day of Little Big Horn, General Custer was really supposed to be on KP?

The contemporary reminder, which should be contemplated along with the words of the Founding Fathers contained in this chapter, comes from former Senator Wayne Morse, one of the two U.S. Senators who voted against the adoption of the Gulf of Tonkin resolution in 1964. Two U.S. destroyers were allegedly attacked by North Vietnamese torpedo boats in 1964, and the Senate passed the resolution that empowered the President to "repel any armed attack against the forces of the United States and to prevent further aggression." The vote was 88 to 2. President Johnson ordered a bombing of North Vietnamese PT-boat bases in retaliation. Senators Wayne Morse and Ernest Gruening sensed the broader implications of the resolution and voted against it. They were subsequently ousted by the voters. On June 24, 1970, the Senate voted to repeal the Gulf of Tonkin resolution with the support of the Nixon administration, which said it did not need that resolution to justify American involvement in Vietnam.

While the legal battle was in process to determine the right of the newspapers to continue publishing the Pentagon study, Wayne Morse spoke with his usual candor and insight, offering words that bring any survey of political life in America quite up to date.

"We are dealing here with violations of the very basic abstract principles of a free society and democratic government," Citizen Morse insisted. "You cannot have a free society without a free press. I know my colonial history—the men of that time knew the value of a free press. After much controversy and debate, they had the appropriate guarantees written into the Constitution."

Speaking of life in America today, Mr. Morse said, "What you are faced with is the steady erosion of the constitutional safeguards of the American people. The result is that we are fast approaching a police state; we are getting ominously close to where the German people stood just before Hitler's Third Reich."

Finally, he took a look into the future and spoke in words reminiscent of the Founding Fathers: "The only hope is that the Nixon policies will result in millions of young people rushing to deliver the message that it is the right and duty of free men to rebel against tyranny. The ultimate check is the right of free people to overthrow tyrannical government."

The words of Wayne Morse may indeed prove to be the most appropriate toast at the bicentennial birthday party.

1

When people today refer to something being "Communist-inspired," they are usually talking about:
  a. the Bolshoi ballet
  b. the exploration of outer space
  c. the May Day parade in Moscow
  d. the music of Peter Tschaikovsky
  e. none of the above.

2

Define welfare. Define subsidy. What is the difference between the two? Cite examples.

3

Read the Declaration of Independence. Make a list of the charges against "the present King of Great Britain" contained in the Declaration. Do you see any similarity to charges now being made against the present government of the United States? What does the Declaration of Independence say people should do when the government becomes "destructive" of "life, liberty and the pursuit of happiness"?

Lesson One
That Long, Hot
Summer–1787

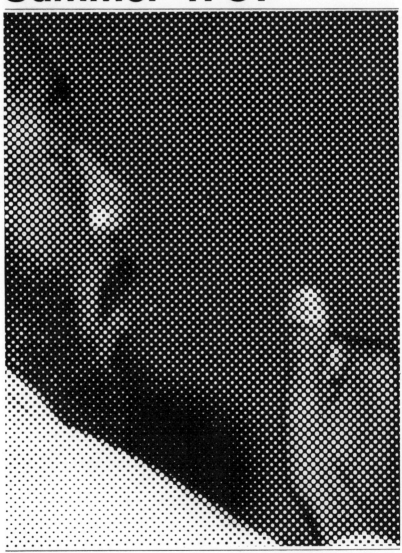

There are two important things to remember about the birth of our nation's government. It began in compromise and it grew out of a long, hot summer. Thus a pattern was established which became reversed over two hundred years. In 1787 the long, hot summer created a compromise government. Today governmental compromises create long, hot summers.

But first a look at the American scene going into the long, hot summer of 1787. At the time of the American Revolution, each of the thirteen colonies was an independent state unto itself, and as such each colony had all of the highest powers of government. Each colony or state called itself "sovereign," which meant it could levy taxes, raise an army and build a navy, enter into treaties with foreign nations, and make war and peace. Thus, the Declaration of Independence proclaimed in 1776 "that *these* United Colonies are, and of right ought to be, free and independent *States.*"

Each colony had its own legislature which made the laws and chartered local government. The Governor of each of the Royal Colonies (Delaware, Georgia, Massachusetts, New Hampshire, New Jersey, New York, North Carolina, South Carolina, and Virginia) was appointed by the King of England. In the proprietary colonies (Maryland and Pennsylvania) the Governor was duty bound to the proprietor of the colony in the same way Royal Governors were to the King. In the corporation colonies of Connecticut and Rhode Island the Governor was elected by the colonial legislature and was really a tool of that body.

Royal Governors were the chief executive officers of their colonies and could recommend and initiate laws, exercise absolute veto over acts of the legislature, control the frequency and length of sessions of the legislature, and could dissolve the legislative assembly and order a new election.

But the colonists took pride in a form of government which allowed the few colonists qualified to vote to choose representatives to the legislature, the body which touched their lives most crucially in the levying of taxes. It was when the Parliament of England attempted to impose taxes upon the colonies, a body in which the colonies had no representation, that the spirit of Revolution took hold and burst forth in the words of the Declaration of Independence.

You Get What You Pay For

During the American Revolution the central legislative body which held the colonies loosely together was the Continental Congress. The Continental Congress was like the Assembly of the United Nations today. It was a gathering of ambassadors from each of the sovereign colonies. But it did not represent a strong central government with any authority or clout.

The First Continental Congress was called in 1774, meeting in Philadelphia, when the impending conflict with England was growing to revolutionary proportions. It was really an official gripe session, and it adopted a Declaration of Rights and Grievances and called another session for 1775, again in Philadelphia.

By the time the Second Continental Congress met in May 1775, the battles of Lexington and Concord had been fought and the colonies were at war with the British government. With the shooting war already under way in Massachusetts, the Second Continental Congress assumed the right to govern the colonies and raise a national army. The Congress appointed George Washington Commander in Chief.

In 1776 the new Congress voted the Declaration of Independence and the following year, 1777, adopted a proposal for a loose federal union of the thirteen colonies. The document was known as the Articles of Confederation and it was sent out into the colonies to be ratified. At that time our word "federal" was still commonly spelled "foederal," which came from the Latin word *foedus* meaning "treaty." So the Articles of Confederation really represented a treaty agreement of sovereign states—thirteen little nations acting in concert. By 1781 all the states had ratified.

The Articles of Confederation had some obvious defects, weaknesses inevitable because of the conditions imposed in Article II: "Each State retains its sovereignty, freedom, and independence, and every power, jurisdiction and right, which is not by this confederation expressly delegated to the United States, in Congress assembled." Thus there was no really strong central government which could speak with authority to the colonies. The Continental Congress had to rely on the individual states to enforce its policies, and it had no way to force the states to do so. Not only was there no sanction in the Articles of Confederation for such enforcement, but the national army was at the mercy of how many men the individual states were willing to provide.

The financial problem of the Continental Congress was a real one. The Articles provided that the Congress could borrow money but did not have the power to levy taxes. It had to rely on contributions from the states. Congress could enter into commercial treaties with foreign countries and could regulate trade with the Indians, but it could not control other aspects of foreign commerce and it could not control commerce between the states.

As usual, while the war was going on, business was good. But when the American Revolution was over and the peace was established in 1783, the colonies plunged into one of the most depressing Depressions in America's history. Colonies began importing goods from Great Britain once again, but they were bringing in more than they could pay for. There was no standardization of money, and each state issued its own paper money. Nobody knew what a New York dollar was worth in comparison to, say, one from Pennsylvania or Rhode Island. Continental money was so inflated it was practically worthless, and trade between the states fell to an all-time low. The phrase "not worth a continental" comes from this period of American history.

So money problems led to the first long, hot summer of 1787, just as money problems (unemployment et al.) bring on long, hot summers today. Two interstate conferences of businessmen preceded the long, hot summer of 1787, the first held in 1785, and the second held the following year in Annapolis, Maryland.

Nine states accepted invitations to the Annapolis meeting. But only twelve men, representing five states, showed up. The colonial situation was rapidly worsening. Farmers could hardly support themselves. Moneylenders were seizing farms all over the place. A new revolution was brewing in Massachusetts led by Daniel Shays, a former captain in the American Revolution, who had now become a poverty-stricken farmer. Again we see a parallel to the United States today. The United States takes young black Americans, trains them to be experts in guerrilla warfare, sends them ten thousand miles to Southeast Asia to apply their training, and then returns them to a hopeless cycle back home of unemployment and poverty. It is little wonder that some returning black soldiers get the urge to apply their training at home, just as Daniel Shays applied his Revolutionary War training back home in Massachusetts.

With only a dozen men at the Annapolis conference, there was not much the delegates could do. One of the delegates was Alexander Hamilton, a young man about thirty years old, whose ghetto upbringing in the Virgin Islands had made him sensitive to the problems of poverty and whose later education at King's College (now Columbia University) had given him political sophistication. Hamilton insisted that the situation in the colonies was really bad and demanded that a call of alarm be sent out to the colonies to dispatch representatives to another meeting the following year in Philadelphia. The call went out and the stage was set for that first long, hot summer.

Sweating Out Sovereignty

On May 25, 1787, fifty-five delegates from twelve states met in the State House (Independence Hall) in Philadelphia. Rhode Island ignored the Convention, causing a Boston newspaper to call it "Rogue's Island." The delegates were lawyers, businessmen, and landowners—men who were concerned about establishing a government that would help business. It is important to remember that the men who wrote the Constitution were primarily concerned about helping business; and helping business has remained a vital governmental concern to this day. There were only one or two representatives of wage earners or small farmers, and there were none representing the pioneers of the frontier. The delegates wanted a government that would be responsible to the "people," but they had no intention of granting "power to the people" in the form of letting the masses elect the President or even the Congress.

D. W. Brogan described the interests represented at the Philadelphia Convention in 1787 as follows:

It was a group of men who wanted a stronger government or, as they would have said, a *government,* for they regarded the Confederation as not being a government in any real sense of the term. It included the public creditors. It included all the possessors of titles to money threatened by the new plague of paper money. It included men who had titles to western lands which were nearly worthless as long as there was no effective government in the western territories. It included merchants and shipbuilders who, as good mercantilists, thought that only a strong federal government could, by navigation acts and commercial treaties, break into the European and Caribbean markets.

The delegates argued and debated the whole hot summer until September 17. At first it was not at all clear what they were supposed to do, since they had not met for the expressed purpose of writing a new Constitution. They thought they were gathering to amend the Articles of Confederation. And what they did do is not absolutely clear, since the delegates initiated that long-standing American tradition of meeting behind closed doors. The delegates decided in advance to keep everything they said a secret, but men of that time were great note takers and letter, diary, and memoir writers, so the word got out.

Delegates were divided, of course, in interests and sensibilities. There were those like James Madison who saw a need for some "power to the people" in whatever structure was developed and saw the dangerous division between the haves and the have-nots which persists today. Writing in *The Federalist,* Madison said: "The most common and durable source of factions has been the various and unequal distribution of property. Those who hold, and those who are without property, have ever formed distinct interests in society. Those who are creditors, and those who are debtors, fall under a like discrimination. A landed interest, a manufacturing interest, a mercantile interest, with many lesser interests, grow up of necessity in civilized nations, and divide them into different classes, actuated by different sentiments and views." Hamilton distrusted "the people" and was to say: "Your people is a great beast."

George Washington presided over the Philadelphia Convention; with a successful revolution under his belt, he enjoyed enormous respect and prestige, and thus was able to keep the delegates from each other's throats and down to business. The good-humored octogenarian Ben Franklin was there and kept spirits high and optimism alive. Franklin was so enthusiastic about the United States Constitution when it was finally hammered out that he wrote to a friend in France: "If it succeeds, I do not see why you might not in Europe carry the project of good Henry the 4th into Execution by forming a Federal Union and One Grand Republic of all its different States and Kingdoms." You can see what a jokester he was!

So when the delegates got down to business during the long, hot summer of 1787, they soon realized that amending the totally inadequate Articles would not do, and they settled on writing a new Constitution. The Great Compromise and debate was over representation in the central government. Both the terms "federal" and "national" were avoided in the final draft of the new Constitution, so that when reference was made to the new government it was simply called "the United States." The terms "federal" and "national" waved red flags in front of delegates who were more than a little uneasy about the powerful new government with headquarters outside their own state telling them what to do. After all, a revolution had just been fought against King George III and the British Parliament because that was a powerful government with headquarters out of the country telling the colonies what to do!

Then there was the problem of the big states and the little states getting pushed around by one another. If all representation in the new government was to be equal, then the tiny states with little to lose—even Rhode Island if it ever noticed a Constitution had been written—could lord it over the larger states. If, on the other hand, representation was to be unequal, based on the size and wealth of a state, then the bigger states could whip the little ones into line any time they got the urge.

The Convention was presented two plans: "The Virginia Plan," representing the interests of the larger states, and "The New Jersey Plan," representing the interests of the smaller states. The Virginia Plan called for a Congress of two chambers. One chamber would be made up of representatives elected by the people, and that chamber in turn would elect members of the other chamber from candidates nominated by state legislatures. But in both chambers the states would be represented according to their size and taxes or some combination of the two. Size would prevail.

The New Jersey Plan proposed a Congress of just one chamber. Each state, regardless of size and wealth, would have just one vote, as under the Articles of Confederation.

So the biggies and the tinies fought it out until William Samuel Johnson of Connecticut came up with a solution now known as the "Connecticut Compromise." It was a novel idea which combined both interests. There would be a House of Representatives where representation would be based on population, thereby giving larger states an advantage. The House would have the exclusive right to originate all bills for raising money. Then there would be an upper house, the Senate, in which all states, regardless of size, would have equal representation. In order for a bill to become law, it would have to pass both houses. So smaller states could stand up for their interests in the Senate, and larger states could try to clobber them in the House. The Connecticut Compromise was adopted.

There was also uneasiness and debate about the idea of having a President. To many folks, the office sounded too much like a King. Men like James Wilson of Pennsylvania and Gouverneur Morris of New York argued for a strong executive who could operate with "energy, dispatch and responsibility." Men like Roger Sherman of Connecticut and Edmund Randolph of Virginia feared the kingly overtones of a one-man executive. Randolph saw the office of President as the "foetus of monarchy," which may be the source of the sentiment of those today who see the President's office as an abortive attempt to give the semblance of democracy!

Randolph and Sherman would rather have seen a three-man troika arrangement than a one-man President. And Patrick Henry, who had stirred revolutionary spirits in 1775 with the words "Give me liberty or give me death," described the office of President as an "awful squint toward monarchy."

Probably what saved the day most for the President supporters was the recognition by the delegates that they were describing and creating an office which George Washington was going to fill. Just as a Broadway musical is sometimes written with a specific star in mind, so the office of President was written with George Washington in mind; and the image of Washington was clearly before the Convention, as he was presiding. Unlike the Broadway pattern today, the new political drama *opened* in New York City, then moved to Philadelphia after a year's run, then settled down for a long run in Washington, D.C., after a change of stars (John Adams had replaced George Washington in top billing and the role was about to be given to Thomas Jefferson).

So it was George Washington who was to be Commander in Chief, have the power to make treaties and appoint ambassadors, public ministers, consuls, judges of the Supreme Court, with the approval of two thirds of the Senate, and who would "from time to time give to the Congress Information of the State of the Union, and recommend to their Consideration such Measures as he shall judge necessary and expedient," and "on extraordinary occasions, convene both Houses, or either of them, and in Case of Disagreement between them, with Respect to the Time of Adjournment, . . . adjourn them to such Time as he shall think proper; . . . receive Ambassadors and other public Ministers; . . . take care that the Laws be faithfully executed, and . . . Commission all the Officers of the United States."

After a full summer of sweating out sovereignty, the delegates adopted a Constitution consisting of a Preamble and seven Articles. The most glaring omission was a Bill of Rights, but that oversight was soon to be remedied. It was surprisingly simple in its language, having been drafted in its final form by the one-legged man from New York, Gouverneur Morris. So those who find the Constitution handicapped today might look to its authors' condition for an explanation. It was a document built around the "commerce clause" and supporting clauses, which, after all, was the primary reason for the delegates convening. It was open-ended in critical areas, with a built-in process for amendment, to allow for passage of time and usage. And it contained what the delegates believed to be a proper system of checks and balances: the President holding the power of veto over acts of Congress, and the Congress only able to override the President with a two-thirds majority vote; the Congress holding the President in check by being able to refuse to provide money; and the Senate holding the power of approving Presidential appointments, as well as the power of veto over treaties negotiated by the President. And a Supreme Court sitting in interpretive authority over the whole thing.

The representation issue had been worked out by the adoption of the Connecticut Compromise, with a sizable amount of sovereignty intact. Representatives to the House were to be elected by the "people of the States." Senators were to be chosen by state legislatures. And the states had the authority to decide who could vote, thereby enabling them to impose religious, racial, and property-holding qualifications upon the voters. If you were white, male, well to do, and free, you could expect to have some role in selecting your representatives, if you also, of course, kept the proper faith.

The new Constitution was immediately sent out to the colonies for ratification, and the states took action as follows:

Delaware	7	December	1787	unanimous
Pennsylvania	12	December	1787	46–23
New Jersey	18	December	1787	unanimous
Georgia	2	January	1788	unanimous
Connecticut	9	January	1788	128–40
Massachusetts	6	February	1788	187–168
Maryland	28	April	1788	63–11
South Carolina	23	May	1788	149–73
New Hampshire*	21	June	1788	57–47
Virginia	25	June	1788	89–79
New York	26	July	1788	30–27
North Carolina	21	November	1789	194–77

* The ninth state to ratify, making the U.S. Constitution official.

The new government had already been in operation a year before Rhode Island got around to ratifying May 29, 1790, by a vote of 34–32. George Washington was inaugurated as first President of the United States in New York City on the balcony of Federal Hall, symbolically facing Wall Street, the financial capital of the nation, promising to "preserve, protect, and defend the Constitution of the United

States." There, in the urban center which was to produce a long, hot summer of its own 175 years later, the new government of the United States was born.

The New Revolution

Today the United States Constitution is the oldest written constitution in existence. Though amended twenty-six times, its forms and basic outline have changed little, certainly less than any other political organization since its inception. There have been changes in the United States, of course, beginning with the growth and dominance of the two-party system (which we shall trace in the next lesson). But the oath of office which George Washington took in 1789 on Wall Street is exactly the same as the one recited by Richard Nixon 180 years later on Pennsylvania Avenue. As D. W. Brogan has reminded us, when the Constitution went into effect in 1789, the French monarchy was still standing; there was a "Holy Roman Emperor, a Venetian Republic and a Dutch Republic, an Autocrat in St. Petersburg, a Sultan-Caliph in Constantinople, an Emperor vested with the 'mandate of heaven' in Pekin and a Shogun ruling the hermit empire of Japan in the name of a secluded, impotent and almost unknown Mikado." The ruler with the mandate of heaven is gone, but the Constitution lives on. It kind of makes you wonder. Of course, I have always felt, when reciting the pledge of allegiance, that if the United States is "one nation, under God," I sure would hate to see one that is "under the Devil."

Constitutional Father James Wilson attributed the probable longevity of the Constitution to calm deliberation and application of the science of government. In a speech to the Pennsylvania Convention on November 24, 1787, Wilson said:

Permit me to add, in this place, that the science even of government itself seems to be yet almost in its state of infancy. Governments, in general, have been the result of force, fraud, and of accident. After a period of six thousand years has elapsed since the Creation, the United States exhibit to the world the first instance, as far as we can learn, of a nation, unattacked by external force, unconvulsed by domestic insurrections, assembling voluntarily, deliberating fully, and deciding calmly, concerning that system of government, under which they would wish that they and their posterity should live.

But Wilson's description tends to obscure the fact that the United States was forged in revolution, and that the country was founded on revolutionary theory, quite new in its day, though perhaps passé today. Of course, Wilson is not alone in brushing aside the real revolutionary roots of these United States. The superpatriots have so enshrined the *documents* of the Declaration of Independence and the United States Constitution that the *sentiments* expressed are forgotten. "Revolution" today is a dirty word when used by those who really mean it, and an example of nonpatriotism to those who revere document rather than sentiment. Until 1952 the documents were kept in an illuminated shrine in the Library of Congress. Now they are housed in the National Archives building in a vault believed to be safe not only from moths, rust, thieves, or left-wing militants, but even from nuclear attack. But anyone who reads the documents will find that the spirit of revolution is there, and, as D. W. Brogan has suggested, Jefferson or even Washington would be as out of place at a meeting of the Daughters of the American Revolution or the American Legion today as any old Bolshevik would be in the Kremlin.

Lord Acton knew what kind of revolutionaries the Founding Fathers were. His description of their deeds should cause today's superpatriots to think about who most exemplifies the original Founding Fathers in America today:

The story of the revolted colonies impresses us first and most distinctly as the supreme manifestation of the law of resistance, as the abstract revolution in its purest and most perfect shape. No people was so free as the insurgents; no government less oppressive than the government they overthrew. Those who deem Washington and Hamilton honest can apply the term to few European statesmen. Their example presents a thorn, not a cushion, and threatens all existing political forms, with the doubtful exception of the federal constitution of 1787. It teaches that men ought to be in arms even against a remote and constructive danger to their freedom; that even if the cloud is no bigger than a man's hand, it is their right and duty to stake the national existence, to sacrifice lives and fortunes, to cover the country with a lake of blood, to shatter crowns and sceptres and fling parliaments into the sea. On this principle of subversion they erected their commonwealth, and by its virtue lifted the world out of its orbit and assigned a new course to history. Here or nowhere we have the broken chain, the rejected past, precedent and statute superseded by unwritten law, sons wiser than their fathers, ideas rooted in the future, reason cutting as clean as Atropes.

In his 1971 State of the Union message, President Richard M. Nixon called for a New American Revolution. The President was careful to point out that he was talking about a "peaceful revolution," but one that is designed to accomplish what the first one never really did—namely, turning "power back to the people." Repeated references were made to the Founding Fathers meeting in Philadelphia, leaving us a legacy which "survives today as the oldest written constitution still in force in the world today."

Perhaps that observation held the clue to what President Nixon described as the "long, dark night of the American spirit," a phrase used to spell the mood of contemporary America. Ours is really the oldest written constitution still *to be enforced* in the world—and in the United States—today.

Rather than specifying a "peaceful revolution," decent-thinking Americans could not help but wish the President had instead urged a moral revolution. The term "peaceful" was chosen, of course, as a rejection of the revolutionary tactics of more militant factions in America, tactics learned from the Founding Fathers. In his State of the Union message, President Nixon spoke of cracking down on welfare cheaters as part of his New Revolution: "Let us stop helping those who are able to help themselves but refuse to do so." His words were loudly applauded by the members of Congress.

One could not help but wonder what response the President would have received had he talked about wiping out the tax frauds of big business, the financial waste by Congressional members themselves, or any of the other welfare benefits reserved for those who make their way into the higher income brackets. A moral revolution, which is more concerned with right and wrong than with revolutionary tactics, would certainly address itself to such issues.

"Now we must let our spirits soar again," the President told the joint session of Congress. "Now we are ready for the lift of a driving dream." The fact of the matter is that such a spirit and such a dream have been moving on the college campuses and in the streets of the United States for some time now. And the sad truth is that what the President encouraged in the rhetoric he employed in the halls of Congress, he has allowed to be jailed, shot, and suppressed elsewhere in the nation.

Much of President Nixon's State of the Union message was rhetorically in line with Father Dan Berrigan's open letter to Weathermen, for example. Father Dan said: "No principle is worth the sacrifice of a single human being. . . . We are something far different, we are teachers of the people who have come to a new vision of things. We struggle to embody that vision day after day. . . ." But Father Berrigan remained in jail for his driving dream, soaring spirit, pure vision, and beliefs.

President Nixon also reminded Congress that the American people will not "continue to tolerate the gap between promise and fulfillment in government." And of course he was right. Governmental promises, followed by governmental compromises, cannot help but lead to long, hot summers. So President Nixon may get his New American Revolution, but not on the terms he outlined.

1

Have there been any long, hot summers in Philadelphia since 1787? Have there been any long, hot summers in other American cities since 1787? Since 1887? Since 1967? What issues were debated during these later long, hot summers?

2

Do you think there will always be long, hot summers in the United States? If so, why?

3

George Washington once said, "Unhappy it is, though, that the once peaceful plains of America are either to be drenched with blood or inhabited by slaves." Write an essay telling if you think Washington's statement was really an either/or proposition.

LIBRARY
ALLEGANY COMMUNITY COLLEGE
Cumberland, Maryland

Lesson Two
Parties
Prevail

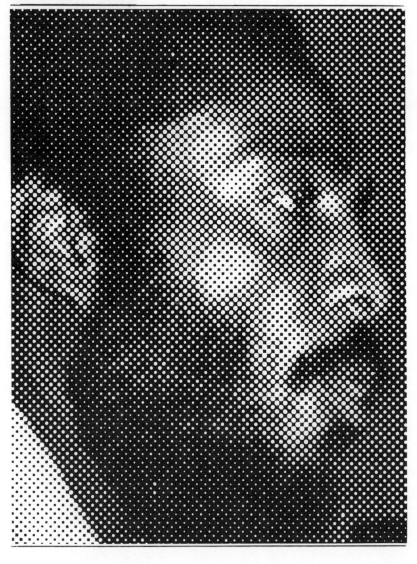

Let me begin this lesson with a warning to the student: it may be very, very confusing. The lesson seeks to explain how the United States moved from a situation where there were no political parties to the contemporary political scene where two parties dominate elections, leaving the voters with little real political choice. On top of that, we will see that the first party which was liberal in orientation, advocating more democratic principles throughout the land, was known as the Republican Party. Years passed, names changed, and today the Republican Party is viewed as the party more conservative in its orientation.

The other party in the two-party structure is the Democratic Party, supposedly more liberal in its outlook and political theory. In practice, the Democratic Party does not want to give the impression of being too liberal, thereby turning off a large number of voters; just as the Republicans do not want to give the impression of being too conservative, thereby turning off a large number of voters. The Republican Party tried going the conservative route in the national election of 1964, under the candidacy of Senator Barry Goldwater of Arizona, and was overwhelmingly defeated at the polls. A safer conservativism was adopted in 1968 under the candidacy of Richard M. Nixon, and the Republicans won the election. However, in states like New York the liberalism of the Democratic Party is distrusted enough for there to be a Liberal Party, and the conservativism of the Republican Party is distrusted enough for there to be a Conservative Party. In 1970 the Conservative Party elected a Senator from New York, James L. Buckley. When Senator Buckley got to the Senate, the Republicans wanted to claim him, thereby keeping the two-party system intact.

The situation is still more confusing when one considers that all Democrats claim to be republicans—that is, concerned with the preservation of the Republic as well as its advancement. And all Republicans claim to be democrats —that is, committed to the true ideals of democracy and operating in the best interests of all the people. So that today candidates wear party labels for identification more than anything else, much like convention delegates wear name tags. The name tag doesn't tell you much about an individual's beliefs, but it lets you know where he is from. Political parties are vehicles for winning elections and gaining control of government.

Feds in Control

From the days of the American Revolution, there were groupings, factions, caucuses, committees of correspondence, or whatever you choose to call them. The Revolution itself grew out of the activities of such groupings, linking sympathizers together from colony to colony. The Whigs or "Patriots" were those who looked with disfavor upon King and Royal Governors calling the shots for the colonies, and who strongly supported local self-government and colonial legislatures. The Tories were the "Toms" of the monarchy and usually sided with the King and the Governors. The Whigs won the Revolution, eliminated the opposition faction, and the leading Tories split to Canada or the Bahamas. Today Canada has become more of a haven for revolutionary spirits, while the Bahamas are the retreat of the wealthy, those more sympathetic toward preserving the status quo and, as we shall soon see, heirs of Alexander Hamilton.

But at the time of George Washington's election to the

Presidency, there were no political parties as such. Again, the debates at the Constitutional Convention had produced two groupings (or factions): the Federalists, basically merchants, landowners, and bankers, who supported the new Constitution; and the anti-Federalists, workers, farmers, and local politicians who feared the loss of state power and local self-government and thus looked with disfavor upon the new Constitution. George Washington was elected unanimously since he was the one man who had the respect and trust of Federalists and anti-Federalists alike, receiving all 69 votes of the first meeting of the electoral college (4 votes were not cast.) John Adams received 34 votes, the second highest number, and thus became the first Vice President.

The electoral-college system for electing President and Vice President, as originally drafted in the United States Constitution, was designed to preserve a partyless situation. Each state was to appoint a number of electors equal to the total number of Senators and Representatives in Congress to which the state was entitled, in a manner to be decided upon by the state legislatures individually. The electors would meet in their respective states and cast their ballots for two people, at least one of them being a resident of another state, and send the lists of names and the number of votes received to the government of the United States. Then the President of the Senate, in the presence of the Senate and the House of Representatives, would tabulate the votes. The candidate receiving the highest number of votes was the President-elect; the person receiving the second highest number of votes would be the Vice President-elect. If more than one candidate had a majority, or if there was a tie vote, the House of Representatives was to vote immediately and choose one of the candidates. If no candidate had a majority, the House of Representatives was to choose among the top five names on the list.

Thus the electoral college represented, as advocated by such Founding Fathers as Alexander Hamilton, an elite group that had complete freedom of choice in Presidential balloting, surveying the entire spectrum of potential leadership in the nation. Such an elitist approach kept the actual election of a President rather remote from the voters themselves.

The system held up through the elections of 1792 and even 1796. George Washington was persuaded to serve again in 1792, and, as usual, he was a sure winner. But the makings of party politics were beginning to take root, and John Adams was the target candidate. The real target, however, was Alexander Hamilton, who was now seen as a super-Federalist. Hamilton had the confidence of George Washington, and although Washington wanted to remain aloof from the parties and party politics, he was identified with the Federalist camp. Adams was accused of being "antidemocratic" and secretly a "monarchist" by the newly forming Republican party, and George Clinton was pushed as a Vice Presidential candidate against John Adams. Adams won by a vote of 77 to 50.

Thomas Jefferson and James Madison were the leading figures in formulating party opposition to the Federalists. Although Jefferson became the main figure, and the party's Presidential candidate, he was really a late recruit to the party, and James Madison was the one who first began to oppose Hamilton and Federalist policies. Hamilton was seen as hiding behind the mantle of George Washington, thereby getting his measures pushed through Congress and making it all but impossible for opponents to criticize him, since they would be accused of committing the unpardonable sin of criticizing George Washington. Norman Small described this technique in his dissertation, "Some Presidential Interpretations of the Presidency":

. . . by shielding his political maneuvres behind the cloak of the President's reputation, Hamilton not only carried out his program with little interference, but practically deprived his opponents of a means of protest; for the latter refused to risk popular condemnation by an attack which, though directed against the Secretary [Hamilton], would have unavoidably included the President. Thus proceeding boldly in pursuit of his policies Hamilton submitted reports to Congress, expounding in detail both the reason why and the manner in which the financial recommendations contained in the President's messages should be adopted, saw to it that party associates in accord with his opinions were appointed to committees deliberating on his measures, and finally when a doubt arose as to the fate of his program, rounded up his political adherents in order to secure a majority vote in favor of his bills. In fact the conduct of the Federalists in Congress was invariably predetermined by the decisions reached in their own secret party meetings at which Hamilton presided.

Not only did George Washington enjoy the enormous prestige he earned in the Revolutionary War, but he consciously tried to enshroud the new office of President with a formality and court etiquette worthy of the trappings of the King of England. Theodore Sedgwick wrote a letter in 1789 describing a dinner with George Washington: "Today I dined with the President and as usual the company was as grave as at a funeral. All the time at table the silence more nearly resembled the gravity of [illegible] worship than the cheerfulness of convivial meeting." In 1793 Thomas Jefferson recalled an observation that James Madison had made to him in 1790, showing that Madison had obviously been to some Presidential dinners too "that the satellites & sycophants which surrounded him [Washington] had wound up the ceremonials of government to a pitch of stateliness which nothing but his personal character could have supported, & which no character after him could ever maintain."

Madison was right, and a dinner recollection of Theodore Roosevelt shows how Presidential eating habits and ceremonies had changed:

When the dinner was announced, the mayor led me in—or to speak more accurately, tucked me under one arm and lifted me partially off the ground, so that I felt as if I looked like one of those limp dolls with dangling legs carried around by small children. . . . As soon as we got in the banquet hall and sat at the head of the table the mayor hammered lustily with the handle of his knife and announced, "Waiter, bring on the feed!" Then, in a spirit of pure kindliness he added, "Waiter, pull up the curtains and let the people see the President eat."

In spite of Washington's attempts at formality, sometimes poor old George couldn't quite pull it off. In his *Journal*, Senator William Maclay described a scene when members of Congress had an audience with President Washington:

The President took his reply out of his coat pocket. He had his spectacles in his jacket pocket, having his hat in his left hand and his paper in his right. He had too many objects for his hands. He shifted his hat between his forearm and the left side of his breast. But taking his spectacles from the case embarrassed him.

He got rid of this small distress by laying the spectacle case on the chimney piece. . . . Having adjusted his spectacles, which was not very easy considering the engagements of his hands, he read the reply with tolerable exactness and without much emotion.

Republican Reform

The party which Jefferson was to head was known by the name of Republicans. As mentioned earlier, it is really the forerunner of today's Democratic Party. But in the 1790s the term "democrat" had the same kind of negative connotations to many folks that the word "radical" has today. A person who was a "democrat" was in favor of mob rule and favored all the head-chopping going on during the French Revolution. So Jefferson would no more run as a "democrat" in 1796 or 1800 than Hubert Humphrey would run as a "radical" in 1968.

It seems to be a recurring theme throughout this primer, and throughout American political history, that money is a source of conflict: how to get it for the have-nots, and how to keep and increase it for the haves. So that first source of opposition to Hamilton and the Federalists was disagreement over his money policies.

Hamilton was interested in developing a plan to pay off the national debt. The Republican opposition was in complete agreement with that goal. The question was how to do it. Madison and others felt that any legislation had to make a distinction between moneyed speculators who had purchased securities from original landholders, usually at a fraction of their original value, and the original holders themselves, who most often were former soldiers in the

Revolution or people who had provided money and supplies when the chips were really down during the darkest days of the Revolutionary War.

There was popular support for the Republican point of view, as well as popular distrust from the common folks toward the Federalists. A farmer wrote in the *Pennsylvania Gazette* in 1790: "The farmers never were in half the danger of being ruined by the British government that they now are by their own." And the *Gazette* also spoke forcefully of the dangers of Hamilton's funding schemes: "Such injustice and oppression may be colored over with fine words, but there is a time coming when the pen of history will detect and expose the folly of the arguments in favor of the proposed funding system as well as its iniquity. . . . If the balance still due the army is paid them, it would spread money through every county and township of the United States, if paid to the speculator, all the cash of the United States would soon center in our cities and later in England and Holland."

But there was Congressional support for Hamilton's schemes which favored speculators, since most of the Congressmen were engaged in the speculation game themselves. Hamilton got his funding program, followed by the Assumption Act, which allowed the federal government to assume the debts incurred by the several states during the Revolution.

Thus the beginning of government control by the wealthy few and the establishment of New England in a favored position, since most of the wealth resided there. With the ball rolling well, Hamilton pushed through an excise tax, which again clobbered the Southern farmers and distillers. In New England only the distillers of West Indian molasses were affected. When Hamilton's "great beast," the people, rose up in Pennsylvania in opposition to the excise tax, Hamilton got his man George Washington to send in government troops. Though the government forces were commanded by Henry Lee, Alexander Hamilton went right along to see that the insurrection was dealt with correctly.

So the establishing of the privilege of the wealthy few at the expense of the many was among the earliest acts of American government. Hamilton's financial programs preceded the ratification of the Bill of Rights by a year, which should stand as a symbolic reminder of the relationship between money and civil liberties in this country. Summarizing Hamilton's career, Joseph Charles has written:

. . . Hamilton put his trust in the privileged classes and considered their interests as inseparable from those of society as a whole. He wanted a close collaboration between this country and England. He aimed at the closest possible union, even a high degree of consolidation, between the different parts of this country, and he wanted a powerful central government. . . . The economic program which he advanced furthered these aims in every respect. It made for the supremacy of the propertied classes; it involved as much consolidation and as great a centralization of power as would have been accepted at that time; and it brought in its train intimate commercial and diplomatic relations with Great Britain. . . .

Of course, Alexander Hamilton's infatuation with the financially blessed is understandable. After all, he was a poor boy from a Virgin Island slum who rose to become the first

Secretary of the Treasury. And in the terms of his first love and interest, Hamilton today enjoys an immortalization ten times that of George Washington. Washington, you will remember, is pictured on the lowly *one*-dollar bill.

The election of 1796 provided the first real contest for the Presidency. Party factions were clearly forming, and Washington, who always abhorred the idea of parties and insisted that he was *not* a Federalist, had said, "If I could not go to heaven but with a party, I would not go there at all." But he was a Federalist in everyone else's eyes, and so Washington refused to consider another term. Hamilton was still very much in the picture, and he favored the election of Thomas Pinckney of South Carolina, ostensibly the Federalist Vice Presidential candidate, over the incumbent Vice President, John Adams. So Hamilton hoped that electors in the South would withhold their votes from Adams, giving Pinckney the majority. Thomas Jefferson was the Presidential hopeful of the Republicans. The in-party bickering among the Federalists led to the unexpected result of Thomas Jefferson receiving the second highest number of votes and becoming Adams' Vice President. Adams polled 71 electoral college votes to Jefferson's 68.

So the people's representative, the democratic Republican, was just a heartbeat away from the Presidency, a reality so eloquently expressed most recently by Chicago's Mayor Richard Daley. Daley was advocating the Vice Presidential candidacy in 1972 of Milwaukee Mayor Henry Maier. Daley said that the cities needed a representative, and Maier would be a good one. And then, mused Mayor Daley, "with the help of God" we might get a city-oriented President. So, as I say, Thomas Jefferson was just a heartbeat away from the Presidency. But God didn't help Jefferson out. He had to win the Presidency later on his own.

Thomas Jefferson was confident that eventually the people would have a true representative in the office of President. Richard Hofstadter has summed up Jefferson's attitude:

Such, then, was Jefferson's view of the Federalists: a small faction creeping into the heart of the government under the mantle of Washington and the perverse guidance of Hamilton, addicted to false principles in politics, animated by a foreign loyalty, and given to conspiratorial schemes aiming at the consolidation of government and the return of the monarchy. It was a faction which, though enjoying certain temporary advantages, would ultimately lack the power to impose its will on the great mass of loyal republicans. Here Jefferson's optimism, as always, sustained him: before long the people through their faithful representatives would take over. And at that point it would be the duty of the Republican party to annihilate the opposition—not by harsh and repressive measures like the Sedition Act, but by the more gentle means of conciliation and absorption that were available to a principled majority party.

During the Adams-Jefferson administration a split began to occur in the Federalist Party. There were the High Federalists and the moderate Federalists. The High Federalists favored a war with France, and they tried to influence President Adams into moving the country in that direction. The Republicans feared that a war with France would bring with it the establishment of a military despotism in the United States. The Alien and Sedition Acts were an example of the kind of repressive regime that could be expected. In the long run, however, it was the moderate

Federalists, rather than the Republican Congressmen, who avoided war with France.

But the hawkish sentiment and the repressive acts of the Federalist administration gave considerable leverage to Jefferson's candidacy by the time the election of 1800 rolled around. The Federalist Congressional caucus met and decided upon Adams and Charles C. Pinckney as the two best men, while the Republican caucus picked Jefferson and Aaron Burr.

The Republicans prevailed over the Federalists, and when the electoral-college votes were counted, Jefferson and Burr were tied. Each had received the same number of votes, since electors could not state a single preference, but rather were required to indicate the *two* men they preferred. There were 73 Republican electors and 65 Federalist. Since all the Republicans voted a Jefferson-Burr ticket, the two were deadlocked at 73 votes, which threw the election into the House of Representatives.

It took thirty-six ballots and seven days of balloting for the House to finally settle upon Thomas Jefferson as the new President and Aaron Burr as the Vice President. Hamilton was strongly opposed to Burr, and favored Adams. But Burr outsmarted Hamilton, took the New York votes away from Adams, and gave them to Jefferson. (Four years later Hamilton used his influence to defeat Burr in his bid for the Governorship of New York. Burr accused Hamilton of publicly calling him a "despicable" person. A duel was fought seven days after Independence Day of 1804, and Burr shot and killed Hamilton. Thus ended Hamilton's last political debate.)

The ridiculous situation of the Jefferson-Burr tie led to the adoption of the Twelfth Amendment to the Constitution, ratified, significantly, the year of Hamilton's death. The adoption of the Twelfth Amendment was also the death of Hamilton's vision of a select assembly choosing the President. The amendment provided that electors would vote separately for President and Vice President, based on the recognition that parties existed, and that electors were merely acting as rubber stamps for the candidates of their party. So less than fifteen years after the Constitution was put into effect, a Constitution which never mentions the word "party" and was designed really to avoid their formation, it was now changed to recognize and accommodate the existing reality of parties in America. And party politics has dominated and directed the American scene ever since. Not only party politics, but *two*-party politics. Although there have been significant third-party attempts, none has displayed any real staying power.

The Democratic-Republicans dominated national elections for the next three decades (now that they were in power the word "Democratic" became respectable). Thomas Jefferson served two terms, followed by James Madison, who served another two. By the time Madison was succeeded by James Monroe, an "era of good feeling" was being touted throughout the land and it seemed for a while that the partyless ideal of the original Constitution had been realized.

By the election of 1828 a new wave of democracy was sweeping the land. More and more white folks were getting the right to vote, as old property requirements for voting were being dropped, and the new Western states were getting started. The Ohio constitution of 1802 gave the vote to almost all adult white men. And the constitutions of other Western states followed suit—Indiana (1816), Illinois (1818), down South in Alabama (1819), and the new Eastern state of Maine (1820). At the same time some of the original thirteen colonies were revising their constitutions, dropping the property requirement—Connecticut (1818), Massachusetts (1821), and New York (1821). Oddly enough, the property requirement as a voting qualification was slow to go in Virginia, the home state of democracy-loving Madison and Jefferson, and it was 1851 before the property requirement was abolished. But by 1828 about twice as many people could vote as could vote twenty years before.

Along with opening up the vote to more people, the right to choose members of the electoral college was being given to the voters themselves, at least indirectly. By 1828 only two states (South Carolina and Delaware) still had their delegates to the electoral college chosen by the state legislature. Thus the time was ripe for a President of the people, representing the new kind of voter, a man not of the aristocracy and proud of the fact that he was not literary and could not spell very good. Such a man was Andrew Jackson, the man who defeated the British in the Battle of New Orleans in 1815, who once said he had no respect for a man who could only think of one way to spell a word.

Jackson was elected President in 1828 as the candidate of the Democratic Party, a split having occurred within the Democratic-Republican ranks, and, democracy swinging full cycle, now the "Republican" was dropped from the party name. Jackson and his Vice President, John C. Calhoun, are considered the first ticket of today's Democratic Party.

Jackson just missed in the election of 1824, running independently. The electoral college failed to give any candidate a majority. Jackson was actually first with 99 and John Quincy Adams second with 84. So the voting went into the House of Representatives. There were twenty-four states at the time, so the winning candidate had to poll 13 votes. It all came down to one state, New York, and one man within the state delegation, General Stephen Van Rensselaer, the largest landowner in the Eastern states. He was a wishy-washy person who usually ended up agreeing with the last person he spoke to. The general had promised to stick with the New York clique controlled by Martin Van Buren, who was not an Adams man.

When the voting got tight, General Van Rensselaer was all shook up over the responsibility. "The election turns on my vote," he worried. "One vote will give Adams the majority. This is a responsibility I cannot bear. What shall I do?" One of Van Buren's men reassured him, and tried to calm him down. But just as the state delegations were ordered to poll their members, the general, seeking some reassurance from Heaven, dropped his head on the edge of his desk in a silent prayer for help from the Almighty. As he removed his hand from his eyes, his glance fell upon a discarded Adams ballot at his feet. Taking this coincidence as an answer to his prayer, the general picked up the ballot and dropped it into the box. Thus did John Quincy Adams become President of the United States in 1824.

It would take a while before the name Republican became entrenched in the American two-party system once again. Against the Democrats were tried the National Republican Party and the Anti-Masonic Party, which claimed that secret societies were dangerous to a republican government. Finally they all got together and came up with the name Whig, hoping to capture some of the aura of the American Revolution which might rub off at the polls. But the new Whigs were conservative, upper crust, in no way representing the revolutionary spirits of 1776. They were more in tune with the Tories. The Whigs remained on the scene until the party disintegrated in 1856, and placed Presidents in office in 1840 (William Henry Harrison and John Tyler) and in 1848 (Zachary Taylor).

In 1856 the Democrats were having trouble getting their Northern and Southern wings together, and the passage of the Kansas-Nebraska Act led to the formation of the Republican Party. The Democrats got through the election with James Buchanan. But in 1860 the Democrats were so badly split up that they failed to nominate a candidate after fifty-seven ballots at the convention in Charleston, reassembled in Baltimore the following month, and finally chose Stephen Douglas of Illinois. The Republicans chose another Illinois man, Abraham Lincoln, and the party was running on the moral issue of slavery, promising to preserve freedom in the territories. Lincoln won the election handily and South Carolina promptly seceded from the Union.

Thus our present two parties prevailed, even as the Union was falling apart, and we've been electing Republicans and Democrats to the highest office in the land for more than a hundred years. And we have been, and still are, electing them by the electoral-college method, as amended by the

Twelfth Amendment. Which means, of course, that the people of the United States do not really elect their President. Though the unit rule applies to all delegates to the electoral college in every state except Maine, according to the Constitution, the electors still maintain their Constitutionally guaranteed independence. The unit rule means that in each state the party candidates for President and Vice President who receive the highest number of votes—whether the margin is one vote or a millon—are awarded all of the state's electoral-college votes.

Thus a Presidential candidate can receive the plurality of the total number of votes cast in the nation and still lose the election. A winning candidate can actually carry only eleven states, those with the largest number of electoral-college votes, and win the election. Fifteen times in our nation's history Presidents were elected who did not receive a majority of the popular vote, and three Presidents—John Quincy Adams, Rutherford B. Hayes, and Benjamin Harrison—actually received fewer votes than their opponents. Andrew Jackson in 1824 received 43.13 percent of the popular vote to Adams' 30.54; Hayes received 48.04 percent to Samuel J. Tilden's 50.99; and Harrison received 47.86 percent to Grover Cleveland's 48.66.

The other Presidents who snuck into office without obtaining a majority of the national popular vote include some of the luminaries of American hero worship: James Polk (49.56), Zachary Taylor (47.35), James Buchanan (45.63), Abraham Lincoln in the 1860 election (39.79), James A. Garfield (48.32), Grover Cleveland in the 1884 election (48.53) and in the 1892 election (46.04), Woodrow Wilson (41.85 in 1912 and 49.26 in 1916), Harry S.

Truman (49.51), John F. Kennedy (49.71), and Richard M. Nixon in the 1968 election (43.16).

The Hayes-Tilden election, which caused the Democrats to feel the election had been stolen (see platform statement in Lesson Five), resulted in a dispute over 19 electoral votes of South Carolina, Florida, and Louisiana. The dispute went on for months until finally Congress appointed an electoral commission to determine the valid returns. The commission consisted of five Senators, five Representatives, and five justices of the Supreme Court (eight Republicans and seven Democrats). The commissioners all voted along strict party lines and Hayes was awarded the Presidency.

Over a century ago a former United States Senator, Thomas Hart Benton, summed up the fallacy in the electoral-college method of selecting a President and the injustice represented in not truly counting the popular vote. Said Benton: "To lose their votes is the fate of all minorities, and it is their duty to submit; but this is not a case of votes lost, but of votes taken away, added to those of the majority and given to a person to whom the minority is opposed."

And Henry Cabot Lodge suggested that the electoral college was to the body politic what the appendix is to the human body. Said Lodge: "While it does no good and ordinarily causes no trouble, it continually exposes the body to the danger of political peritonitis."

So the ongoing lesson of the electoral-college system is that when you vote for a President and Vice President, your personal vote counts only if the candidate you choose happens to receive the majority vote in your state. And your candidate can win only if he or she also receives the majority vote in enough other states to receive a winner-take-all majority in the electoral college. The total number of like-minded voters throughout the nation really has no meaning at all. It's part of what we call the "democratic process."

Yassuh, Boss

The emergence of two-party politics gave rise to a phenomenon with which I am quite familiar personally, since my adopted hometown is Chicago, the political machine. In most places in the country, voting is looked upon as a right and a duty, but in Chicago it's a *sport*. In Chicago not only *your* vote counts, but all kinds of other votes—kids, dead folks, and so on. After a recent election in Chicago the Republicans found that thousands of votes had been recorded of folks who had been dead for years. Chicago is the only place in the United States where, after the election is over and they talk about the "spook" vote, they're not talking about us black folks. In Chicago it is very hard *not* to qualify to vote. Even death is not a prohibitive factor, and for a Republican candidate to accuse the Democrats of talking about "dead issues" just might be pointing a finger at the largest constituency!

"Machine" comes from the Latin word *machina,* which means "device" or "trick." Webster's dictionary offers an archaic definition which is more contemporary in places like Chicago: "handiwork of a divine or supernatural power." But the standard definition of "machine" is "any device consisting of two or more resistant, relatively constrained parts which may serve to transmit and modify force and motion so as to do some desired kind of work." That definition is perfect. The political machine recognizes the existence of "two [or more] resistant" parties which are "relatively constrained" (subject to public opinion, the law, or rebellion in the streets if their actions get too outrageous), and is designed to get out the vote for the candidates the machine supports.

The "desired kind of work" the political machine is constructed to perform is political control, which means "transmitting and modifying force and motion" so as to control nominations and elections. Since the fuel for the political machine is people and their votes, the machines naturally took root in the big cities to which people were immigrating in large numbers. Such immigrants, as D. W. Brogan has described, had "nothing to lose but their chains and little to sell but their votes." Thus the political machine moved in to perform much-needed services for new immigrants in strange surroundings, at the same time organizing newly enfranchised voters.

Political machines served as charitable institutions, providing coal, clothes, and food to families in difficulty; they helped in arranging naturalization; they doled out minor jobs and arranged for licenses; they controlled police departments and thereby could adjust the degrees of law enforcement; and they provided entertainment in the form of parades and outings, thereby completing the total package of provision from bread to circuses.

Our old friend Aaron Burr, sharpshooter from New York, is the man who started the machine as a fixed political reality. Under his leadership, the most famous of all machines, Tammany Hall, took root on Manhattan Island in the nation's largest city. New York has reformed and re-reformed ever since.

Back in 1789 Tammany Hall began as a patriotic society whose patron was St. Tammany, a Delaware chief of whom it was said in the eloquence of the era: "There was no force, no violence, in his measures, but general consent and concurrence of sentiment conferred on him all the authority he possessed. . . . If he obtained influence, that influence was conferred on him by the citizens, and they trusted him with power because they were confident he would not abuse it."

The Society of St. Tammany had branches in Philadelphia, Washington, and Ohio, but only the New York "Wigwam" endured. Under Burr's leadership, it became an organization of the Republicans, and it remained attached to the party which is really the heir of the Republicans, namely the Democrats. And it was Burr's use of the Tammany machine which gave rise to some of Alexander Hamilton's most critical remarks. Hamilton saw machine politics as the ultimate in political corruption. He called attention to that conviction in quite unguarded terms. And, as we have seen, he was shot. So we might say that the fate of Alexander Hamilton provides the basic tenet of machine operation which remains true to this day: Speak out against the machine and you are sure to be dealt with.

Aaron Burr was really the first modern politician, if not big-city boss. He ran things from his law office, developed popular tickets of candidates, settled internal party disputes, and set up a finance committee which would be a pretty good model today. Without the use of computers, Burr made a card file of all the voters in the city. Each card listed the voter's political history, his views, his habits, his temperament, his health, and how easy or hard it would be to get him to the polls. So the computerized voter profiles and opinion polls today would not be "new" politics for Aaron Burr.

An interesting aside to this lesson is that Tammany Hall was indirectly responsible for the now famous emblems used to depict the Democratic and Republican parties. After the Civil War, cartoonist Thomas Nast, of *Harper's Weekly,* pictured the elephant to portray the Republicans, the donkey to portray the Democrats, and the tiger to portray Tammany Hall. The tiger had been the emblem of the volunteer fire department to which Boss Tweed of Tammany Hall belonged. It was seen by Nast to be a fitting symbol to depict the viciousness of Tammany Hall toward its prey, the people of New York City. All three symbols stuck.

George Washington Plunkitt, a ward boss of Tammany Hall at the turn of the century whose political "philosophy" was made famous by journalist William L. Riordon in 1905 in his book *Plunkitt of Tammany Hall,* gave the answer to those ideological heirs of Alexander Hamilton who see Machine politics as corrupt:

Everybody is talkin' these days about Tammany men growin' rich on graft, but nobody thinks of drawin' the distinction between honest graft and dishonest graft. There's all the difference in the world between the two. Yes, many of our men have grown rich in politics. I have myself. I've made a big fortune out of the game, and I'm getting richer every day, but I've not gone in for dishonest graft—blackmailin' gamblers, saloonkeepers, disorderly people, etc.—and neither has any of the men who have made big fortunes in politics.

There's an honest graft, and I'm an example of how it works.

I might sum up the whole thing by sayin': "I seen my opportunities and I took 'em."

Just let me explain by examples. My party's in power in the city, and it's goin' to undertake a lot of public improvements. Well, I'm tipped off, say, that they're going to lay out a new park at a certain place.

I see my opportunity and I take it. I go to that place and I buy up all the land I can in the neighborhood. Then the board of this or that makes its plan public, and there is a rush to get my land, which nobody cared particular for before.

Ain't it perfectly honest to charge a good price and make a profit on my investment and foresight? Of course, it is. Well, that's honest graft.

Some six decades later another journalist, Mike Royko, in his book *Boss: Richard J. Daley of Chicago,* was describing the Tammany philosophy translated to Chicago:

Ward bosses are men of ambition, so when they aren't busy with politics or their outside professions, they are on the alert for "deals." At any given moment, a group of them, and their followers, are either planning a deal, hatching a deal, or looking for a deal.

Assessor Cullerton and a circle of his friends have gone in for buying up stretches of exurban land for golf courses, resorts, and the like. Others hold interests in racetracks, which depend on political goodwill for additional racing dates.

The city's dramatic physical redevelopment has been a boon to the political world as well as the private investors. There are so many deals involving ranking members of the Machine that it has been suggested that the city slogan be changed from *Urbs In Horto,* which means "City in a Garden," to *Ubi Est Mea,* which means "Where's mine?"

Of course, Chicago has a long history of machine corruption. In 1903, in his *Shame of the Cities,* Lincoln Steffens described Chicago as: "First in violence, deepest in dirt, lawless, unlovely, ill-smelling, irreverent, news; an overgrown gawk of a—village, the 'tough' among cities, a spectacle for the nation."

Perhaps Steffens was familiar with the backgrounds of the delegates to the 1896 Cook County Convention held in Chicago. Robert White reported in his book *American Government: Democracy at Work* that 644 out of 723 delegates to that particular convention, or 89 percent, were ex-convicts (130), saloonkeepers (265), persons who had been on trial for murder (17), of no occupation (71), political employees (148), or vagrants, ex-prizefighters, or gamblers (13)!

Of course, the party in power makes little difference in Chicago history. Mike Royko was describing the current Democratic machine, and the Democrats were also in power when Steffens described Chicago. But in 1927, when Republican Mayor William Hale Thompson was running for his last term, Al Capone was operating full-swing, and the Chicago Crime Commission estimated that Capone and other gangsters put more than $300,000 in the Thompson campaign. That election day was described as rather quiet by authors Lloyd Wendt and Herman Kogan:

In the early hours two Democratic precinct clubs on the North Side were bombed, two election judges were kidnapped and beaten, half a dozen voters were driven from the polls by pistol-waving thugs and five shots were fired into a West Side polling booth. Little violence occurred during the rest of the day, with police squads cruising the city, machine guns in their laps and tear bombs in their pockets.

The 1968 election in Chicago was an interesting example of machine over party. Alderman Joe Burke of the 14th Ward had died, and John Patrick Tully, who had lived most of his life in that ward, decided to run for the post. He was a Democrat, but the machine picked Edward Burke, son of the departed alderman, as the candidate. So Tully ran as an independent.

William H. Rentschler in his column, "Viewpoint from Mid-America," dated March 22, 1969, reported how the machine dealt with opposition even within its own party ranks. Lugs were removed from the front wheels of a car driven by a Tully volunteer. Tully volunteers distributing posters and literature were pelted with bricks from the top of a building plastered with Burke posters. A student teacher passing out Tully literature was chased by a car, two men got out, grabbed her, took away her brochures, and ordered her to stop what she was doing. The lady said one of the men was Candidate Burke. A hardware-store owner put up a Tully sign and immediately got threatening phone calls saying, "Take down that sign or we'll close your store for good."

All big cities have had their machines and bosses. In 1905 John F. Kennedy's grandfather "Honey Fitz" Fitzgerald went after the mayorship of Boston. A colorful figure, known for his boutonnière, his Irish tenor, and his less than rigorous political ethics, "Honey Fitz" went Sweet Adelining down the campaign trail. Louis D. Brandeis, who later became a distinguished Supreme Court justice and the first Jew nominated to the Court, called JFK's granddaddy "one of the worst types" of machine politicians. And Brandeis fought unsuccessfully to keep him out of City Hall.

The Tom Pendergast machine in Kansas City, operating in the late 1930s, was a good example of machine devices and tricks. A crusading district attorney named Maurice M. Milligan took after the corrupt organization and ended up hauling nearly three hundred members of the Pendergast machine into federal court.

What had happened in Kansas City allowing the machine to win elections year after year? One audit showed that $68 million had been diverted from the city funds. The number of persons on the city payrolls was double the number of actual workers. City and county employees had from two to eight false names on the voter registration rolls under which they could vote, and vote, and vote . . . Vacant lots were listed as residences for thousands of voters. Voter registration in many precincts was larger than the population of the precinct. Small houses accounted for the place of residence for a hundred or more voters. The total registration of voters in Kansas City exceeded the city population by 200,000.

Students interested in seeing a contemporary political machine in operation should plan a visit to Chicago on election day, or St. Patrick's Day, or even a side trip to the Illinois State Fair, where they will witness scenes so graphically described by Mike Royko:

On certain special occasions, it is possible to see much of the Machine's patronage army assembled and marching. The annual St. Patrick's Day parade down State Street, with Daley leading the way, is a display of might that knots the stomachs of Republicans. An even more remarkable display of patronage power is seen at the State Fair, when on "Democrat Day" thousands of city workers are loaded into buses, trains, and cars which converge on the fairgrounds outside Springfield. The highlight of the fair is when Daley proudly hoofs down the middle of the grounds' dusty racetrack in ninety-degree heat with thousands of his sweating but devoted workers tramping behind him, wearing old-fashioned straw hats and derbies. The Illinois attorney general's staff of lawyers once thrilled the rustics with a crack manual of arms performance, using Daley placards instead of rifles.

So, in conclusion, the prevalence of the two-party system has produced two distinctly contradictory political institutions: the electoral college (in its present form), in which the vote of the individual voter does not really count, and the machine, in which the vote of the individual voter (if it is the vote the machine advocates) is likely to count over and over again.

Presidents and Their Parties

President	Party	Presidential Terms
1. George Washington	Partyless though identified with Federalist	April 30, 1789– March 3, 1793 March 4, 1793– March 3, 1797
2. John Adams	Federalist	March 4, 1797– March 3, 1801
3. Thomas Jefferson	Republican (Democratic)	March 4, 1801– March 3, 1805 March 4, 1805– March 3, 1809
4. James Madison	Republican (Democratic)	March 4, 1809– March 3, 1813 March 4, 1813– March 3, 1817
5. James Monroe	Republican (Democratic)	March 4, 1817– March 3, 1821 March 4, 1821– March 3, 1825
6. John Quincy Adams	Republican (Democratic)	March 4, 1825– March 3, 1829
7. Andrew Jackson	Democratic	March 4, 1829– March 3, 1833 March 4, 1833– March 3, 1837
8. Martin Van Buren	Democratic	March 4, 1837– March 3, 1841
9. William Henry Harrison	Whig	March 4, 1841– April 4, 1841
10. John Tyler	Whig	April 6, 1841– March 3, 1845
11. James K. Polk	Democratic	March 4, 1845– March 3, 1849
12. Zachary Taylor	Whig	March 4, 1849– July 9, 1850
13. Millard Fillmore	Whig	July 10, 1850– March 3, 1853

Presidents and Their Parties

President	Party	Presidential Terms
14. Franklin Pierce	Democratic	March 4, 1853–March 3, 1857
15. James Buchanan	Democratic	March 4, 1857–March 3, 1861
16. Abraham Lincoln	Republican	March 4, 1861–March 3, 1865 March 4, 1865–April 15, 1865
17. Andrew Johnson	Republican	April 15, 1865–March 3, 1869
18. Ulysses S. Grant	Republican	March 4, 1869–March 3, 1873 March 4, 1873–March 3, 1877
19. Rutherford B. Hayes	Republican	March 4, 1877–March 3, 1881
20. James A. Garfield	Republican	March 4, 1881–Sept. 19, 1881
21. Chester A. Arthur	Republican	Sept. 20, 1881–March 3, 1885
22. Grover Cleveland	Democratic	March 4, 1885–March 3, 1889
23. Benjamin Harrison	Republican	March 4, 1889–March 3, 1893
24. Grover Cleveland	Democratic	March 4, 1893–March 3, 1897
25. William McKinley	Republican	March 4, 1897–March 3, 1901 March 4, 1901–Sept. 14, 1901
26. Theodore Roosevelt	Republican	Sept. 14, 1901–March 3, 1905 March 4, 1905–March 3, 1909
27. William Howard Taft	Republican	March 4, 1909–March 3, 1913

Presidents and Their Parties

President	Party	Presidential Terms
28. Woodrow Wilson	Democratic	March 4, 1913–March 3, 1917 March 4, 1917–March 3, 1921
29. Warren G. Harding	Republican	March 4, 1921–Aug. 2, 1923
30. Calvin Coolidge	Republican	Aug. 3, 1923–March 3, 1925 March 4, 1925–March 3, 1929
31. Herbert Hoover	Republican	March 4, 1929–March 3, 1933
32. Franklin D. Roosevelt	Democratic	March 4, 1933–Jan. 20, 1937 Jan. 20, 1937–Jan. 20, 1941 Jan. 20, 1941–Jan. 20, 1945 Jan. 20, 1945–April 12, 1945
33. Harry S. Truman	Democratic	April 12, 1945–Jan. 20, 1949 Jan. 20, 1949–Jan. 20, 1953
34. Dwight D. Eisenhower	Republican	Jan. 20, 1953–Jan. 20, 1957 Jan. 20, 1957–Jan. 20, 1961
35. John F. Kennedy	Democratic	Jan. 20, 1961–Nov. 22, 1963
36. Lyndon B. Johnson	Democratic	Nov. 22, 1963–Jan. 20, 1965 Jan. 20, 1965–Jan. 20, 1969
37. Richard M. Nixon	Republican	Jan. 20, 1969–

1

Would you like to be invited to a political party?

2

Would George Washington like to be invited to a political party? Would John Adams? Would Alexander Hamilton? Would Thomas Jefferson? Why or why not?

3

In an essay of five words or less, state clearly the differences between the Democratic and Republican parties today.

Lesson Three
The Primary
Objective

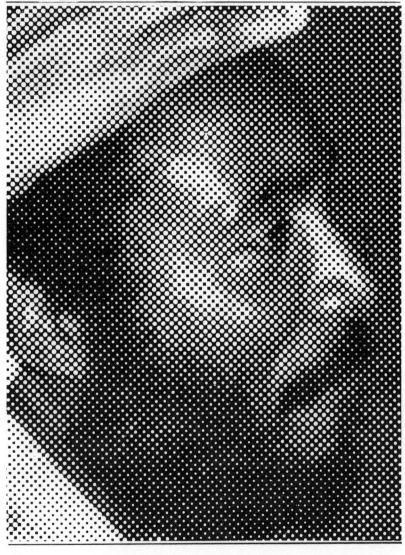

The primary objective of a political party is to win an election, and the objective of the primary is to select the candidate who will win for the party. Both primary elections and national conventions are products of the two-party system and have no mention or precedence in the United States Constitution, since the Constitution neither favored nor intended the growth of parties. But as we have seen in the last lesson, parties *did* prevail, and with them other institutions to make them function.

In the earliest days of party formation, nomination of Presidential and Vice Presidential candidates was handled by "Congressional caucuses," members of Congress who sympathized with a particular party drawing aside to select the candidates. From 1800 to 1824 there was basically uncontested apostolic succession to the Presidency, the gentlemen from Virginia known as the Virginia Dynasty, two terms for Jefferson, two terms for Madison, and two terms for James Monroe. With the election of 1824 the common folks began to want their representative in the form of Andrew Jackson. And emerging party leaders out in the boondocks, who were not members of Congress, also wanted to have a say in who would be the Presidential candidate. The Republican (Democratic) Congressional caucus really messed up with such elements by failing to nominate Andy Jackson in the 1824 election. Jackson had to run on his own and, as we have seen, almost made it (but for a prayer).

The Republican (Democratic) caucus tried to remedy their mistake in 1828 by nominating Jackson, but the damage was already done and the stage was set for the development of national party conventions and the further development of primary elections. By the time the 1832 national elections rolled around, the major parties were holding national conventions.

A form of primaries had already taken root, again because party politics had become a reality. The growth of cities meant the growth of politics, politics of the Burr-type machine orientation. Folks in the cities were close at hand. They were relatively easy to organize, could be called together for meetings rather quickly, could meet candidates face to face, hear debates, and discuss issues, and parades and demonstrations could be organized. But in the rural areas news traveled slower, it was harder for people to get together, and a different brand of political participation was developed.

Drawing up party tickets of candidates was done in state conventions. Delegates to these conventions were chosen by a meeting of party members. Once the delegates were chosen, the stage was set for the state conventions. By the late 1820s and 1830s state party conventions were being held all over the country. And especially in the rural areas they were big events. With no radio, television, movies, or the like, the state convention was the best entertainment going. It was like a church picnic and a state fair all rolled up into one. Farmers had an excuse to go to the big city, and politics became the delight of all.

Of course, as party politics thrived, party organizations grew. The primary objective of each major party became more and more institutionalized. A look at the organizational structure of today's two major parties shows how thoroughly party politics dug into the national body and all its appendages. At the head of the party are a national committee and a national chairman, usually chosen at the national convention. The national chairman is actually named by the Presidential nominee.

Meanwhile, down in the states there are state central committees, state chairmen, and various subcommittees and offices. Then there are county committees and central committees in large cities. Cities are broken down into wards and precincts, so that city central committees are usually composed of the chairmen of ward committees, or else include all ward and precinct committeemen. At the base of the party organization is the precinct leader, captain, or committeeman, as the role is variously called. And at the very bottom of the party organization, of course, is the voter. The success of the total structure is based on what the voter says at the polls, but the structure itself is designed to get the voter to say what the party needs and wants.

There is no direct line of authority which runs down from the national committee to the local precincts, or which flows from the base back on up to the top. Thus, in United States politics, whatever real dispute and opposition exists at all exists internally within the party structures. And in most states a voter must be a party member to participate in primary elections. The voter declares party allegiance and then votes for candidates representing that party. The independent voter, then, is structurally excluded from the election process until the final elections, when party candidates have already been chosen. At best the independent voter has the right to choose between party members' earlier choices.

Primary elections, then, are old institutions in most American states—that is, elections to choose the delegates who will then choose the candidates. Direct primary elections,

elections where the voters themselves vote for the candidates who will represent the party in the general election, did not take root until the beginning of the twentieth century.

Today there are basically two types of primary election: the closed primary and the open primary. The closed type is the most common. Voters must declare their party and, in most cases, show that they are registered under that party label. Then the voter is free to choose between candidates competing for nomination in the later general election under the party to which they belong. In the open primary the voter can decide to vote for candidates in whatever party he or she chooses. The voter still, of course, must stick to voting among candidates of one party. The state of Washington offers a variation of the open primary where the voter may choose between candidates of one party for a particular office and then cross over and choose between candidates of another party for another office.

Because of the limitations on choice, and the dominance of the party system in primary elections, voter turnout is usually low, frequently falling to about a third of those eligible to vote. And in most cases voters are merely confirming the choice of party leaders and party financial backing, though occasionally a candidate can come up with the money, personality, and use of the media to buck the regular party choice in the primary.

In most cases the candidate who gets the greatest number of votes is the party nominee in the general election. In eleven Southern and border states, where the Democrats have dominated for over a century, a majority is required. If no candidate receives a clear majority during the first primary election, a second primary or runoff election is held to choose between the two candidates who received the largest pluralities.

All of the above is merely a detailed aside to the crucial reality that the primary objective is to maintain the two-party tradition, and primaries are merely a way of deciding which candidates will represent the major parties. Those who fought for the direct-primary system early in this century saw it as a way of reforming, if not destroying, the party system (at least the party system as it had grown over a hundred years). Governor "Fighting Bob" La Follette in Wisconsin got the ball rolling by getting his legislature to adopt the direct-primary system in 1903.

What the appearance of the direct primaries did was to make the primary elections the real contest, particularly in those states where one political party held overwhelming dominance. Even in states where neither the Democratic nor the Republican party can claim a sure victory, the primaries provide the really hot contests, and the general elections basically boil down to choosing between the two-party candidates who have made it through the primaries. Thus, by focusing on struggles within the parties, the direct primaries served to allay possible other party movements which would break up the dominance of the two-party system. Rather than reforming the two-party system, direct primaries rejuvenated it.

All of which brings us to the Presidential primaries. Presidential candidates of the two major parties are still chosen by delegates to the national convention. In 1910 the direct-primary concept was first extended into national politics. Oregon adopted a plan for "Presidential preference primaries." The people of the state expressed their choice of the man they wanted to see nominated by their party delegates. By 1912 a dozen states had adopted the system.

At one time or another, twenty-four states have used Presidential preference primaries to elect delegates to the national party conventions. By 1968 the number had been reduced to fifteen and the District of Columbia. The states still using the primary method of selecting delegates to the party convention are California, Florida, Illinois, Indiana, Massachusetts, Nebraska, New Hampshire, New Jersey, Ohio, Oregon, Pennsylvania, South Dakota, West Virginia, and Wisconsin. In Alabama the system is used only by the Democrats. States that have tried the system and then abandoned it through the years are Georgia (Democrats), as well as the states of Iowa, Michigan, Minnesota, Montana, New York, North Carolina, North Dakota, and Vermont.

But it is very rare that Presidential preference primaries are actually a determining factor in the choices finally made in the national party conventions. At best, a primary gives a candidate who chooses to enter it a kind of exposure and test of the public reaction which might influence delegates at the convention. It was good, for example, for Richard Nixon in 1968 to enter the primaries and show that not everyone thought he was a total loser (since he had lost one bid for the Presidency and a later bid for the Governorship of California). For the most part, the big-city bosses and the party politicos who control the conventions keep their eyes on primary results to see if a hand-chosen candidate does really have appeal. Such was the case with John F. Kennedy in 1960, when he came through the West Virginia primary and convinced the party bigwigs that folks *would* accept a Roman Catholic for President.

But the fact remains that even if a candidate wins a Presidential primary, delegates are not bound to cast their ballots for him when the voting gets rough at the convention. What happens there we will see in the next lesson. So Presidential hopefuls are accustomed to gather in New Hampshire, the most significant of all Presidential primaries. In 1971 a Republican hopeful who, having defeated Shirley Temple, was encouraged to try to unseat President Nixon said he will be found "where the fish are," and that is understandable, since he, like the trout, was swimming upstream. At the same time five Democratic hopefuls surveyed the territory, quoting the incumbent President's rhetoric of three years before and saying, "I told you so."

New Hampshire, you see, enjoys the status of being the first Presidential primary to record the emerging national sentiment. Primaries in New Hampshire have always been held in March. During the 1972 Presidential election year they had to move the date up from March 14 to March 7 because Florida had a primary coming on March 14. It is important to New Hampshire to be the first state on record. Probably New Hampshire feels a special obligation because it was the state whose ratification made the Constitution official.

At least one New Hampshire party official felt that 1972 would be the end of the New Hampshire primary. So many Democrats were in the running that the New Hampshire vote would not leave a clear impression, and the returns from Florida would be more important than the vote in New Hampshire.

He needn't have worried, of course. A candidate could sweep all the Presidential primaries and it wouldn't mean anything when the convention delegates sat down to play. Not unless the candidate was wise enough to have already made his peace with the convention controllers.

Tuning in on voter sentiment is always nice, but the primary objective is getting that nomination.

1

True or False: "The direct primary election is the best assurance the voters have that they are truly selecting the men and women who will represent them in government"?

2

What are closed primaries? What are open primaries? What is a closed society? What is an open society? How do all of these compare?

3

Have you ever known an open society? Give examples.

Lesson Four
Politics
on Parade

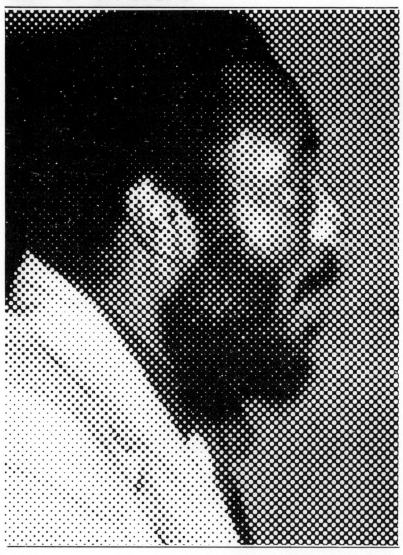

The political parade is best observed during the Presidential election year. National party conventions portray American politics inside and out. *Inside* the convention hall will be found balloons, placards, costumes, live entertainment, bands, loud demonstrations, muffled obscenities, and a more dignified form of obscenity, political oratory. *Outside* the convention hall may be found demonstrations of a different sort, peace officers ready to club participants in the demonstrations and unleash tear-gas canisters which will pollute the convention site for blocks around, occasional street rebellions which may inspire gunfire—in short, everything you would expect to happen when voters are denied the right to choose their President.

The election of 1840 really got the American political parade under way. The incumbent Democratic President, Martin Van Buren, was renominated to carry the banner of his party. The Whigs chose the military hero, winner of the Battle of Tippecanoe against the Shawnees, William Henry Harrison. Oddly enough, the candidate of the old party of the common man, Andrew Jackson, was now portrayed as an aristocrat out of touch with the common folks, while the Whig candidate won the honor of being the people's real representative. Van Buren, the dignified New York lawyer, given to fancy clothes and expensive tastes, was the delight of opposition political cartoonists. He was pictured as sitting at an expensively decorated table drinking champagne from a crystal goblet. An anti-Harrison newspaper in Baltimore countered the description, unintentionally giving the Whigs their campaign tactic. The paper suggested that Harrison really didn't want to be President at all, but would rather sit in his log cabin with a barrel of hard cider to get drunk on.

The Whig battle cry: Hurrah for the log cabin and hard cider! That's where common folks live and what they drink. The preference for both only indicated that Harrison was the real representative of the common man. And such common tastes were no disgrace.

So the Whigs held a big rally in Baltimore on May 4, 1840. They started out by firing a cannon. With 25,000 people marching and another 75,000 watching, eight log-cabin floats moved along in procession pulled by horses. Out of one log-cabin chimney puffed a cloud of smoke, supposedly indicating that a squirrel was roasting inside, and in front of the cabin door several Harrison supporters drank hard cider from a barrel. Banners waved and campaign buttons were worn. The slogan was born: "Tippecanoe and Tyler Too!"—in honor of Harrison's greatest victory and his Vice Presidential runningmate, John Tyler. Another, more direct slogan against the Democratic opponent was coined: "Little Van, the Used-Up Man."

The theme of the Baltimore rally was to show that a ball was rolling and picking up momentum in favor of Harrison. In the parade, men pushed balls taller than themselves. Another group arrived at the rally pushing an enormous ball they had pushed for over a hundred miles—all the way from Allegheny County in far western Maryland. The ingredients for today's political parades were all there in 1840—gunshot, balloons, campaign buttons, slogans, music, booze, and *lies*. Actually, Harrison was born of an old well-to-do Virginia family who lived in a mansion at the time. But his supporters soon found a log cabin that he was supposed to have been born in.

Harrison won overwhelmingly, but the campaign effort was too much for him. One month later he was dead of pneumonia. The campaign was prophetic. Indeed the country got Tippecanoe—and Tyler too!

National nominating conventions were first held in 1832. Baltimore quickly became the favorite convention site. New American-style hotels were beginning to appear throughout the land, called "Palaces of the Public," and one of the finest, Barnum's City Hotel, an elegant six-story building with two hundred apartments, was located in Baltimore. Until 1856 nominating conventions were held in that city, with two exceptions: the Whig Party gathered in Harrisburg, Pennsylvania, in 1840, and at Philadelphia in 1848. After 1856 Baltimore was honored only three times with national conventions: the Republicans in 1864, and the Democrats in 1872 and 1912. (The Democrats reconvened in Baltimore in 1860, but Charleston was the convention site.)

Beginning in 1860, Chicago became the favorite gathering place for delegates to the national party conventions. Since that date Chicago has hosted nominating conventions twenty-four times. One can only speculate concerning the attraction of Chicago for political parties. First of all, party leaders know what they are up to at party conventions, and the very name "Chicago" is most descriptive of their endeavors. Chicago was originally a trading post on the shores of Lake Michigan which the Indians called *Es-chi-ka-gou,* or "place of bad smells." Chicago returned to its historical roots most dramatically during the 1968 Democratic convention as the tear gas used to dispel peace demonstrators left a nauseating aroma hanging over the town.

Also, even though Chicago is called a "city," it has all the elements of a town. It is really a big town. It's a town where one can have fun, hence the expression "There'll be a hot time in the old town tonight." But that jingle refers to a very embarrassing moment in Chicago history when a cow kicked over a lantern and burned the town down. But Chicago has gotten its revenge. Since the cow burned the town down, Chicago has become the meat-packing center of the country. It's not to make money, really, it's to get back at that cow's cousins.

Chicago's machine politics are also good for providing exciting conventions. The machine can use little tricks that would be hard to pull off in any other city. During the 1940 Democratic convention the anti-third-term forces who were opposed to Franklin D. Roosevelt's candidacy were done in by a cunning trick of Chicago's strong third-term mayor, Edward J. "Ed" Kelly. He put the superintendent of sewers in a small basement room with a secret microphone and instructed him to shout "We want Roosevelt" and "America needs Roosevelt" at appropriate times. A faulty public-address system magnified the shouts to inhuman proportions, but the convention was amused and delighted, and Roosevelt got the nomination.

Chicago is always a good place for packing galleries and arranging "spontaneous" outbursts of affection. During the 1860 convention "Honest Abe" Lincoln used the technique effectively. William H. Seward was the front runner for the nomination, but Lincoln's managers got ahold of some counterfeit admission tickets, always easily available in Chicago for the "right" persons. Packing the galleries with Lincoln supporters, the gate-crashers yelled and yelled for their man. While the yelling was going on, Lincoln's managers were running around making deals, and Lincoln won the nomination on the third ballot.

One hundred and eight years later the Chicago galleries were again being packed to stage a display of "affection." This time it was for a Democrat, Mayor Richard J. Daley, host of the convention and proud presider over the "place of bad smells." Wednesday night of convention week Mayor Daley's police had launched a brutal attack upon demonstrators in front of the Hilton on Balbo Drive. Heads were mercilessly clubbed in full view of national television cameras. While the Battle of Balbo was going on, the convention delegates sat in not-so-solemn deliberation. Senator Abraham Ribicoff of Connecticut rose to nominate Senator George McGovern for President and he referred to the Chicago police as "Gestapo." Mayor Daley responded with a flurry of suspected obscenities the content of which still remains in dispute.

Mike Royko describes Daley's gallery-packing activities the following evening:

. . . On Thursday the word went out to precinct captains in Bridgeport and several other South Side wards that each of them should bring ten people to ward headquarters. They were loaded on buses, given "Daley" signs, noisemakers, and special over-sized passes to the gallery. Daley was going to pull the oldest convention stunt of them all—packing the gallery. It was a strange time to do it, since the choice of a candidate for President had already been made, but he was packing the gallery for himself. Now, if there was anybody shouted down, his people would do the shouting.

That night, when he entered the hall, the chant "We love Daley, we love Daley," rolled down from the gallery, most of it filled with his patronage workers. Throughout the evening, he turned them on and off like an orchestra conductor. After seeing a film about Sen. Robert Kennedy, delegates emotionally sang the "Battle Hymn of the Republic," until Daley thought it was time to stop and he used his gallery to drown out the singing. The New Hampshire delegation tried to make speeches about the arrest of their chairman, who had been collared and taken to Daley's neighborhood police station when he tried to show that the hall's ID checkers were rigged, but their words were lost in the chants of Daley's gallery. Wisconsin nominated Julian Bond for vice-president and Daley, to cut off the speeches, gleefully led the gallery in singing "God Bless America."

Considering all the other activities going on at a convention, a long demonstration on the floor is sometimes dangerous and can work against the candidate for whom the demonstrators are yelling. In 1912 the Democrats were again meeting in Baltimore, and on the tenth ballot Champ Clark had more than a 200-vote lead on Woodrow Wilson. Clark managers allowed a long demonstration on his behalf, which gave Wilson's backers the time they needed to run around dealing with delegations. Wilson came back strong and won the nomination. Many historians feel that Clark could have won on a fast eleventh ballot.

And sometimes the best of gimmicks can backfire. During the 1948 Republican convention in Philadelphia the supporters of Senator Robert Taft of Ohio carried a huge inflated rubber elephant, the emblem not only of the Grand

Old Party (GOP) but also of Taft himself, who was heralded as the party's true representative. Almost as an omen of what was to happen on the convention floor, the elephant collapsed before the voting began. Some folks suggested that a Democrat stuck a pin into it. Governor Dewey of New York won the nomination.

Despite all the show of support, the whooping it up in demonstrations, the posters, balloons, songs, and slogans, most of the really important activity is going on elsewhere. And the most important activity has taken place long before the delegates assemble in the convention city. Presidential preferential primaries are but one small ingredient in that preconvention strategizing.

Richard M. Nixon put four years into plotting his 1968 Presidential nomination. John F. Kennedy was at work five years building up a majority for the Democratic convention of 1960. The necessary groundwork for getting Franklin D. Roosevelt nominated in 1932 began two years before. Immediately after Roosevelt was reelected Governor of New York, James A. Farley, the Democratic state chairman, sent a little booklet to state chairmen, vice chairmen, national committeemen, and party workers around the country. It was intended to arouse interest in what was happening in New York and to initiate further correspondence. Then Farley sent the tabulation of Roosevelt's vote in the 1930 gubernatorial election, comparing it to the record of other Democrats.

Next, financial backers were approached, and as money came in, a headquarters was opened in New York City a full year before the Presidential campaign began to get hot. Roosevelt scouts with their expenses paid moved through the Rocky Mountain and Southwestern states to recruit delegates. In July 1931 Mr. Farley said he was going to attend an Elks convention in Seattle. All along the way, he talked to important party people in eighteen states, made a pitch for Roosevelt, and gathered vital information. Farley estimated that he had talked to 1,100 party folks. Thus by convention time the solid Roosevelt organization was set. It takes a lot of balloons and some heavy slogans to counteract that kind of organization.

Barry Goldwater began his bid for the 1964 Republican nomination three years in advance of the convention. F. Clifton White, a public-relations man in New York, gathered together twenty-two men from sixteen states. He gave them a course in practical politics: how to build an organization from the precinct up, and how to influence the selection of delegates to the nominating convention. White's students were to get Goldwater people on the committees at the bottom of the party. A state chairman later remarked: "We are having people show up in district conventions that we never heard of and know nothing about. The party is being taken over by people who are strangers to us. We don't know where they are coming from."

By 1962, when thirty members of White's team gathered in a Minnesota hunting lodge, a plan was in effect for a Goldwater leader in every county and Congressional district in the country. A detailed study was made of the way states choose delegates to the convention, and regional directors were instructed to master those rules and regulations. Such was the "spontaneity" of delegate affection for Goldwater in the San Francisco Republican convention in 1964.

The highly inbred, undemocratic method of selecting delegates to the national party nominating conventions makes it quite convenient for a wise candidate with good organization men to build the kind of machine Barry Goldwater and others have done. And it further removes from the voters themselves any choice at all in determining Presidential candidates. It has been estimated that ninety-seven percent of the voters have no choice at all in determining two thirds of the delegates to nominating conventions. The majority of states use the convention method of choosing delegates. As mentioned earlier, fifteen states choose delegates in Presidential preferential primaries.

So in thirty-five states the choice of delegates to the nominating convention really begins at the precinct level. The precinct leader calls together party people to pick delegates to a county or Congressional convention, who in turn pick the delegates to the national convention. Some states have laws regulating the holding of such precinct meetings, so it is conceivable that the ordinary voter would know about their being held. But in most instances attendance at such meetings is a handful of party regulars who happen to be within whispering distance of the call of a meeting. There are just too many precincts for any kind of realistic regulation. Chicago alone has 3,500.

A 1967 survey by the League of Women Voters documented the sad reality of a few folks hand-picking those who will hand-pick the major Presidential nominees. In Arizona a county committeeman once sent out five hundred invitations to a meeting for choosing convention delegates. Twelve people showed up. In Colorado typical attendance at caucus meetings to pick delegates to the county convention was six to eight persons. In Idaho delegates to the county central committee were picked two years prior to the Presidential election. In Minnesota only one half of one percent of the voters had ever attended a precinct meeting. In New Mexico county chairmen forgot to call precinct meetings, so they simply picked delegates themselves. The overwhelming conclusion of the survey was that party regulars pick delegates. And when the general election rolls around, after the nominating conventions have played their elaborate games, the voter is left with a choice of the lesser of two evils, which, of course, is no choice at all.

At the nominating conventions themselves, the real choice of a Presidential candidate is in the hands of a few party leaders from states with big blocks of delegates. Generally, a state is allotted twice as many delegates as the state has electoral votes—that is, two times the number of Senators and Representatives. Sometimes states that have turned out the vote for the party in the past are rewarded with "bonus" delegates. So California, Illinois, Michigan, New York, Ohio, Pennsylvania, and Texas can be keys to the final choice of a party nominee. These are the delegations with which a particular candidate's representatives wheel and deal to swing the vote to their man.

If an incumbent President is seeking renomination, he is almost sure to win, though in past years conventions rejected incumbents Tyler in 1844, Fillmore in 1852, Pierce in 1856, Andrew Johnson in 1868, and Arthur in 1884. All were defeated in the bid for renomination. Though there is frequently talk of "dumping" a President, twentieth-century precedent is against its happening, though there was some threat to Truman in 1948.

And the talk about "dark horse" candidates slipping through is quite exaggerated. Franklin Pierce, James Buchanan, Rutherford B. Hayes, and Benjamin Harrison are among those cited as "dark horses," but they were all highly available to the convention. D. W. Brogan suggests that Warren G. Harding was the only true dark horse. He had three chief competitors, General Leonard Wood, Governor Frank Lowden, and Senator Hiram Johnson, who canceled each other out. There was no spontaneous outburst for Harding, but rather a general weary feeling among delegates that there was nothing much wrong with Harding's candidacy. He was the best in sight from the point of view of the delegates, who were eager to get home.

Until 1932 the candidates themselves always stayed away from the nominating conventions, unless they happened to be part of a delegation. After a candidate was nominated, he waited for about a month until he was formally notified of the nomination before the campaign trail was blazed. Franklin D. Roosevelt changed the whole tradition by flying to Chicago to accept the convention nomination on the spot.

The political parading at the national conventions merely sets the stage for the parading which will continue throughout the country. The campaign bears the same stamp as the convention, with parades and motorcades accompanying candidates wherever they appear, banners, placards, balloons, slogans, songs, and rhymes.

At least one candidate chose not to blaze the campaign trail. William McKinley, during the election of 1896, conducted a "front porch" campaign. Instead of the candidate going to the people, the people were invited to come and see the candidate. Railroads cooperated by giving excursion rates so inexpensive that one newspaper said visiting McKinley was "cheaper than staying home." McKinley's opponent, Democrat William Jennings Bryan, made a record number of appearances during the campaign. Perhaps too many, since McKinley won the election.

During the campaign almost anything is fair game which will help one candidate and damage the other. A candidate must be careful that mud-slinging tactics do not get him dirtier than his opponent. During the campaign of 1884 the word went out that the Democratic candidate, Grover Cleveland, had had an affair with a young widow and had fathered a child. Cleveland accepted the responsibility, and the Republicans had a field day. They developed the campaign chant: "Ma; Ma; Where's my pa? Gone to the White House. Ha! Ha! Ha!"

But the Republican candidate, James G. Blaine, had some usable flaws also. Just before the Republican convention a Congressional investigating committee had charged Blaine with using political influence to aid railroads in which he had a personal interest. Key testimony was given by James Mulligan, who had some letters written by Blaine to a Boston businessman. Blaine got ahold of the "Mulligan letters" and refused to give them up. So the countering Democratic slogan in the 1884 election was "Blaine, Blaine, James G. Blaine, the continental liar from the State of Maine, *Burn this letter*."

An unknown candidate is sure to be the object of opposition scorn. During the election of 1844 the Whig Party used the campaign slogan: "Who is James Polk?" The Whig candidate was the very well-known Henry Clay. Polk's fellow Democrats countered with a slogan of their own, "54–40 or Fight!" referring to the entire Oregon Territory, which it was felt the United States ought to own even at the expense of war with Great Britain. The advocating of violence made up for the lack of prominence, and Polk won the election. During the Presidential campaign of 1968 Democrats were asking the question "Who is Spiro Agnew?" referring to the little-known Republican Vice Presidential nominee. They need never ask that question again.

Though slogans like "I Like Ike" (Dwight D. Eisenhower) and "All the Way with LBJ" (Lyndon B. Johnson) are usually cooked up to be taken out onto the campaign trail, sometimes the campaign itself produces better propaganda devices than could ever be contrived by a candidate's staff. Richard M. Nixon was greeted at a whistle stop by a little girl carrying a sign reading "Bring Us Together" and a campaign slogan was born. Vice Presidential Nominee Edmund S. Muskie was interrupted by young protesters during a campaign speech. He responded by turning the microphone over to one of their representatives, thus demonstrating a quality which could never have been created by even the cleverest slogan of how he had "bridged the Generation Gap."

The business started by the nominating convention and conducted by the campaign closes out when the general-election votes are tabulated. When the network news teams go on national television on election night to quickly project the winners after a minute percentage of the vote has been counted, it is but one more reminder of the insignificance of the individual grass-roots voter. That voter has not had a hand in saying who will be nominated to choose the delegates who will attend the convention to nominate the candidate. And in the long run his vote will only count if he happens to cast it for the winning candidate in his state.

So why wait a long time for all those individual votes to be counted? Turn off the TV set early and go to bed. You needn't worry. The electoral college will give you a President, and a Vice President too!

1

Does a national nominating convention differ from a circus? If so, in what ways?

2

Would George Washington have enjoyed attending a national nominating convention? Why or why not?

3

True or false: "The process of choosing a nominee for President begins when the national nominating convention convenes"?

Lesson Five
Pounding Out
Platforms

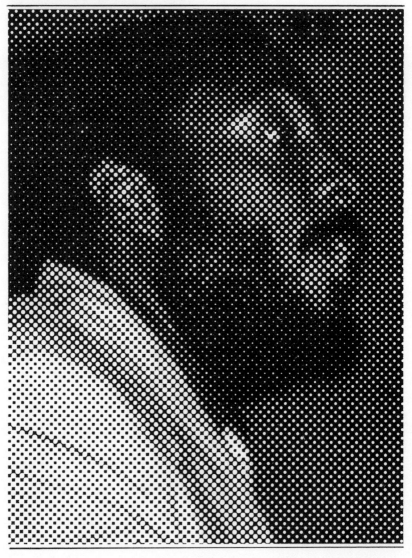

The platform is a statement of the beliefs of a particular political party, highlighting what it sees to be the major issues confronting the nation. By reading the platform, a voter is supposed to have a pretty good idea of how a candidate will act if he or she gets into office.

The platform of the party in power will emphasize the virtues and accomplishments of the incumbent President and his administration. The platform of the party out of power will point out the follies and foibles of that administration, and tell what must be done to save the nation from utter disaster. The platforms of the lesser parties (other than the two dominant political parties) tend to be more visionary and bold, reflecting a particular ideology upon which the party is based and which would present an alternative solution to world and national ills.

Campaign rhetoric and slogans usually come from the platform. Since most voters do not read the party platforms, the campaign speeches and statements of a Presidential candidate during a national election become the working party platform. There is good reason, of course, for the voters' not taking the time to read party platforms. They are wordy and cumbersome. And platforms tend to be dismantled immediately after the election is over. So platforms are more an aid to getting into office than they are an indication of what can be expected during a particular administration.

The practice of pounding out platforms did not really begin until the election of 1840, and only the Democratic Party seems to have written one. On December 13, 1831, the National Republican Party held a convention in Baltimore, Maryland, and nominated Presidential and Vice Presidential candidates. No platform came from that gathering, but the following May 11 a group of "young men" from the party met in Washington, D.C., and drafted a series of resolutions which some people called the platform of the National Republican Party.

By 1844 the platform-pounding process was well established and the Democratic Party, the Whig Party, and the Liberty Party all had official platforms. The Liberty Party (the first anti-slavery party, which later merged with the Free Soil Party in 1848) had a platform about three times the length of the other two party platforms, and its successful splitting of the Whig vote brought Democrat James K. Polk through the 1844 election.

A thorough study of all the party platforms since 1844 is beyond the scope of this lesson. Anyone interested in such a study should see the book *National Party Platforms: 1840–1964*, compiled by Kirk H. Porter and Donald Bruce Johnson (Urbana and London: University of Illinois Press, 1966). But focusing on a few selected platforms will give an idea of the reliability of platforms in making predictions.

War: Keep Out

Woodrow Wilson was first inaugurated President on March 4, 1913. In his inaugural address he sounded the high note of statesmanship: "Here muster not the forces of party, but the forces of humanity." One would assume that "the forces of humanity" would be opposed to war and killing, and President Wilson's conduct during his first term in office indicated that he shared that assumption. When faced with the problem, immediately after taking office, of recognizing the government of General Victoriano Huerta in Mexico, who had overthrown the reform government and assassinated its leader, Francisco Madero, President Wilson decided to recognize only those governments resting on the undoubted consent of the governed. He adopted a policy of "watchful waiting" toward Mexico until the people chose a government for themselves. Some American business interests didn't appreciate the watchfulness and wanted Wilson to recognize the Huerta regime.

Maintaining a stance of neutrality became more and more difficult as Wilson's first term wore on. World War I exploded in August 1914, and as German submarines began to ravage the high seas (especially the sinking of the British passenger liner *Lusitania,* resulting in a heavy loss of American life) Wilson's policy of neutrality was described by some U.S. hawks as being "too proud to fight."

So when election time rolled around in 1916, the Democrats ran their incumbent President with the slogan: "He kept us out of war." Wilson himself declined to use neutrality as a campaign promise. The Republicans included it in their platform, while at the same time talking about the need for military preparedness. Only the Socialist and Prohibition parties offered an expansive peaceful vision. The Democrats felt the best idea was to remain noncommittal, to remind the voters that Wilson had kept the country out of war so far, and let them draw their own conclusions.

The 1916 Democratic platform began by "endorsing the administration of Woodrow Wilson. It speaks for itself. It is the best exposition of sound Democratic policy at home or abroad." Typical of the pattern of platform-pounding, the Republicans began their platform by refuting the Democratic claim. The Republicans insisted that the Democrats had violated their promises of four years earlier and had been too soft on "combatism."

We declare that we believe in and will *enforce* the protection of every American citizen in all the rights secured him by the Constitution, by treaties and the laws of nations, at home and abroad, by land and by sea. These rights, which in violation of the specific promise of their party made at Baltimore in 1912, the Democratic President and the Democratic Congress have failed to defend, we will unflinchingly maintain.

The Socialists, on the other hand, left all the party bickering to the Democrats and Republicans. They offered a systems analysis. As the Socialists saw it, the issue was capitalism. Capitalism produces both combat and profit.

In the midst of the greatest crisis and bloodiest struggle of all history the socialist party of America re-affirms its steadfast adherence to the principles of international brotherhood, world peace and industrial democracy. . . . *The great war which has engulfed so much of civilization and destroyed millions of lives is one of the natural results of the capitalist system of production.* [Italics mine.]

After the preliminaries, the Democrats, Republicans, and Socialists offered their solutions. Both the Democrats and the Republicans echoed the same sentiments of military preparedness, while the Socialists insisted the war preparation must be dismantled. The Democrats used a favorite platform-pounding technique of claiming to be above party interest while outlining the programs which would advance the interest of their party. Building up America's military might was seen as "an issue of patriotism" and a demonstration of national character. "To taint it with partisanship," said the Democrats, "would be to defile it. In this day of test, America must show itself not a nation of partisans but a nation of patriots."

Voters who read the 1916 Democratic platform carefully would have seen immediately that the slogan "He kept us out of war" was only a reminder of past performance and not a comforting word for the future. The platform clearly suggested that maintaining a stance of neutrality would be almost impossible, and that it is the duty of America to protect the rights of people around the world.

The Democratic administration has throughout the present war scrupulously and successfully held to the old paths of neutrality and to the peaceful pursuit of the legitimate objects of our National life which statesmen of all parties and creeds have prescribed for themselves in America since the beginning of our history. *But the circumstances of the last two years have revealed necessities of international action which no former generation can have foreseen.* [Italics mine.] We hold that it is the duty of the United States to use its power, not only to make itself safe at home, but also to make secure its just interests throughout the world, and, both for this end and in the interest of humanity, to assist the world in securing settled peace and justice. . . .

Incidentally, while the Democrats were condemning as unpatriotic any person or group which arouses "prejudices of a racial, religious or other nature," they slipped and included a phrase in their platform with overtones of white supremacy worthy of Adolf Hitler. "There is gathered here in America," said the Democratic platform, "the best of the blood . . . of the whole world, the elements of a great race. . . ."

The Republicans went much further than the Democrats

in promising a continued neutral status for the United States, writing into their platform a belief "in maintaining a strict and honest neutrality between the belligerents in the great war in Europe." The Republicans further stated their belief that peace and neutrality, "as well as the dignity and influence of the United States," could not be "preserved by shifty expedients, by phrase-making, by performances in language, or by attitudes ever changing in an effort to secure votes and voters." By using such techniques, the Republicans insisted, the Democrats had not only ruined the influence of the United States overseas but also "humiliated us in our own eyes."

How was the United States to preserve a stance of continued neutrality? According to the Republicans, by being strong enough to clobber any would-be aggressors. Although the Republicans gave passing lip service to the idea of a world court, their real solution was in terms of building up American military strength. Just in case belligerents would not come to a world court, America had to be able to flex her muscle and do the belligerents in if necessary.

In order to maintain our peace and make certain the security of our people within our own borders the country must have not only adequate but thorough and complete national defense [sic] ready for any emergency. We must have sufficient and effective Regular Army and a provision for ample reserves, already drilled and disciplined, who can be called at once to the colors when the hour of danger comes.

We must have a Navy so strong and so well-proportioned and equipped, so thoroughly ready and prepared, that no enemy can gain command of the sea and effect a landing in force on either our Western or our Eastern coast. To secure these results we must have a coherent continuous policy of national defence, which even in these perilous days the Democratic party has utterly failed to develop, but which we promise to give to the country.

And, eight years after the birth of former Representative Adam Clayton Powell, Jr., the 1916 Republican platform ended by urging all Americans "to keep the faith."

Whereas both the Democrats and Republicans saw the answer in terms of building up military strength, the Socialist and Prohibition parties saw the answer in terms of dismantling it. The Socialist platform would make good copy for underground newspapers today. It talked about imperialism and militarism going hand in hand, and portrayed the United States as an imperialist power whose involvement in world war will be inevitable.

An armed force in the hands of the ruling class serves two purposes: to protect and further the policy of imperialism abroad and to silence by force the protest of the workers against industrial despotism at home. Imperialism and militarism plunged Europe into this world war. America's geographical and industrial situation has kept her out of the cataclysm. But Europe's extremity has been the opportunity of America's ruling class to amass enormous profits. *As a result there is a surfeit of capital which demands the policy of imperialism to protect and further investments abroad. Hence the frenzy of militarism into which the ruling class has made every attempt to force the United States.* [Italics mine.]

Since the imperialistic interests of the ruling class will inevitably plunge the nation into world war, the Socialists felt such chaos could only be avoided by action on the part of the nonruling class—namely, the workers. It was too late for the workers of Europe, but there was still a chance for concerted action by the workers of the United States.

The workers in Europe were helpless to avert the war because they were already saddled with the burden of militarism. The workers of the United States are yet free from this burden and have the opportunity of establishing a working class policy and program against war. They can compel the government of the United States to lead the way in an international movement for disarmament and to abandon the policy of imperialism which is forcing the conquest of Mexico and must, if carried out, eventually plunge the United States into a world war.

To avoid the clear and present danger of all-out war, the Socialists offered a mind-expanding vision of peace, totally the opposite of the muscle-flexing proposals of the Democrats and Republicans. They called for checks on the power of the President to involve the nation in war, a halt to military build-ups, and a world congress to rationally arbitrate disputes among the belligerents. Thus the 1916 Socialist "demands" included:

That all laws and appropriations for the increase of the military and naval forces of the United States shall be immediately repealed.

That the power be taken from the president to lead the nation into a position which leaves no escape from war. No one man, however exalted in official station, should have the power to decide the question of peace or war for a nation of a hundred millions. To give one man such power is neither democratic nor safe. Yet the president exercises such power when he determines what shall be the nation's foreign policies and what shall be the nature in tone of its diplomatic intercourse with other nations. We, therefore, demand that the power to fix foreign policies and conduct diplomatic negotiations shall be lodged in congress and shall be exercised publicly, the people reserving the right to order congress, at any time, to change that foreign policy.

That no war shall be declared or waged by the United States without a referendum vote of the entire people, except for the purpose of repelling invasion.

That the government of the United States shall call a congress of all neutral nations to mediate between the belligerent powers in an effort to establish an immediate and lasting peace . . . based on a binding and enforceable international treaty, which shall provide for concerted disarmament on land and at sea and for an international congress with power to adjust all disputes between nations and which shall guarantee freedom and equal rights to all oppressed nations and races.

So even in 1916 it was clear to the Socialists, at least, that the President had begun to usurp powers of foreign-policy determination which the Constitution had placed under the jurisdiction of Congress. The Socialist "demand" was really a demand that the letter of the Constitution be followed and that the spirit of the Constitution be honored in the United States' calling a congress of neutral nations.

Looking back at the 1916 election year, perhaps the Prohibition Party was the most enlightened of all. They felt that if Americans would stop drinking and start thinking, a lot of problems could be solved. When we consider that there are 10 million alcoholics in the country today, directly affecting the lives of 85 million people, and that 28,000 people are killed on the highways of America each year by drunken drivers, the Prohibition Party platform had a good point. The first step was to clear the heads of the American people from the drug of alcohol: "We will not allow the country to forget that the first step toward physical, economic, moral and political preparedness is the enactment of National Prohibition."

The Prohibition Party was to see its vision enacted (but not realized) in 1919 with the 18th Amendment to the Constitution and repealed in 1933 with the 21st Amendment.

The clear-headed Prohibitionists saw the nation's military obsession as dangerous. They were also hip to the developing military-industrial complex. Thus their platform called for immediate disarmament. The Prohibitionists wanted Americans to lay down both their bottles and their guns.

We are committed to the policy of peace and friendliness with all nations. We are unalterably opposed to the wasteful military programme of the Democratic and Republican parties. Militarism protects no worthy institution. It endangers them all. It violates the high principles which have brought us as a Nation to the present hour. . . . We will support a compact among nations to dismantle navies and disband armies. . . . We are opposed to universal military service and to participation in the rivalry that has brought Europe to the shambles and now imperils the civilization of the race. . . . Private profit, so far as constitutionally possible, should be taken out of the manufacture of war munitions and all war equipment. . . . We condemn the political parties, which for more than thirty years have allowed munition and war equipment manufacturers to plunder the people and to jeopardize the highest interest of the Nation by furnishing honeycombed armour plate and second rate battleships which the Navy League now declares are wholly inadequate. . . .

But the drinkers and the capitalists prevailed, and Woodrow Wilson was elected in a close race against Republican

Charles Evans Hughes. Weeks before his second inauguration, Germany resumed unrestricted submarine warfare against all shipping, including American ships. On April 2, 1917, the man who "kept us out of war" went before a joint session of Congress to request the declaration of a state of war against Germany, saying that "the world must be made safe for democracy."

That phrase has enjoyed great popularity in the United States, and each time America marches into another area of the world, displaying the imperialistic tendencies which the 1916 Socialist Party platform so clearly described, the excuse is given that the world is being made safe for democracy.

Rascals and Rece$$ion

The Presidential campaign of 1928 provided some of the most graphic platform rhetoric on record. Calvin Coolidge was the incumbent Republican President. He had been presiding over a country in high economic spirits, though officially low on alcoholic spirits. Prohibition was in effect, with all of the crime, corruption, and racketeering that accompanied "outlawing" alcoholic beverages. Coolidge had declared that "the business of America is business," and stock-market speculation was rampant among a nation of big spenders. Republicans felt the country had never had it so good, but the Democrats saw things in a much different light.

After invoking the memory of Woodrow Wilson and Thomas Jefferson, the 1928 Democratic platform quickly moved into a biting condemnation of the Coolidge administration. It was clear to the Democrats that the performance of public officials had reached an all-time low in human history.

Unblushingly the Republican Party offers as its record agriculture prostrate, industry depressed, American shipping destroyed, workmen without employment; everywhere disgust and suspicion, and corruption unpunished and unafraid.

Never in the entire history of the country has there occurred in any given period of time, or, indeed, in all time put together, such a spectacle of sordid corruption and unabashed rascality as that which has characterized the administration of federal affairs under eight blighting years of Republican rule. Not the revels of reconstruction, nor all the compound frauds succeeding that evil era, have approached in sheer audacity the shocking thieveries and startling depravities of officials high and low in the public service at Washington. From cabinet ministers, with their treasonable crimes, to the cheap vendors of official patronage, from the purchasers of seats in the United States Senate to the vulgar grafters upon alien trust funds, and upon the hospital resources of the disabled veterans of the World War; from the givers and receivers of stolen funds for Republican campaign purposes to the public men who sat by silently consenting and never revealing a fact or uttering a word in condemnation, the whole official organization under Republican rule has become saturated with dishonesty defiant of public opinion and actuated only by partisan desire to perpetuate its control of the government.

As in the time of Samuel J. Tilden, from whom the presidency was stolen, the watchword of the day should be: "Turn the rascals out."

"We endorse without qualification the record of the Coolidge administration," began the Republican platform in 1928. "By unwavering adherence to sound principles, through the wisdom of Republican policies, and the capacity of Republican administrations, the foundations have been laid and the greatness and prosperity of the country firmly established." The Republicans insisted that the Coolidge administration had stood for "honesty in government" and "for the appointment of officials whose integrity cannot be questioned." And, in answer to the Democratic plea to "turn the rascals out," the Republicans insisted that "the Government today is made up of thousands of conscientious, earnest, self-sacrificing men and women, whose single thought is service to the nation." So the Republicans promised to guarantee "contentment among all our people at home" by a continuation of the noble policies of the Coolidge administration.

But Calvin Coolidge himself would not be the Republican candidate. He had shocked the nation on August 2, 1927, when he handed the press a slip of paper on which was written: "I do not choose to run for President in 1928." So the Republicans nominated Herbert Hoover, a wealthy man who had demonstrated administrative capability and economic success. He was highly touted as the ideal man to carry on the prosperity and bulging economy of which the Republicans were so proud and promised to maintain in the future. With all their talk about rascals and corruption, the Democrats were not able to defeat Herbert Hoover.

Seven months after Hoover took office, the stock market crashed. People lost fortunes overnight. By November 13, 1929, $30 billion in the market value of listed stocks had been wiped out; by mid-1932 the losses had increased to $75 billion. As the bread lines, soup lines, and unemployment lines grew, the Republican promise of "contentment among our people at home" hovered over the nation as a cruelly mocking reminder of the absurdity of believing political platforms. And the Republican Party was not entrusted again with the high office of President for two decades.

World War Again

Six Presidential elections after Woodrow Wilson was being heralded as the man who "kept us out of war," war clouds were gathering again. Franklin Delano Roosevelt, the man who had been given the job of picking up the pieces during the Great Depression, was the incumbent Democratic President. In 1940, after two terms in office, Roosevelt was breaking tradition and trying for an unprecedented third term, causing some uneasiness within the Democratic Party and, of course, great concern among Republicans.

Once again the question loomed whether or not the United States would get itself involved in world war. The 1940 Democratic platform made it clear that Americans did not want war and the United States would become involved only in case of attack.

The American people are determined that war, raging in Europe, Asia and Africa, shall not come to America.

We will not participate in foreign wars, and we will not send our army, naval or air forces to fight in foreign lands outside of the Americas, except in case of attack. We favor and shall rigorously enforce and defend the Monroe Doctrine.

The direction and aim of our foreign policy has been, and will continue to be, the security and defense of our own land and the maintenance of its peace.

As in 1916, the Democrats saw the solution for maintaining peace to be in the size of America's military strength. If the United States was not going to be involved in war except in case of attack, part of keeping the peace was to make any foreign power afraid to risk attacking us.

Weakness and unpreparedness invite aggression. We must be so strong that no possible combination of powers would dare to attack us. We propose to provide America with an invincible air force, a navy strong enough to protect all our sea coasts and our national interests, and a fully-equipped and mechanized army. We shall continue to coordinate these implements of defense with the necessary expansion of industrial productive capacity and with the training of appropriate personnel. Outstanding leaders of industry and labor have already been enlisted by the Government to harness our mighty economic forces for national defense.

The Republican stance was the same as the Democrats. The Republicans also pledged to keep the United States out of foreign war, promised to strengthen America's military preparedness, and chastised the Democrats for miserable failure in that regard.

We are still suffering from ill effects of the last World War: a war which cost us a twenty-four billion dollar increase in our national debt, billions of uncollectible foreign debts, and the complete upset of our economic system, in addition to the loss of human life and irreparable damage to the health of thousands of our boys.

The present National Administration has already spent for all purposes more than fifty-four billion dollars;—has boosted the national debt and current federal taxes to an all-time high; and yet by the President's own admission we are still wholly unprepared to defend our country, its institutions and our individual

123

liberties in a war that threatens to engulf the whole world; and this in spite of the fact that foreign wars have been in progress for two years or more and that military information concerning these wars and the rearmament programs of the warring nations has been at all times available to the National Administration through its diplomatic and other channels.

The Republican Party stands for Americanism, preparedness and peace. We accordingly fasten upon the New Deal full responsibility for our unpreparedness and for the consequent danger of involvement in war.

But the Communist Party saw things differently. Its 1940 platform offered the same kind of analysis the Socialist Party platform gave in 1916. The Communist Party platform insisted that American business interests were hungry for war, that some way or other the United States would get involved, and that all the talk of the Democrats and Republicans was just a smoke screen to cover the truth of the matter —namely, that Wall Street wanted war.

The predatory war unleashed by the imperialist ruling classes of Berlin, London, Paris, Rome and Tokyo is a worldwide struggle for the division of the world among imperialist bandits—a struggle for the right of capitalist imperialist exploitation of the world by sacrificing the freedom of all peoples and the national independence of all nations.

Therefore the richest and most predatory of international bankers and trust heads of the whole world—those of Wall Street —are determined to enter into this worldwide, military contest in order to claim for themselves a share in proportion to their gigantic wealth. While their war profits pile high they deliberately seek to prolong the war and feverishly prepare to enter it. They have already transformed our country into an arsenal for one side of the predatory European conflict, and into a chief source of war materials for the Japanese adventures in Asia—thus making the United States, while still a non-belligerent, nevertheless a participant in the worldwide military conflict.

Aspiring for world dominion, the American finance capitalists strive to drag the American people into the European war on the side of Great Britain. They work for a continuation and extension of that war and share guilt for the fate of those countries already conquered in Europe, Asia and Africa. But the same American imperialists have not closed the door to possible temporary agreements with the German and Japanese conquerors for the establishments of the "new orders" in Europe and Asia, if only the terms be advantageous to the bankers of Wall Street.

So what the Democrats were describing as "enlisting labor and industry in the interests of national defense," and what the Republicans were saying was totally inadequate in that regard, the Communist Party saw as an imperialist Wall Street strategy to eventually involve the United States in World War II.

Wendell Willkie was chosen by the Republicans to oppose President Roosevelt. Willkie blew a lot of potential votes by waving the warning flag of war a little too close to Roosevelt. Many folks thought it was an unfair accusation. The Democratic platform had been translated in Roosevelt's speeches to "American boys will not fight another war in Europe." Willkie suggested that if Roosevelt didn't honor that pledge any "better than he did the platform of 1932," American boys "better get ready to get on the transports." Of course Willkie was absolutely right, but there are some things you can't say before the event. It looks like dirty pool. For example, President Harry Truman was treading on dangerous campaign ground when he compared the mustache of his Republican opponent, Thomas E. Dewey, to Hitler's during the 1948 campaign.

Roosevelt defeated Willkie, but his majority at the polls was reduced considerably over his first two elections. And the following year the Democratic platform was enacted, though not in the way the average voter had expected. The Japanese attacked the United States naval base at Pearl Harbor by surprise on December 7, 1941, at 7:55 A.M. local time (1:00 P.M. Washington time), wiping out the entire Pacific battle fleet and half of the planes on the island. Nineteen battleships were sunk or disabled, 150 planes were destroyed, and 2,335 soldiers and sailors were killed. Civilian casualties numbered 1,200, including 68 deaths.

December 8, the United States Congress declared war on Japan. December 11, Germany and Italy declared war on the United States, and Congress immediately returned the favor. The United States had been attacked and the Democratic platform promise was fulfilled. And so too were the predictions of the Communist Party platform.

In retrospect, one cannot help wondering the extent to which the United States government knew the Japanese plans in advance. It is known, for example, that the blue code, the most advanced intelligence code of the time developed by the Japanese, had been broken by the United States some time before the Pearl Harbor attack. But the commanders at the base, Rear Admiral Husband Kimmel and Lt. General Walter Short, were not informed that the Japanese code had been broken, nor apprised of the intelligence gained. They were later blamed for not having adopted adequate defense measures.

And since the Japanese did not have planes which could

fly all the way to Pearl Harbor from Japan, the attack was launched from aircraft carriers. With all the friends the United States was supposed to have around the world, you would think someone would have noticed all those Japanese ships steaming toward Hawaii and let the President know about it.

Perhaps, then, the 1940 Democratic and the Communist platforms give us a clue. An incident like Pearl Harbor was the only way the United States could get involved in World War II. Yet involvement in that war was inevitable even as the platform words were being pounded out. Harsher judgments of Franklin Delano Roosevelt suggest that he welcomed the Pearl Harbor attack precisely because it permitted entry into World War II (see *Air Raid—Pearl Harbor!* by Theodore Taylor, New York: Thomas Y. Crowell Co., 1971). Not that FDR welcomed the tragic results of the Pearl Harbor incident, only the triggering incident itself.

President Nixon recently shed light upon the Pearl Harbor incident when he sent American forces into Laos. He redefined accepted military terminology by telling us that the United States was not invading Laos, since no ground combat troops were being used. The action in Laos was an *incursion,* employing only air power. So an invasion requires the use of ground combat troops. If the President's terminology is correct, it would seem that the United States owes Japan a retroactive apology. The Japanese did not employ ground troops at Pearl Harbor. They just used air power to bomb it to bits. But the United States misinterpreted (by President Nixon's definition) the action as an invasion and declared war on Japan. And Hawaii wasn't even a state at the time.

Boys Will Be Boys

Let us end this lesson by looking at more recent platform statements from the '60s. In 1964 incumbent Democratic President Lyndon B. Johnson sought reelection, running against Republican Barry Goldwater. LBJ easily won that election, amassing the largest vote plurality in American history (61.4 percent of the more than 68 million votes cast). In view of subsequent events, it is surprising how little mention was made of Vietnam in the 1964 Democratic platform.

Passing reference was made to the Gulf of Tonkin incident in a section which extolled Presidents Johnson and John F. Kennedy as having used power with restraint against Communist aggression.

President Kennedy and Vice President Johnson set out to remove any question of our power or our will. In the Cuban crisis of 1962, the Communist offensive shattered on the rock of President Kennedy's determination—and our ability—to defend the peace.

Two years later, President Johnson responded to another Communist challenge, this time in the Gulf of Tonkin. Once again power exercised with restraint repulsed Communist aggression and strengthened the cause of freedom.

The Democratic platform also said that the citizens of the United States are "determined that it be the most powerful nation on earth" and insisted "that this power be exercised with the utmost responsibility." The Democrats pledged to "strengthen further our forces for discouraging limited wars and fighting subversion," as well as to "oppose aggression and the use of force or the threat of force against any nation."

On the campaign trail, however, Democratic pledges concerning American involvement in Southeast Asia were more specific. Campaign oratory insisted: "We are not about to send American boys nine or ten thousand miles away from home to do what Asian boys ought to be doing for themselves."

The 1964 Republican platform was more specific concerning the war in Vietnam, and the party purchased a war-mongering image as a result. The Republicans accused the incumbent Democratic administration of being too soft on Communism and allowing an increase of aggression in South Vietnam.

[This Administration] has abetted further Communist takeover in Laos, weakly accepted Communist violations of the Geneva agreement, which the present Administration perpetrated, and increased Soviet influence in Southeast Asia.

It has encouraged an increase of aggression in South Vietnam by appearing to set limits on America's willingness to act—and then, in the deepening struggle, it has sacrificed the lives of American and allied fighting men by denial of modern equipment.

This Administration has permitted the shooting down of American pilots, the mistreatments of American citizens, and the destruction of American property to become hallmarks of Communist arrogance.

Beyond criticizing the Democrats for their past weakness, the Republicans made it clear that they would take whatever steps were necessary to win in Vietnam.

In diverse regions of the world, Republicans will make clear to any hostile nation that the United States will increase the costs and risks of aggression to make them outweigh hopes for gain. It was just such a communication and determination by the Eisenhower Republican Administration that produced the 1953 Korean Armistice. The same strategy can win victory for freedom and stop further aggression in Southeast Asia.

We will move decisively to assure victory in South Vietnam. While confining the conflict as closely as possible, America must move to end the fighting in a reasonable time and provide guarantees against further aggression. We must make it clear to the Communist world that, when conflict is forced with America, it will end only in victory for freedom.

One further item in the 1964 Republican platform is curious in view of the later revelations of the "top secret" Pentagon study. In a section entitled "Trusting Ourselves and Our Friends," the Republicans stated: "Secrecy in foreign policy must be at a minimum, public understanding at a maximum. Our own citizens, rather than those of other nations, should be accorded primary trust."

During the campaign of 1964 many people began to fear that Candidate Goldwater might be inclined to unleash nuclear weapons in Southeast Asia, especially as the Republican platform was being interpreted in his campaign rhetoric. Thus President Johnson was elected to pursue his more "sane and reasonable" course.

Almost immediately after the votes were counted, American involvement in Vietnam began to escalate. From sixteen thousand men in Vietnam at the time President John F. Kennedy was assassinated in 1963, American involvement rose to more than a half-million men by the end of 1968. Whatever the "Asian boys ought to be doing for themselves," a whole lot of American boys were making that long trip.

The publication of the "secret" Pentagon study in June-July 1971 indicates that the Republican platform pledge

130

concerning secrecy and public trust was in no way a major concern for the incumbent Democratic administration. Even as Democratic oratory insisted that American boys would not be sent to do the job of Asian boys, plans were in the making for bombing North Vietnam as an "inducement" to those Asian boys to fight better. The bombing of North Vietnam was put into effect in 1965, beginning the major escalation of American involvement, to (according to the Pentagon study) prevent collapse of the war in the South. Those Asian boys were just not doing what they "ought to be doing." Therefore, by the traditional twists of campaign pledges, American boys must be sent to do it for them. One cannot help wondering why those Asian boys needed more of an "inducement" than the promise of "freedom."

All of which brings us to the 1968 platform pledges of the Republican Party. This lesson ends with one pledge which helped to bring President Richard Nixon to the White House.

Under the Johnson-Humphrey Administration we have had economic mismanagement of the highest order. . . . New Republican leadership can and will restore fiscal integrity and sound monetary policies, encourage sustained economic vitality, *and avoid such economic distortions as price and wage controls.* [Italics mine.]

The entire Republican platform makes good reading for the currently unemployed. And if all the unemployed took to reading it, the platform would hit the best-seller lists overnight.

1

True or false?
  a. Woodrow Wilson promised to keep the United States out of World War I.
  b. Franklin Roosevelt promised that American boys would not be sent to fight a foreign war.
  c. Lyndon Johnson promised that American boys would not be sent nine or ten thousand miles to fight a war that Asian boys ought to be fighting.
  d. Woodrow Wilson kept the United States out of World War I.
  e. Franklin Roosevelt kept the United States out of World War II.
  f. Lyndon Johnson kept American boys out of Southeast Asia.

2

Why do you think political parties write platforms?

3

Do people read them? Why or why not?

Lesson Six
Promises,
Promises

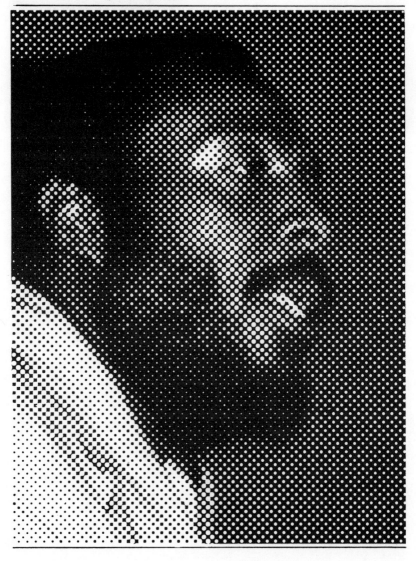

There are two major kinds of promises in politics: the promises made by candidates to the voters and the promises made by the candidates to persons and groups able to deliver the vote. Promises falling into the latter category are loosely called "patronage," and promises falling into the former category are most frequently called "lies."

As we have seen in Lesson Two, political parties prevailing in the United States have made both kinds of promises necessary: promises to the voters are necessary to lure them from the opposition candidate; and patronage is a means of keeping the machine oiled.

Then there are other types of promises: promises made by Presidents in private, promises made after successful candidates get into office, and promises to explain why earlier promises are not being kept (each time President Nixon appears on television, for example, it is to explain why the promise to bring the Vietnam war to a halt is being forestalled).

Oh, Promise Me

Sometimes a President's enactment of promises can get him into real trouble, in spite of the best intentions. Andrew Jackson was the "people's candidate" and the promise of his candidacy was "Let the people rule." Jackson attempted to institute that promise immediately after his inaugural address. He invited the people into the White House for the reception. Jackson's crowd "worked out," grabbing food and drinks, knocking furniture around and climbing all over it, breaking White House china, and otherwise enjoying themselves. The hilarity of the party and the pressure of the crowd became so great that President Jackson had to split through a window.

A candidate like Zachary Taylor is the cleverest of all, running on the promise not to make any promises. Such a promise is called nonpartisan by the candidate, and noncommittal by those less sympathetic to his views.

Perhaps the quieter the promise, the more chance there is that it will be realized. James K. Polk made a quiet personal promise to the historian George Bancroft that he would try to do four things as President: reduce the tariff, reestablish the independent treasury, settle the Oregon dispute, and acquire California. Polk did them all in just one term in office.

President Polk must have been a model for Governor Ronald Reagan. Reagan acquired California and has done a lot to establish his own independent treasury, since it was recently revealed that he did not pay personal income taxes. Many people were surprised at that revelation, but I knew something was up when I saw Governor Reagan slip during a television interview and refer to April 15 as Christmas! And, by the way, I don't know if you have realized that "Reagan" pronounced backwards is "nigger." That's why I've always hoped Governor Reagan would pull himself together and get elected President. Then we could say we have a backward nigger in the White House.

Theodore Roosevelt came up with a promise during his time in the White House which has really dug into the American governmental psyche. Known as the Roosevelt Corollary to the Monroe Doctrine, the United States promised it was prepared to exercise "an international police power" in instances of "wrongdoing or impotence." And the United

States has been policing the world ever since. The problem is that the U.S. police force is representing the wrongdoing against the supposedly impotent. Brother Teddy was fond of pushy promises. He said the office of President was a "bully pulpit," and so he advocated "carrying a big stick" as a good bully should. Roosevelt's rhetoric took root, and some six decades later Author Norman Mailer was describing the United States involvement in Vietnam as representing "a bully with an Air Force."

A President's inaugural address is usually a good place for making or reaffirming promises, unless, of course, you happen to face a most difficult situation like Rutherford B. Hayes. Folks were so upset about the dubious way Hayes copped the election from Samuel Tilden that Hayes didn't face the masses on Inauguration Day, but rather canceled the parade and the ball and took the oath of office in private.

Votes and Vocations

The Roman Catholic Church has provided us with the patronage concept, which was used to describe the transfer of power by the Pope to his natural sons, called "nephews" (hence the word *nepotism*), and the Pope's other relatives. The Catholic Church was the only institution to sanction patronage by law (*jus patronatus*), though many other governments and institutions have practiced patronage since ancient times.

Patronage represents the jobs and favors which a candidate can promise to bestow upon those who help him get elected, and promise to withhold after he is elected if he needs to pressure lesser office-holders into doing his bidding. Presidents, Governors, Senators, Representatives, Mayors, and many other public officials have patronage powers which can be effective in the hard task of persuasion.

Governor Nelson Rockefeller of New York provides a good example of using the power of patronage after election. During the 1968 New York legislative session Governor Rockefeller threatened to withhold "personal favors" from legislators unless they switched their votes to allow the passage of a $6-billion slum-clearance bill. The bill had been defeated early in the afternoon. Then came the Governor's threat. By 11:30 that night the decision was reversed and the bill was passed. Thirty-four legislators who knew they would be needing some "personal favors" from the Governor changed the votes.

The bestowing of patronage jobs and favors by successful candidates is known as the "spoils system," an idea coined by New York Governor William Learned Marcy, who once exclaimed: "To the victor belong the spoils of the enemy." Governor Marcy was extolling the era of Andrew Jackson, whose administration is generally credited with formalizing the spoils system and the practice of patronage. When Jackson was defeated in 1824 by John Quincy Adams, he charged that Adams was dealing in patronage and had traded the post of Secretary of State for the electoral votes controlled by Henry Clay. But when Jackson finally made it into the White House, he enjoyed seeing all the patronage applicants personally and passing out jobs.

The whole patronage thing was part of Jackson's desire to bring the common folks into government. He felt the aristocracy, the privileged money and propertied class, had held the reins of public office too long. But, for all his talk, Jackson really didn't do that much removing of people from office and putting his own folks in. Only 252 of 612 executive appointees were removed to make way for Jackson patronage beneficiaries, and about 600 postmasters out of 8,000.

Abraham Lincoln, on the other hand, used his patronage powers to their maximum. In 1860, 1,195 out of 1,250 Presidential appointees were fired to make way for supporters of Lincoln. The large number of federal office-holders led to ensuring Lincoln's renomination, and historians have stated that Lincoln's thorough and expert use of patronage powers is what held the Union together. Lincoln didn't get the kick out of handing out jobs that Jackson did. One time Lincoln came down with smallpox, and he told his secretary: "Tell all the office seekers to come at once, for now I have something I can give to all."

The Congressmen soon caught on to the idea of patronage powers, and they began to get fees for voting legislative privileges to railroads, oil, coal, and timber interests, and the like. America's greatest social satirist, Mark Twain, looked at all the goings-on and observed: "I think I can say, and say with pride, that we have legislatures that bring higher prices than any in the world."

So that the patronage system today has moved far beyond the earlier distribution of jobs and salaries to include defense contracts, construction contracts, banking and insurance funds, all of the myriad ways persons can make a profit from government spending and the allocation of tax revenue. Patronage, then, is the life blood of politics in the United States, from the local clubhouse all the way up to the White House and the Capitol building, which stands not far away. It is patronage, special interest, the spoils of government, which determine governmental decisions and actions more than anything else, including the selection and election of candidates.

Martin and Susan Tolchin summarize the contemporary truth about patronage:

The major hazard of patronage, however, is not that it builds political empires or private fortunes, but that it encourages public officials to compromise the public interest for private gain, and to sacrifice the national interest for the needs of their regional constituencies. This begins with the selection of presidential candidates at national conventions, and includes every aspect of public policy and government funding. How much of the $80 billion defense budget is actually used to protect the country, for example, and how much is allocated for military installations and defense contracts intended to win the support of various legislators, anxious to obtain more jobs and money for their districts? "I am convinced that defense is only one of the factors that enter into our determinations for defense spending," charged Mississippi Representative Jamie L. Whitten. "The others are pump priming, spreading the immediate benefits of defense spending, taking care of all services, giving military bases to include all sections. . . . We see the effects in public and Congressional insistence on continuing contracts, or operating military bases, though the need has expired." . . . One wonders how long the Vietnam war would continue if it were *against* the patronage interests of our national political leaders, and if a reduction in military installations and defense spending enriched, rather than impoverished, their constituencies and themselves. . . . To what extent has tax reform been evaded because of the patronage needs of Congressmen, and to what extent has pollution been ignored because the polluters had more favors to dispense than did those who opposed pollution? What would be the national commitment to the war on poverty if the principal recipients of anti-poverty patronage were rich and influential, instead of poor and disenfranchised? And how is national policy affected by the 183 House members who have a financial or management interest in companies doing business with the federal government or subject to federal regulatory agencies?

Office-holders who say they are not engaging in patronage and special interest are either lying, not functioning, employing patronage and calling it by another name (like "good government policy" or "reform tactics"), or are so out of touch with what is going on that they actually don't know what their underlings are up to.

Since patronage is the oil in the political machine, it is seen in its rawest expressions where the machine is most visible. Once again Chicago is the laboratory for patronage research. The Cook County machine, controlled and operated by Mayor Richard J. Daley, gives him control of county jobs in the courts, sheriff's offices, jails, and hospitals, and city agencies taking care of services like parks, sanitation, sewers, recreation, and health. And that's just jobs. All related enterprises, like contracts, franchises, etc., also pass through the fingers of the machine's Top Mechanic. Alderman Leon Despres has said that Mayor Daley controls some thirty-five thousand city and county jobs, which does not even take into consideration jobs made available to him from private industry.

And a well-oiled machine is slick enough to accommodate even the best of reforms. Like the reform of placing jobs in the Civil Service category. The *Christian Science Monitor* reported that 97 percent of the city government jobs in Chicago fell under that category. But the machine avoids that hangup by listing at least 40 percent of the jobs as "temporary," which could mean a 180-day limitation. But you pile enough 180 days on end and you have twenty-year employees, which is how long some of the more politically active and productive Daley "temporaries" have been holding down their jobs.

It takes the veteran machine-watcher in Chicago, Mike Royko, to give an adequate laboratory analysis:

Another reason the size of the patronage army is impossible to measure is that it extends beyond the twenty to twenty-five thousand government jobs. The Machine has jobs at racetracks, public utilities, private industry, and the Chicago Transit Authority, which is the bus and subway system, and will help arrange easy union cards.

Out of the ranks of the patronage workers rise the . . . fifty ward committeemen who, with thirty suburban township committeemen, sit as the Central Committee. For them the reward is more than a comfortable payroll. If they don't prosper, it is because they are ignoring the advice of their Tammany cousin George Washington Plunkett, who said, "I seen my opportunities and I took 'em." Chicago's ward bosses take 'em, too.

Most of them hold an elective office. Many of the Daley aldermen are ward bosses. Several are county commissioners. Others hold office as county clerk, assessor, or recorder of deeds and a few are congressmen and state legislators. Those who don't hold office are given top jobs running city departments, whether they know anything about the work or not. A ward boss who was given a $28,000-a-year job as head of the city's huge sewer system was asked what his experience was. "About twenty years ago I was a house drain inspector." "Did you ever work in the sewers?" "No, but many a time I lifted a lid to see if they were flowing." "Do you have an engineering background?" "Sort of. I took some independent courses at a school I forget the name of, and in 1932 I was a plumber's helper." His background was adequate: his ward usually carries by fifteen thousand to three thousand votes.

The moral of patronage is as follows: the spoils system benefits the few and makes them rich. But a spoiled system infects us all.

1

If a President fails to keep a political promise:
  a. the Senate Majority Leader washes the President's mouth out with soap;
  b. the voters tend to overlook it because they didn't expect the promise to be kept in the first place;
  c. the President feels very bad;
  d. all of the above;
  e. none of the above.

2

Many times at nominating conventions Governors' names are placed in nomination as "favorite son" candidates. Using this lesson as a guide, especially the section on patronage, what do you think "favorite son" means?

Lesson Seven
The High Cost
of Conviction

Dwight David Eisenhower, our thirty-fourth President, had all the proper qualifications for a Presidential candidate. He was the product of the small Kansas town of Abilene. He came from a modest family background, went to work after high school, then went on to West Point (though disappointing his deeply religious and pacifist parents), and later became one of our nation's greatest military heroes. "Ike" fitted right in with the other common folks in the White House—"Old Hickory" (Andrew Jackson), "Old Rough and Ready" (Zachary Taylor), "The Farmer of North Bend" (William Henry Harrison), and "Honest Abe, the Rail Splitter" (Abraham Lincoln).

But in 1968 General Eisenhower was upset about politics in America. The former President said: "We have put a dollar sign on public service, and today many capable men who would like to run for office simply can't afford to do so. Many believe that politics in our country is already a game exclusively for the affluent. This is not strictly true; yet the fact that we may be approaching that state of affairs is a sad reflection on our elective system."

It sounded as though the general had just begun to realize the "high cost of political conviction" in the United States. One would hardly suspect that at least $140 million had been spent on campaigning during the 1952 election, when the general was first elected President. Or that the general himself had raised $4 million for his own campaign, speaking on closed-circuit television to a fifty-three-city, $100-a-plate Republican dinner.

Nor would one suspect that Winthrop W. Aldrich, a New York banker, had headed the Republican 1952 finance committee which is credited with having produced $2,250,-000 for the campaign. Less than a month after the general became President, Mr. Aldrich was rewarded for his efforts with an appointment as Ambassador to Great Britain.

But the general knew more about the prior costs of conviction than he was letting on. He knew that folks giving big dough must be rewarded. In his reelection campaign in 1956, $26,500 was given by the owner of a chain of dress shops. A few months later the contributor was appointed Ambassador to Ceylon. During public hearings by a Senate committee trying to determine whether or not the appointment should be confirmed, the proposed appointee could not name the prime minister of India or of Ceylon.

The issue the general raised is quite real, and it puts to shame the old American myth that every little boy can dream of being President someday. And the myth is even more shameful for politically minded, ambitious little girls. Somewhere along the line he or she must tie into some big dough, which means selling out to rich individuals, corporations, the party machine, or preferably all of them together.

Mayor Richard Daley of Chicago is a poor boy who made good in politics. He sold newspapers as a youngster, then worked in the stockyards by day and went to DePaul University by night. With a law degree in hand, he tied into the Democratic machine, got into the state legislature, was beaten in his bid for sheriff, and then got an appointment from Governor Adlai Stevenson as director of the state department of finance. Daley moved into the Stevenson organization, got himself elected Cook County Clerk, and four years later he was Mayor of Chicago with his hands on the nation's most powerful political machine. Perhaps he could not dream of becoming President, but he could certainly dream of controlling the nominations of those who would.

Had Richard Daley been content simply to save his newspaper money, he couldn't have gotten very far. That $140 million spent in election campaigning in 1952 was up to at least $327 million by 1968. A hard-working kid dreaming of being President one day would have to make $1 million a year from the moment of birth to the age of qualification, *and not spend a penny,* to have even an outside chance at the office! And certainly it would be an outside chance. Figures of *reported* campaign expenditures indicate that it costs anywhere from $35 million to $60 million to become President (an estimated $100 million was spent to elect a President in 1968), $50,000 to $6 million to become Governor, $250,000 to $5 million to become Senator, and $30,000 to $300,000 to become a member of the House of Representatives. And, of course, reported figures do not even begin to tell the whole story of campaign spending. Local committees can bury funds, and Senators and Congressmen can conceal campaign income and expenditures by only acknowledging money collected and disbursed with their "knowledge and consent."

Of course, if a kid is born with enough money, he can let his dreams run wild. The kid can not only dare to dream, but his family fortune can afford to pay the fare of his particular political fantasy. Governor Nelson Rockefeller of New York is a good example. He reported that he spent $5.2 million in 1966 to get reelected to a $50,000-a-year job. His next reelection bid, in 1970, cost him $6.8 million, according to his own figures. Estimates of Rockefeller's *actual* spending range from $10 million up to $20 million. With that kind of money, I could run for God—and win!

But even rich kids can have their well-financed fantasies frustrated. Richard L. Ottinger used the resources of a family fortune to run for the Senate on the Democratic ticket in the 1970 New York election. Ottinger took the primary, continued to spend more and more bread on the general election, and ended up losing to the Conservative Party candidate, James L. Buckley. Ottinger reported spending $2 million to lose, but the actual spending was double the report.

The Republican opponent of Ottinger, incumbent Senator Charles E. Goodell, reported that he spent $1.3 million to lose, while the winning candidate, James Buckley, reported spending about $2 million.

Losing can be very expensive, and not just on the Presidential level. It cost former Senator Albert Gore more than $500,000 to lose to Representative William E. Brock III in the 1970 Senatorial election in Tennessee. That was more than five times the amount Gore had spent in either of his two successful Senatorial bids (1958 and 1964). Brock spent over $1 million to win, at least three times the amount spent by any previous Republican candidate in the history of Tennessee.

In Pennsylvania, in 1966, Democrat Milton Schapp spent $1.4 million to win his party's nomination for Governor. He spent another $1.1 million in the general election. But his Republican opponent, Raymond P. Shafer, won the election. Perhaps Mr. Schapp saw it as an investment in the future, for he won the Governorship in the 1970 election. Also in 1966, Haydon Burns spent $1.6 million trying to get the Democratic primary nomination for Governor of Florida, but he lost.

If you have a good emotional issue going for you, so that the voters persuade themselves and don't have to be convinced by radio, television, newspaper advertising, and the like, you can get by relatively cheap. Riding the surf of a wave of segregationist sentiment, Lester Maddox became Georgia's Governor and supposedly only spent about $40,-000. But in the same election it cost Ellis Arnall more than $1 million to lose the Democratic nomination to Maddox, and Howard H. Callaway, a Republican, the same amount to lose the general election.

So Maddox only spent his first year's salary. A Georgia Governor makes the same as a Congressman, $42,500 a year. But even with segregationist sympathy going for you, campaigning can be expensive. The late Lurleen Wallace spent half a million dollars to become Governor of Alabama, even with the strong prestige and backing of her husband, George.

A large part of the high cost of political conviction is getting the message aired on television. Since a large portion of the electorate spends a good deal of its leisure time in front of the television tube, a candidate must pay for a part of the potential voter's viewing time.

Just after the 1970 mid-term elections a team of *Washington Post* reporters looked into the matter of campaign television spending. They found:

That in California, Representative John V. Tunney, Democratic nominee, spent $800,000 in his successful Senatorial race against incumbent Republican Senator George Murphy, who spent about $500,000 on television advertising.

That incumbent Democratic Senator Vance Hartke of Indiana spent $246,000, quite a bit less than the $441,000 spent by his Republican opponent, Representative Richard L. Roudebush. That election was so close that it remained in dispute for some time after the votes were counted. But Hartke returned to the Senate.

That in Texas, at just five major stations in Dallas and Houston, Democratic Candidate Lloyd M. Bentsen, Jr., spent $115,540 to win a Senate seat. His Republican opponent, George Bush, now the Ambassador to the United Nations, spent $68,000 more at the same five stations, or a total of $184,000.

That at the six major television stations in New York City, files showed that winning Senatorial Candidate James L. Buckley spent $310,557; Democrat Richard L. Ottinger spent $554,740; and incumbent Republican Senator Charles E. Goodell spent $463,854.

Of course, the obvious question is where does the money come from? It certainly does not come from a spontaneous display of financial affection from the rank-and-file voter. In 1964 in Saginaw, Michigan, a community-wide experiment was conducted to see what kind of campaign revenue could be raised. There was wide publicity, detailed planning, and civic and political support for a door-to-door canvass. The canvass of 6,830 voters raised a total contribution of $410.86 from 372 donors.

In Chicago, Illinois, and in many other states Two-Percent Clubs are standard procedure, which means that those holding down government jobs kick back two percent of their monthly salary into the party machine. With the rise in the cost of living, some clubs have been inflated to Five-Percent Clubs.

A study of Indiana's financing of campaigns showed that the Democrats have installed a collector in each state agency to pick up employee contributions at each pay period. Sometimes employees were required to give another one or two percent of their income to county chairmen. From the 1930s to the 1960s, when the Republicans were in power in Indiana, workers were usually required to give one week's pay a year to the Republican state committee. The system applied to about 6,350 government workers.

Indiana also has a party practice of assessing candidates for statewide offices, the money obtained going into a common campaign fund. Thus candidates for Senator or Governor must pay $2,500. A place on the ticket for a Supreme Court judge costs $2,000; $1,250 for Lieutenant Governor and Appellate judges; $1,000 for attorney general; $750 for secretary of state, auditor, treasurer, and court reporter.

So there is a very high cost involved in getting the chance to express one's political convictions in public office. And both the underworld criminals and the corporation criminals are eminently able to underwrite that cost. The Kefauver hearings of the 1950s paraded leading underworld figures before the national television-viewing public, and their links to leading politicians became clear. With regard to campaign spending, for example, the Kefauver Committee discovered that a service which provided racing news for illegal bookmakers and gamblers paid $600,000 in political contributions over a three-year period. A Chicago and Miami race-track operator, closely associated with gangland operations, gave $100,000 toward the campaign of a Governor of Florida.

Probably the most thorough study of campaign contributions was done in 1956, the year General Eisenhower was elected once again to the Presidency. One presumes the general knew how much money was coming in, where it was coming from, and what it was being spent on. So even then the "dollar sign on public service" was rather pronounced. Morton Mintz and Jerry S. Cohen in their book *America, Inc.* summarize some of the findings of the 1956 Congressional study:

For example, contributions of $500 or more yielded to the Republicans $8,064,907, and of $5,000 or more $2,894,309, compared with $2,820,655 and $860,380, respectively, for the Democrats. Twelve selected families gave the Republicans $1,040,526 (with the du Ponts accounting for $248,423, the Pews $216,800, the Rockefellers $152,604 and the Mellons $100,150) and the Democrats $107,109. Officials of the 225 largest corporations gave the Republicans $1,816,597, the Democrats $103,725. For officials of the 100 largest military prime contractors the figures were $1,133,882 versus $40,975; for officials of the 29 largest oil companies $344,997 versus $14,650; for officials of the 10 leading radio and television station licensees, $37,800 versus $1,000; for officials of 17 certificated airlines, $132,150 versus $31,609; for officials of 37 leading advertising agencies $51,600 versus $0; for officials of 47 leading underwriters of investment bonds, $237,800 versus $2,000; for officials of 13 professional, business and other selected groups, $741,189 versus $8,000, and for officials of 88 corporations participating in the atomic energy program, $387,342 versus $34,700.

That, of course, was an election year when President Eisenhower was a sure winner. But the 1956 study is a reminder today of who not only puts men in office, but calls the shots after they get in, a topic which will be discussed in the next lesson. The high cost of conviction is not only the financial price tag involved in running for office, but the sad fact that convictions themselves must be sold to the highest bidders. *What gaineth a man if he sell his own soul?* Most of the time, public office.

**A Guide for Ambitious and
Dedicated Kids Interested in
Fulfilling Some American Dreams**

(A sample survey of what you can
expect to spend and what you *may* get
in return, brought to you through the
courtesy of the American political system)

Expenditure	Realization
PRESIDENT	
$60 million	$200,000 a year salary, or 3/10 of 1 percent back on what you spent
GOVERNOR	
In New York, if you are running against a Rockefeller, $7 million to $20 million	$50,000 a year salary, or 7/10 to 1/5 of 1 percent back on what you spent
In North Carolina, at least $1 million	$35,000 a year salary, or 3.5 percent back on what you spent
In Pennsylvania, $1 million to $2 million	$45,000 a year salary, or 2.25 to 4.5 percent back on what you spent
In Georgia, $40,000 to $1.5 million	$42,500 a year salary. It helps to have segregation on your side. You might make money
In Arkansas, why bother?	$10,000 a year salary
U.S. SENATOR	
Anywhere from $250,000 to $5 million. (Pick your state carefully. By all means, stay away from New York, especially if you hear a fellow named Ottinger is running. He'll run your bill up considerably.)	$42,500 a year salary, or the best you can do is get back 17 percent of what you spent
U.S. REPRESENTATIVE	
Anywhere from $30,000 to $300,000. (Unless you are an incumbent of long standing, better count on the higher figure.)	$42,500 a year salary, so if you're really lucky, you can make some money

156

1

Using this lesson as a guide, write an essay interpreting the familiar phrase "The price one must pay for freedom."

2

Using this lesson as a guide, write an essay interpreting the familiar phrase "You get what you pay for."

3

Using this lesson as a guide, write an essay interpreting the not-so-familiar phrase "It matters not so much that a candidate win or lose, but how he *pays* the game."

Lesson Eight
Power to
What People?

There is no denying that politics as currently practiced in the United States represents "power to the people." The question is, what people?

The "high cost of conviction" should make the answer quite obvious. Power to the people who have the money to buy the power! That is the name of the political game in America, and certainly elections themselves are a game. The political game in the United States is sort of a combination of Monopoly and chess. There are the wealthy brokers who advance the candidates on the game board. And there are also pawns—namely, the voters.

Consider for a moment the actual running of elections in the United States. First of all, as we have seen, they are expensive. Technological advancements in the mass media have ballooned the expense out of any reasonable proportion. So the first consideration of the realistic candidate is how to finance the campaign. Costs are so high that there are very few people able to supply the kind of money needed. They are the wealthy businessmen. The wealthy businessmen represent businesses which need governmental favors so that they can stay wealthy. Thus the wealthy businessman will invest in a candidate's campaign so that favors, concessions, and appropriate protective legislation can be assured once the candidate gets into office.

The catch is, of course, that technically the voters have to record their opinion. It would be so much easier for the businessman if he could just buy an office directly and put the candidate in it. But I imagine most businessmen feel that those bothersome elections are the price they must pay for freedom. So the money must be placed in the party-machine coffers, or in the campaign of an individual candidate, in large enough proportions to finance a campaign able to overwhelm voter sentiment. Smart businessmen, of course, realize the margin of possible error and invest in the campaigns of both major parties. No matter who wins, the businessman can claim he helped win the election.

Mintz and Cohen, in *America, Inc.,* put the process as follows:

It costs money, more all the time, to seek elective public office. The money is obtained from where it's at, which is primarily large corporations and financial institutions. Their campaign "contributions" are really not that at all; they are investments in licenses to govern the government, or if you prefer, to translate economic power into political power. Being prudent, the investors take out insurance by, for example, investing in both political parties at once. The investors get all that money can buy from candidates and parties, which is not to say they get *everything* they want. As compared with corporations, those who cannot afford such investments, or who are unorganized to make them—the poor, the blacks, Puerto Ricans, Spanish-speaking and Spanish-surnamed Americans, Indians, workers displaced by advancing technology and retreating resources, much of the middle class, even professional men—generally get bad deals. "Under the circumstances, it is utterly amazing that the public makes out as well as it does," Senator Russell B. Long (D-La.) once said.

So just as there are party machines and bosses who run them, those bosses of machines know who their bosses are— the financiers who keep the machine operating. Senator Robert A. Taft found that out in the election of 1952. He was in battle with Dwight Eisenhower for the Republican nomination for President. Then he ran up against the New York financiers. He later said that New York financial interests and the businessmen subject to their influence had chosen Mr. Eisenhower as their candidate more than a year before the convention.

Senator Russell Long is chairman of the Senate Finance Committee, and thus he is very familiar with the practices of those who invest in government. And he has some personal dealings which further familiarize him with the process. He receives a large income from his own oil and gas interests, and he has been a champion in protecting the oil industry from the burden of fair taxes and fair competition.

In 1967 Senator Long spoke on the floor of the Senate concerning a proposal to permit the individual taxpayer to earmark $1.00 of his income tax to be used for a Presidential campaign fund. Long offered an illustrative list of campaign-funding procedures, part of which follows (as excerpted by Mintz and Cohen):

Most campaign money comes from businessmen. Labor contributions have been greatly exaggerated. It would be my guess that about 95 percent of campaign funds at the congressional level are derived from businessmen. At least 80 percent of this comes from men who could sign a net worth statement exceeding a quarter of a million dollars. Businessmen contribute because the Federal Corrupt Practices Act prohibits businesses from contributing. . . .

A great number of businessmen contribute to legislators who have voted for laws to reduce the power of labor unions. . . .

Many businessmen contribute to legislators who have voted to exempt their businesses from the minimum wage.

Businessmen contribute to legislators who have fought against taxes that would have been burdensome to their businesses, whether the tax increase was proposed as a so-called reform, a loophole closer, or just an effort to balance the Federal budget.

Power company officials contribute to legislators who vote against public power. . . .

Bankers, insurance company executives, big money lenders generally contribute to legislators who vote for policies that lead to high interest rates.

Many large companies benefit from research and development contracts which carry a guaranteed profit, a so-called fixed fee of about 7 percent of the amount of the contract. Executives of such companies contribute to those who help them get the contracts or who help make the money available. . . . Research contractors contribute to legislators who vote to permit them to have private patent rights on government research expenditures.

Drug companies are often able to sell brand-name drug products at anywhere from twice to 50 times the price of identical nonbranded products for welfare and Medicare patients if the companies can prevail upon government to permit their drugs to be prescribed and dispensed by their private brand names rather than by the official or generic name of the product. Executives of drug companies will contribute to legislators who vote to permit or bring about such a result.

Many industries are regulated. This includes the railroads, the truckers, the airlines, the power companies, the pipelines, to name but a few. Executives of regulated companies contribute to legislators who vote to go easy on the regulation, and ask no more questions than are necessary about their rates.

Companies facing threat of ruinous competition from foreign sources have executives who contribute to those who help protect them from competition by means of tariffs and quotas.

Many industries are subsidized . . . the merchant marine, the shipbuilders, the sugar producers, the copper producers and a host of others. Executives in such industries contribute to those who help keep them in business.

Campaign spending and fund collecting have gotten so far out of hand that there is not even a pretense of enforcing the regulations on the books. Even if there was, parties and politicians have developed skills in avoiding such regulations. The Corrupt Practices Act places an upper limit of spending by any one committee at $3 million, and a maximum contribution of $5,000 by an individual to a single committee. So the major parties set up scores and scores of committees, none of them spending $3 million and all able to collect $5,000 from a single donor, so that a larger donation can be split up.

Power to the special people is aided by the fact that some three fourths of the seats in the House of Representatives, for example, are held by reelected incumbents, and the incumbents continue to win, piling up seniority and protecting the interests of their financiers. Campaign costs feed the process, because the incumbent Representative will naturally have a more direct access to the large special-interest contributors. And after an incumbent Senator or Representative has been around Capitol Hill long enough, he can learn little tricks like getting members of the federal bureaucracy to help a reelection effort. Federal departments and agencies can grant or withhold federal contracts, appointments, and other little political favors.

Writing in the September 1971 issue of *Playboy* magazine, *New York Times* White House Correspondent Robert Semple calls this federal bureaucracy the "hidden government." Not only hidden, but the real government when it comes to governmental functioning. The most noble legislative acts cannot make an impact on the national body unless the federal bureaucracy can be mobilized to effect implementation. Said Robert Semple:

The real issue in Government is not between the elected President and the top men he appoints; Cabinet Secretaries and Undersecretaries can be made to serve his purposes. The real issue is broader: the continuing tension between those who are in some sense vulnerable to the wishes of the electorate (Presidents, Congressmen, even Cabinet members who usually leave office when the President who appoints them is defeated or retires) and those who remain insulated from the electorate through seniority, skill, tenacity, influence or simple anonymity. They make up the permanent bureaucracy. Government cannot work unless the men who carry the popular will to Washington every few years can make an impact on them; and so far, our elected officials haven't been very successful.

Sometimes a Presidential candidate who has made some liberal-sounding proposals during the campaign will deal with the problem by appointing a conservative administrator to implement those proposals after he gets in office. Robert Semple cites the example of President Nixon's appointment of Maurice Stans as Secretary of Commerce. Under the leadership of Stans, the highly ballyhooed "black capitalism" program of Nixon's 1968 campaign has amounted to little.

Once again we see that the individual voter in the United States gets the shaft. Whomever the voter decides upon, the candidate is undoubtedly beholden to certain special financial interests. Already the voter's concerns are relegated to at least secondary status. Then the electee who moves into an office in Washington, D.C., is at the mercy of the clogged wheels of the federal bureaucracy. It's worth remembering the next time you are told by a patriotic party worker how much your vote counts!

Along with the campaign financiers, who are most frequently known only to party leaders and sometimes aspiring candidates, there are other, more visible special-interest groups bidding for legislators' and agencies' attention. They are the professional lobbies, sometimes highly organized and bureaucracies in themselves.

The word "lobbying" refers to the early practice of special-interest representatives hanging out in the lobbies of legislative buildings trying to collar lawmakers as they made their way into the chambers to vote. H. L. Mencken says the word was first used in 1829 to refer to "lobby-agents" in the New York State Capitol in Albany.

Considering America's cowboy mentality, it is not surprising that the big lobby which first caused Congressional investigation in 1855 was that of Samuel Colt, inventor of the famous Colt .45 pistol. He had a lobbyist named Alexander Hay, who maintained headquarters in various hotels and freely dispensed food and liquor to Congressmen. Hay also had the services of three ladies called Spiritualists who were skilled, so the report goes, at "moving with the Members." Colt was found to have paid a "contingent fee" of $10,000 to a Congressman to get him a patent extension.

James Buchanan wrote to Franklin Pierce in 1852 expressing alarm at the growth of lobbyists: "The host of contractors, speculators, stockjobbers, and lobby members which haunt the halls of Congress, all desirous . . . on any and every pretext to get their arms into the public treasury are sufficient to alarm every friend of his country." Walt

Whitman had no use for lobbyists. He lumped them in with "kept editors" as "the lousy combings and born freedom-sellers of the earth."

The old-style lobby tactics have changed somewhat, but the purpose of influencing elected officials and federal bureaucrats is still the same. And the "food, booze and lady" syndrome of the old lobbyists is reflected in contemporary practices of providing legal fees for the law firms of Congressmen back home and the handsome "honoraria" provided for Congressmen speaking to interest-group gatherings.

One Senator summed it all up in the early 1960s. A poll was conducted concerning lobbies, asking 175 Senators and Representatives whether there is "some field of interest which is not represented by an organized lobby . . . but which, in your opinion, should be." The Senator pessimistically responded: "One group which will never be adequately represented—the ordinary citizen and taxpayer."

1

Andrew Jackson once said, "There are no necessary evils in government." Do you agree or disagree? Why? Do you think most Congressmen agree or disagree? Why?

2

Using newspaper articles, interviews, and any other materials you can find, make a chart showing who really has power in your community. Is it the mayor? Is it the sheriff? Is it the city council? Is it the bank president? Is it the largest realtor? If you cannot find out who has the real power, what does this suggest to you?

3

Make a similar chart showing who has the least power in your community. Be sure to include such facts as the income of the powerless, the unemployment rate among the powerless, and the ethnic background of those with no power.

4

Today the phrase "power to the people" means (circle the correct answer):

a. The economic and political control of the nation's twenty most wealthy families;

b. The authority of the Federal bureaucracy in Washington, D.C.;

c. The structure of leadership in the Democratic and Republican parties;

d. None of these.

Lesson Nine
Missing
the Party

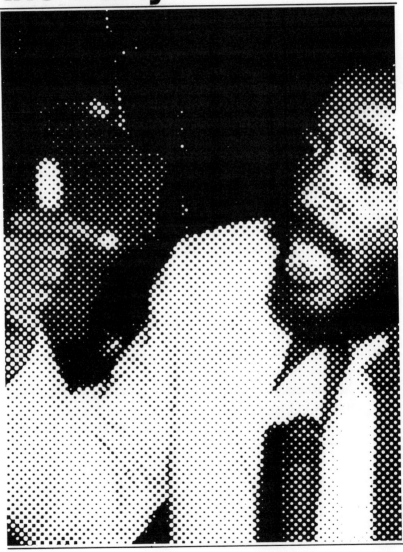

As we have seen, the two major parties, the Democrats and the Republicans, dominate elections in the United States. Yet there are ways in which a voter can choose to "miss the party." The most common way is to register as an independent voter—that is, a voter with no particular allegiance to a particular party. Independents usually end up voting for the candidates of one of the two major parties. And both Democratic and Republican candidates make a bid for the independent vote.

Another way for the voter to exercise true independence is to write in a candidate of the voter's own choosing. However, vote fraud and manipulation being what they are, such evils are magnified when it comes to giving a true count of write-in ballots. I myself have been a write-in candidate twice: for Mayor of Chicago in the 1967 election and for President of the United States in the 1968 election. In both elections I found it impossible to get an accurate count of my total vote.

Or the voter can support a "third party" candidate. The two-party system is so dominant in the political life and thought of the United States that no matter how many other parties there are in a particular national election, each of them is referred to as a "third party."

Finally, the voters can band together and work within the structures of the Democratic and Republican parties to form a counter power bloc to the regular party leadership. Within the Democratic Party in the South, black voters are being effectively organized to challenge traditional party structures.

I'll Do It My Way

Although a national third-party movement has not placed a President in the White House since the two parties became fixed in the United States, third-party candidates can have an effect upon the fate of the two major-party candidates. During the 1968 Presidential election Governor George Wallace of Alabama ran as the candidate of the American Independent Party. He polled nearly ten million popular votes and 46 electoral-college votes (Arkansas, Louisiana, Mississippi, Alabama, and Georgia). The Democratic Party candidate, Hubert Humphrey, received 191 electoral-college votes to President Nixon's 301. Thus, even if Mr. Humphrey had received the 46 additional electoral-college votes which went to Governor Wallace, he would not have had the necessary majority to become President.

But the candidacy of George Wallace had another effect upon the electorate. Governor Wallace inspired excitement and enthusiasm among some voters and curiosity (even when mixed with animosity) among others. Voters who would not bother to watch television appearances of the two major-party candidates, knowing that they are basically the same, turned on their TV sets to see what Governor Wallace was saying. In the process, they found themselves also staying tuned in to the major-party candidates. Governor Wallace forced a comparison and a consideration of the Democratic and Republican candidates which would not have occurred if he had not been a candidate.

There have been times in this century when third-party candidates have made a strong showing. Eugene V. Debs was the Presidential candidate of the Socialist Party in 1900, 1904, 1908, 1912, and 1920. He never made a strong enough showing to receive any electoral-college votes. But his strongest showing in total popular votes came in 1920, when he was running as a candidate from a prison cell where he was confined because of his antiwar activity. He received nearly 920,000 votes. That was about three percent of the total popular vote. In 1912, when he was running against Woodrow Wilson (Democrat), William Howard Taft (incumbent Republican President), and Theodore Roosevelt (third-party Progressive candidate), Debs received six percent of the popular vote.

Theodore Roosevelt received 88 electoral-college votes in that 1912 election, polling over four million popular votes. In 1908 the then President Teddy Roosevelt hand-picked William Howard Taft as his successor. Four years later Roosevelt felt that Taft had reneged on Progressive principles, and, feeling like a Bull Moose, as Roosevelt once put it, he ran as an opposition candidate. Roosevelt's candidacy represented more of a split within the Republican Party than an independent third-party movement, but it was enough to give the White House to the Democrats for two terms.

In 1924 Governor "Fighting Bob" La Follette of Wisconsin stirred the hearts of both the rural and the urban workingman and ran as the Progressive Party candidate for President. He was endorsed by the American Federation of Labor, which had never before endorsed a candidate. La Follette set a third-party record for popular votes, nearly five million (about 600,000 more than Teddy Roosevelt had received as a third-party candidate) and 13 electoral-college votes. The record was broken by Governor Wallace.

The 1948 Presidential election produced two substantial

third parties. Both were splinters from the regular Democratic Party. Several Southern delegations who were critical of the regular Democratic Party's civil-rights platform bolted the party and formed the States' Rights, or "Dixiecrat," Party. The Presidential nominee was Senator J. Strom Thurmond of South Carolina. (Thurmond later became a Republican.) The liberal and left-wing Democrats, who were critical of President Truman's foreign policy, also split away and ran a separate ticket under the banner of the Progressive Party. The Presidential nominee was Henry Wallace, Vice-President under Franklin D. Roosevelt during his third term in office.

Both the Progressives and the Dixiecrats polled 2.4 percent of the popular vote apiece (or a little over a million votes each). Only the Dixiecrats scored in the electoral college, with 39 votes. In spite of the Democratic Party splinter groups, incumbent Democratic President Harry S. Truman won the election, holding almost the entire black and labor votes. The election was a tight one and produced the now famous picture of President-reelected Truman holding the post-election morning edition of the *Chicago Tribune* whose headlines bannered the victory of Truman's Republican opponent, Thomas E. Dewey.

Occasionally electoral-college delegates will conduct their own "third party" movement. When the college met after the 1956 national election, a lone Democratic elector cast his ballot for Walter B. Jones. Four years later fifteen electors—eight unpledged Mississippi Democrats, six unpledged Alabama Democrats, and one Oklahoma Republican—voted for Senator Harry F. Byrd of Virginia, whose name was not even on the national election ballot.

Rather than grasping control of the government, the major victory of third-party movements is to affect national policy. The Populists of the late nineteenth century, angry farmers of the West and South, as well as the Socialists and Progressives of the twentieth century, have seen most of their policies and programs incorporated into the actions of the two major parties. This was particularly true of the visions of the persistent six-time candidate of the Socialist Party, Norman Thomas.

So missing the party can succeed in nonetheless making a point.

From Huey P. Long to Huey P. Newton

Huey P. Long, Jr., was born in 1893, during the era of the Populist movement, in a small, poor rural area in north-central Louisiana known as Winn Parish. It was a strange little plot of American soil, having both expressed Union sentiment during the Civil War and supplied soldiers for the Union Army.

After the Civil War was over and the era of Reconstruction had come to a close, Louisiana politics became the special possession of a privileged group of wealthy planters and lumber, railroad, sugar, and oil tycoons. New Orleans had a well-oiled political machine which served the interests of the wealthy few, and the poor masses were neither considered nor solicited for their votes. The machine not only controlled the state patronage, but also had the press in its pocket.

Huey Long decided to try to upset the control of the privileged few and provide for the needs of the masses. His particular brand of "missing the party" was to build a machine of his own, using the same tactics against his wealthy political enemies that they had been using against the masses. Said Huey Long, "I'm fighting a crooked machine in the Old Regulars and have to fight fire with fire." He was successful, got himself elected Governor, then Senator, and was being spoken of as a possible third-party Presidential candidate in the 1936 election when he died of an assassin's bullet in 1935.

Describing Huey Long's political career, T. Harry Williams has written, "Huey Long was the first Southern mass leader to leave aside race-baiting and appeals to the gold-misted past and address himself to the social and economic ills of his people." Thus in the year Huey Long became Governor, there were in Louisiana 296 miles of concrete roads, 35 miles of asphalt roads, 5,728 miles of gravel roads, and 3 major bridges. Seven years later, the year Huey Long was shot down, there were 2,446 miles of concrete roads, 1,308 miles of asphalt roads, 9,629 miles of gravel roads, and 40 major bridges. Of course, such massive highway construction efforts left ample room for political patronage favors, but the roads were built just the same. Beyond road building, Long provided such necessities as free textbooks in the schools and free night schools for illiterate adults.

Some thirty years after the death of Huey P. Long an independent party movement, the Black Panther Party, took root under the leadership of another Louisiana-born Huey—Huey P. Newton. The Newton family moved to California when little Huey, born in 1942, was only a year old. In the fall of 1966, in Oakland, Huey P. Newton and Bobby G. Seale organized the Black Panther Party for Self-Defense (Huey was Minister of Defense and Bobby was Chairman).

Whereas Huey P. Long was concerned with building *roads* in the state of Louisiana, Huey P. Newton was concerned with making *inroads* into the black community in every state. Whereas Huey P. Long provided free textbooks and free classes for illiterate adults, Huey P. Newton provided free breakfasts for hungry black ghetto children and free instruction in how to be free.

Other comparisons could be made between the political activities of the two Hueys. Whereas Huey P. Long stated he had to "fight fire with fire," Huey P. Newton insisted, along with the United States Constitution, that oppressed black people have the right of self-defense, or the right to (paraphrasing Long) fight firearms with firearms. When firearms and physical brutality are used against the black community by agents of the ruling system, either official or self-appointed guardians of white supremacy, the Black Panther Party advocated the right and duty of protection of life, family, and property.

The very name "Black Panther" was chosen because the panther has a reputation for never making an unprovoked attack but will defend itself ferociously when it is attacked. The black panther, accompanied by the slogan "Move On Over or We'll Move On Over You," was originally the emblem of the Lowndes County Freedom Party in Alabama, organized in 1965. The panther then became a symbol of black militancy and was copied throughout the nation.

The assassination which befell Huey P. Long had its counterpart in the numerous assassinations which cut down leaders of the Black Panther Party as the party began to make inroads all across the country. The killings of Chicago Panther leaders Fred Hampton and Mark Clark in

December 1969 were but the most dramatic and publicized examples of such assassinations.

As Mr. Williams described Huey P. Long as putting aside "racing-baiting" and "appeals to the gold-misted past," so Huey P. Newton and the Black Panther Party rejected "racist" thinking (though the ruling system labeled them racist) and entered into coalitions with persons and movements truly concerned with addressing social and economic ills of their people, seeing the struggle for human liberation as a much broader movement than anything which could be defined by narrow racial distinctions. And Huey P. Newton and his followers rejected the "gold-misted" past by refusing to accept the myths of life in America and constructed a program which tried to deal with the realities.

Finally, a comparison of Huey P. Long's "Share the Wealth" program and the Black Panther Party's Ten-Point Platform provide some interesting similarities. Both speak of a fair distribution of wealth, of closing the gap between the haves and the have-nots, and of making government serve the needs and aspirations of the common folks.

Huey P. Long's program called for limiting poverty by allowing all families to share the wealth of America for not less than one third of the average wealth—that is, to possess not less than $5,000 free of debt. Fortunes would be limited to such few millions that most of the wealth and profits of the land could be shared by the balance of the American people. Taxes to run the government would first of all be supported by reducing big fortunes from the top, allowing also for employment in public works when unemployment became a problem.

Such concerns were echoed in the Panther Party platform. The party of Huey P. Newton recognized the need for full employment, stating that it is the responsibility of government to provide either employment or a guaranteed annual income. The Panther Party platform stated:

We believe that if the white American businessmen will not give full employment, then the means of production should be taken from the businessmen and placed in the community so that the people of the community can organize and employ all of its people and give a high standard of living.

The Panther platform also recognized the imbalance of the tremendous fortunes amassed by the haves, purchased at the expense, labor, and *misfortunes* of the masses of black people, and called for a restitution of "payment in currency" to "be distributed to our many communities."

The Panther Party inroads into the black community are not as easily measured in tangible statistics as Huey Long's road-building program in Louisiana. But those who apply another standard of measurement than cold statistical figures can see a tremendous impact of the Black Panther Party and the uncompromising stance of black militancy it fostered.

In the fall of 1969 many Americans were wondering why the anticipated riots and rebellions that had been expected to occur in the black ghettos during the summer had failed to materialize. In comparison to previous summers, the summer of 1969 had been quite calm. Those seeking an enlightened explanation found an ironic circumstance. The militants in the black ghettos, who were usually accused of *causing* disturbances, were really the prime movers in a riot-free summer. Thus the militants were the real peace-makers, though they continued to be harassed by peace officers.

To understand what happened, one has to be familiar with life in the black ghetto. Though black militants have a profound disrespect for the corrupt racist system in the United States, they have an equally profound passion for oppressed black people. In ghetto after ghetto across the country, militant organizations were opening storefront offices, setting up community organizations, and establishing a new rapport with ghetto dwellers. For the first time in their lives, residents of the black ghetto had someone to turn to, someone who really understood their problems, organizations sincerely committed to seeking real solutions.

It was an entirely new situation in the black ghetto. The militant organizations which took root in the black ghettos of the nation were truly *of* and *for* black people, and rep-resented a dramatic break from the paternalistic patterns of social-service agencies and government programs, and from the machine political patterns of black wards and black politicians. While black machine politicians did give black people someone to turn to, and did assist in getting services and a governmental hearing for ghetto dwellers, such politicians always owed primary allegiance to serving the interests of the white-controlled machine.

Thus earlier programs did not speak the language of the ghetto, nor serve the real needs as seen and felt by the black ghetto residents themselves. In the absence of com-munication and understanding, open revolt is inevitable. Bricks and Molotov cocktails are sure attention-getters and represent the outraged cry of those who have been totally abandoned.

The political and social system in America places ghetto residents in a mental and physical pressure-cooker which demands some kind of release. I remember once seeing a tragic scene in New York City's black ghetto of Harlem which illustrated well the pressures of ghetto life. A little black boy stood on the Harlem street with a seashell held to his ear. Trying to escape the unbearable pressures of his immediate environment, the little boy tried to hear the roar of the sea, and in his mind, at least, he would be enjoying the natural freedom of surf and sand.

How tragic it was to realize that the little boy was only a seashell's throw away from the sea itself! Yet his life had been so confined, pressured, and programmed by ghetto imprisonment that he didn't seem to realize that Harlem was so close to the Atlantic Ocean.

Such a black child, pressured in the ghetto and cut off from understanding and freedom of movement (the ocean was as inaccessible to him as if he had lived in the Midwest), must seek relief from ghetto oppression. And the growing number of militant organizations, spawned by the activity of the Black Panther Party and such programs as the break-fast program, provided the understanding, leadership, and avenues of expression which any black ghetto child must have, and which at least make total destruction an *option* rather than the *only resort*.

Thus Huey P. Long chose to "miss the traditional party structure" by using the machine tactics against it. Huey P. Newton chose to avoid the corrupt practices of party politics, and began to build community-based organizations where ghetto residents would no longer be seen as pawns serving political party interests but would rather have the power to determine their own destinies.

And the Panther Gave Birth to the Eagle

An excellent example of organizing voters to present a counter power bloc to traditional party leadership is the National Democratic Party of Alabama (NDPA), under the leadership of its chairman, Dr. John Cashin. The NDPA is a counter structure to the "regular" Alabama Democratic Party, and has adopted the emblem of the eagle just as the "traditional" Democrats have always used the rooster.

The party was really born in 1968, when Dr. Cashin led an attempt to get the nationwide Democratic Party to recognize the Eagle party as the official affiliate from Alabama to the Democratic national nominating convention in Chicago. The NDPA rightfully claimed to be the true representation of loyal Democrats, since about three fourths of the Democratic Party members in Alabama are black voters. Dr. Cashin's efforts were rebuffed and the old-line Rooster party was recognized as Alabama's official delegation.

But the 1970 Alabama elections indicated the strength the NDPA had been able to muster. Twenty-one black people were elected to office in Alabama in 1970—12 from the Eagle party, 6 from the Rooster party, and 3 with both Eagle and Rooster backing. Dr. Cashin himself was the NDPA candidate for Governor, and he was soundly defeated by Governor George Wallace. Dr. Cashin received about sixteen percent of the total Alabama vote. But his candidacy was largely responsible for bringing out the vote in the Black Belt counties of Alabama where other NDPA candidates won.

The attitude of the Rooster party toward the NDPA was a good indication that its potential strength was being recognized. During the 1970 elections, increased efforts were made to enter into deals to buy off black votes (NDPA began in the first place because of such buying and selling out of black votes), instances of voter intimidation were stepped up, cheating at the polls was resorted to, and the campaign efforts of the regular Rooster Democrats were greatly increased. A primary reason for the Roosters running scared was that important offices were in contest, such as sheriff or probate judge. Two years earlier, in 1968, Rooster efforts were not as intense because lesser offices (constable or justice of the peace) were at stake.

Efforts to discredit the Eagle party were also increased. The NDPA was portrayed as an organization of "separatists," the implication being that support of Eagle party candidates would be a step backward from the desired goal of integration. Actually, the real "separatist" party was the white-controlled Rooster party and always has been. Membership in the NDPA is about 90 percent black and 10 percent white.

Though the NDPA is still in its embryonic stages, it does represent a sound strategy for "missing" the traditional party structures. For one thing, the emblem itself is most important, making it much less complicated for the black voters and their white voting allies to mark their ballots or pull the voting-machine levers "for the Eagle." And the NDPA represents the organization of a voting bloc that can both build up a significant total of votes for its candidates and withhold a significant number of votes from other would-be "regular" candidates. As such, it indicates a kind of strategy which an organized black vote can use on a nationwide basis within the Democratic party.

A solid "outside the party" organizational effort rallied behind black Presidential and Vice Presidential candidates would serve two potential purposes. It could be used as a threat to the leadership of the regular Democratic Party. And it could be the basis of a third-party ticket outside the two-party system, in case the regular Democratic Party leadership failed to respond to black demands and aspirations. With the rise in black voters, regular Democratic leaders should realize that such a decision could very well mean missing a chance of victory.

So the Panther gave birth to the Eagle, and who knows where the genealogy will end?

1

What was the difference between the road- and bridge-building activities of Huey P. Long and Huey P. Newton?

2

True or false: "There was a summer of relative calm in the United States in 1969 because all of the black militant leaders were in Northern Ireland serving as 'technical advisors' "?

3

An Eagle is:
   a. two shots under par in golf;
   b. a gold coin;
   c. the seal of the United States;
   d. the emblem of the National Democratic Party of Alabama;
   e. all of the above.

Lesson Ten
The Constitution's Institutions

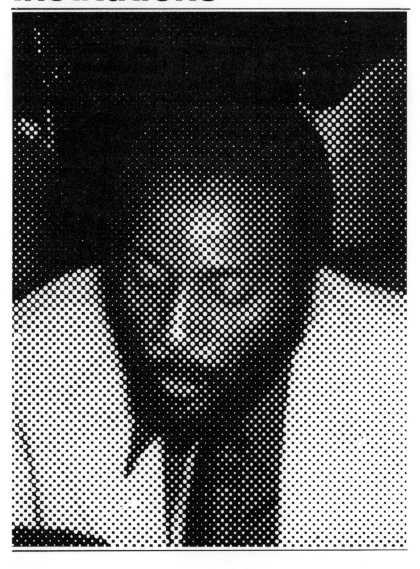

The three basic institutions of the United States Constitution are Congress, representing legislative power; the office of President, representing executive power; and the Supreme Court, representing judicial power. The function of each branch of the federal government is quite simply laid out in the Constitution, but custom and practice over the years have complicated the roles considerably. Like political parties, the Constitutional institutions have burrowed into the American body politic and have become fixed and rigid beyond the point of original recognition.

The Congress

To become a Senator, a man or woman must be at least 30 years of age, have been a citizen for nine years, and be a resident of the state represented. A member of the House of Representatives must be at least 25 years of age, have been a citizen for seven years, and be a resident of the state represented. Custom has also determined that the Representative must reside in the Congressional district represented, but that is not a Constitutional requirement. Senators and Representatives alike receive a salary of $42,500 a year, plus expense and travel allowances, free mailing privileges, long-distance phone calls for themselves and staff, stationery allowances, and all sorts of other fringe benefits many members of Congress would call "creeping socialism" if they were being extended to just ordinary citizens.

The youngest member of the current session of the Senate is 36 years old; the oldest is 80. Over in the House the youngster is 29 and the old-timer is 83 (Emanuel Celler of Brooklyn, New York). So that the average age of Congress is 56.4, just a year and a half younger than President Nixon at the time of this writing. The average age of the new Senators is 44.8 and of the new Representatives is 45.0.

Thus there is some relatively young blood flowing through the veins of Congress, but institutional habits effectively clot the Congressional arteries. The actual functioning of Congress is in the hands of standing committees, and these committees are controlled by their chairmen. There are twenty-one standing committees in the House of Representatives and seventeen in the Senate. The chairmanship of standing committees is decided according to the seniority rule. That is, the member of a particular committee who has the longest consecutive service becomes the chairman if his political party is the majority party. The member of the minority party with the longest period of consecutive service is recognized as the ranking minority member, which means that member will become the chairman if there is a shift in majority parties.

Thus the old-timers control the Congress. Not necessarily the elder statesmen of the country, they are the Senators and Representatives who have been able to appease the voters and accommodate to political-party leadership enough to keep getting elected time and time again. And since the South has traditionally been a stronghold of the Democratic Party, so that the two-party system is not at all competitive, Congressmen tend to pile up seniority, giving committee control to Southern legislators.

Thus in the Senate 58-year-old Herman Talmadge of Georgia chairs the Agriculture and Forestry Committee; 81-year-old Allen J. Ellender of Louisiana chairs the Appropriations Committee; 70-year-old John Stennis of Mississippi chairs the Armed Services Committee; 72-year-old John

Sparkman of Alabama chairs the Banking, Housing and Urban Affairs Committee; 53-year-old Russell Long of Louisiana chairs the Finance Committee (a youngster, really, by seniority standards); J. W. Fulbright of Arkansas, who does not give his birth date in the current Congressional Directory but who was elected to the Senate in 1944, chairs the Foreign Relations Committee; 75-year-old John McClellan of Arkansas chairs the Government Operations Committee; 68-year-old James Eastland of Mississippi chairs the Judiciary Committee; 70-year-old Jennings Randolph of West Virginia chairs the Public Works Committee; and 75-year-old B. Everett Jordan of North Carolina chairs the Rules and Administration Committee.

Over in the House, Texas Representatives ride herd over five committees, with Banking and Currency Committee Chairman Wright Patman leading the age group at 78. W. R. Poage (Agriculture) and George Mahon (Appropriations) are both in their 70s. Octogenarian Emanuel Celler chairs the House Judiciary Committee; and the House Armed Services Committee is headed by 70-year-old F. Edward Hébert of Louisiana, the first Louisianian in history to serve twenty-five consecutive years in the House of Representatives.

It would seem, of course, that in spite of the old folks in control of standing committees, the youngsters could get together and vote on legislation. After all, legislative acts are what is important. But it is not that simple. A proposed bill must travel an unbelievable route before (or if) it is voted upon. And, sure enough, it has to pass through committees, where it can get choked in a stranglehold of senility.

Let us trace the usual route of a bill through the labyrinth of Congressional procedure. A House member introduces a bill by placing it in the "hopper," a box on the Clerk's desk. It is then numbered and sent to the Government Printing Office and made available the next morning at the document room. Then the bill is referred to a standing committee. The standing committee, or subcommittee thereof, examines the bill and decides upon its merit. Bills not approved by the standing committee usually "die" at this stage, though it is conceivably possible for the House to compel a committee to discharge a bill. The procedures governing such compulsion are extremely difficult, and the action is never taken.

If a bill gets the green light from the standing committee, it is "reported" back to the House, either as it was originally introduced or with recommended amendments. Then the bill is placed on the calendar in accordance with the kind of bill it is. This is the second stage where a bill may be killed. Many bills appearing on the calendar never get considered.

But if a bill does get considered, there is a second reading, at which time the bill is open for amendment and debate. At the end of discussion and proposed amendments, if any, which occur on the second reading, the question is put to the House: "Shall the bill be engrossed and read a third time?" An engrossed bill is a bill in the form in which it finally is adopted by the House of Representatives.

If the question is answered favorably, the bill is read a third time (usually by title only) and if adopted, it is signed by the Speaker of the House and the Clerk and passed on to the Senate.

In the Senate the bill goes through the same procedure. The bill gets passed on to another committee, and the committee has the power to kill bills at this stage by refusing to report them. If a bill does get to the floor of the Senate, debate can be prolonged because Senators are permitted to speak at length on any subject. Opposition Senators can engage in a filibuster, talking for days and weeks on end, and they can only be stopped by cloture proceedings. Cloture requires sixteen Senators filing a petition and a two-thirds vote in favor of cloture within two days after filing the petition.

If the bill gets by the Senate, with or without amendments, it is passed on back to the House, where the amendments proposed by the Senate are considered. The bill is referred to a conference committee, customarily including ranking majority and minority members of the standing committees in the Senate and the House who handled the bill in the first place. The conference committee tries to settle the differences. Conference committees function in secret, and no minutes or formal record is kept of their proceedings.

After the autopsy in conference committee, the bill is enrolled on parchment, examined by the chairmen of the appropriate House and Senate committees, and signed by the Speaker of the House and the President of the Senate. Then the bill is ready to be sent to the President for his signature or his veto. The President usually refers the bill to another department or committee for recommendation. The President has ten days to act upon a bill. If he does not act, the bill becomes law.

If the bill is vetoed by the President, it must pass a two-thirds majority vote of the members present in each House of Congress at the time voting occurs, provided a quorum is present. The House or Senate may consider the veto of a President at once, postpone consideration to another day, or refer the matter to a committee. If the bill fails to get a two-thirds vote, the whole process is over with.

If the above sounds unduly complicated, it is because it is. One wonders if it is really what the Founding Fathers had in mind when, in writing the Constitution, they said, "Each House may determine the Rules of its Proceedings."

But even when the Founding Fathers were very clear about the separation of powers in government, the "course of human events" has reversed their best intentions. The long, hot summer of debate in Philadelphia in 1787 produced a Constitution which made it very clear that the Senate, rather than the President, was to be predominant in determining foreign policy. True, the President (George Washington) was to be Commander in Chief, was to appoint ambassadors, consuls, and the like. *Congress* was to have the exclusive power to declare war. The Senate in particular was granted the power to advise, consent, and approve all foreign-policy commitments. The President could initiate treaties, for example, with other countries. But those treaties were not binding without Senate approval. In all matters of foreign policy, neither the President, the Secretary of State, nor any other official can commit this country without the agreement of the Senate. Any resurrected Founding Father would have to marvel at how we got involved in the war in Southeast Asia in the absence of approval by the Senate.

The late Clem Miller, Representative from California, whose chartered campaign plane crashed into the side of a mountain in 1962, described well the feeling of a fresh young Congressman faced with the rigidity of Congressional procedure:

No man, when chosen to the membership of a body possessing great powers and exalted prerogatives, likes to have his activity repressed, and himself suppressed, by imperative rules and precedents which seem to have been framed for the deliberate purpose of making usefulness unattainable by individual members. Yet such the new member finds the rules and precedents of the House to be.

And no less a figure than Woodrow Wilson labeled Congressional procedure "our disintegrate methods of legislation." He was talking about power being distributed among standing-committee chairman. And these "petty barons," as Wilson called them, have only found more opportunities to wield control as government has grown.

The Shadow Congress

Who knows what evil lurks in the hearts of men? The Shadow Congress knows.
The cumbersome stalling and delay tactics of traditional Congressional procedure, the maneuvering to protect special interests, and the power plays by senior citizens of Congress to cater to their Golden Age concerns have produced concerned individuals and committees of individuals within Congress itself who take it upon themselves to do the kinds of things standing committees ought to be doing.

One of the earliest such groupings was the Democratic Study Group, a group of Northern liberals trying to use their power more effectively. The DSG over the years has developed task forces which almost duplicate Congressional committees and which gather information to be made available to members of Congress, thereby giving a point of view other than the "official" one. Another Shadow in Congress is the group Members of Congress for Peace Through Law, which, among other things, has issued studies and reports on war spending. That MCPL is taken seriously is attested by the Pentagon rebuttal to the Shadow findings.

And individual Congressmen take it upon themselves to conduct hearings on burning issues which the regular channels refuse to deal with. One outstanding example was California Congressman Ronald Dellums' hearings on war crimes.

The newest and most promising grouping within the Shadow Congress is the fourteen-member Black Congressional Caucus, a united black legislative front comprising twelve members of the House of Representatives and the nation's only black Senator, Senator Edward Brooke of Massachusetts. They are joined by Walter Fauntroy, black nonvoting Congressman representing the District of Columbia.

These twelve members of the House of Representatives are: William "Bill" Clay from St. Louis; Ronald Dellums and Augustus Hawkins from California; John Conyers and Charles Diggs from Detroit; Shirley Chisholm and Charles Rangel from Brooklyn and New York City; Ralph Metcalfe and George Collins from Chicago; Robert N. C. Nix from Philadelphia; Louis Stokes from Cleveland; and Perren Mitchell from Baltimore. The members of the Congressional Black Caucus have openly and unapologetically rallied around their blackness.

The real promise of the emergence of the Black Congressional Caucus in 1971 is that it is a reflection of a change in attitude in the black community in recent years. There was a time when black folks wanted and admired *Negro* politicians. Now the black community is demanding *black* politicians. There is a big difference between the two. The Negro politician merely demonstrated that a white-dominated and -directed legislative mentality could come in different colors. The black politician challenges the assumptions and structure of white dominance and verbalizes the deepest yearnings and insights of the black mind at the highest levels of government.

The Black Congressional Caucus really began March 25, 1971, when a long-awaited meeting with President Nixon was finally granted by the White House. The Caucus presented some sixty demands, which the President "heard" with predictable appreciation and then proceeded to ignore as part of the administration program. So the Caucus held a subsequent press conference and expressed their understandable indignation that once again the black voice of the land had not been truly listened to and much less "heard."

But no President, incumbent or future, will be able to dismiss that voice so easily. Even President Nixon admitted that he was impressed by the homework the Caucus had done. And that homework is just beginning, strategically and legislatively. It's nothing new for black folks. We've been keeping close watch over white folks for four hundred years. Even the old "house niggers" during the days of slavery were doing their homework in more ways than one, and they certainly knew their "masters" better than the "masters" knew them.

Taking stock of the House, the Black Caucus realizes that their strength and influence reach far beyond the number thirteen. There are presently some seventy-five white Congressmen who owe their seats in the House of Representatives to the votes of a black constituency, and the Caucus is not about to allow them to forget it. Add to that a determination on the part of each member of the Black Caucus to get two voting friends each time the roll is called, and a very substantial voting bloc is established.

And that voting bloc is certain to grow with each new election from now on. Black voter registration in the South has nearly tripled over the past decade, due both to the 1965 Voting Rights Act and the new pride and determination developed through the work and sacrifices of such men as Dr. Martin Luther King, Jr., Medgar Evers, and countless others. Surely the next election, or two at the most, will produce the first black member of Congress from the South since the days of Reconstruction.

In responding to the President's lack of responsiveness to the demands laid before him, Caucus Chairman Charles Diggs of Detroit referred to the familiar phrase that has described America's social and political attitude since the birth of the nation: "If you're black, get back!" Now the black community is rephrasing that slogan, especially now that the young blacks have the right to vote. They're saying to their elected representatives in Congress, "If you're black, we'll send you back."

So the days of the Negro politician are over, and the days

of the black politician are just beginning. The black community knows it, and it will soon become evident to white legislators, party power wielders, and even the old men who guard the chairmanships.

There was a day when white politicians could hand-pick their favorite Negro politicians, incorporate them into the machine, and offer them to the black community as candidates. But now white folks have abandoned the cities. They've even relinquished the nation's capital to black folks. The 1970 census shows that 22 million blacks are concentrated in fifteen cities. That leaves an increasing majority in large urban areas to do the selecting *and* electing. And, believe me, the resulting successful candidates will be *black*.

The Shadow not only *knows,* but also *grows.*

The President

To become President, a man or woman must have reached the age of 35 and be a native-born citizen. Precedent indicates that life really begins at 40 for Presidential hopefuls. The youngest President was Teddy Roosevelt at 42. John F. Kennedy came next at 43; Ulysses S. Grant at 46; Grover Cleveland at 47; Franklin Pierce at 48; and James Polk and James Garfield at 49.

We have already seen how the original Constitutional method for electing a President, the electoral-college system, has been maintained. The Founding Fathers also provided that Senators would be elected by the legislatures of the various states. But the 17th Amendment in 1913 changed that Constitutional process, so that now Senators are elected by direct popular vote. The ancient method of electing a President still hangs on.

Once again the Constitutional description of the duties of the President is quite simple:

The President was to be commander in chief of the army and navy.

He could require the opinion of every principal officer in each of the executive departments in writing.

He could make treaties, with the advice and consent of the Senate.

He could appoint ambassadors, Supreme Court judges, and other public ministers and consuls, again with the advice and consent of the Senate.

He could give a state-of-the-union message to Congress from time to time, recommending legislation.

Time, custom, the growth of political parties and the nation have added enormously to the President's role. Yet as late as the latter part of the 1930s the President's staff still reflected the rather simple Constitutional description of his function. (Though there is no Constitutional requirement that the President be a man, everywhere in the Constitution the President is referred to as "he.") So that the President's staff consisted of a couple of career clerks, as well as assorted personnel borrowed from old-line departments around Washington, D.C. With the coming of Roosevelt and the New Deal, braintrusters with or without official status settled down in the White House. Then in 1939 the Executive Office was established, providing for three secretaries and six administrative assistants. During the time of the Eisenhower administration, White House and Executive Office personnel climbed to a total of 2,730. Today the budget for the White House alone is $3,229,000. Another $2,503,-000 is expended for Secret Service and White House police.

In January 1970, as a kind of bicentennial preview and a demonstration of how far this country had moved away from England's Buckingham Palace and the monarchy, the White House guards appeared all decked out in bright new uniforms. The costume was described as including

double-breasted white tunics festooned with gold braid and alive with gold buttons, black trousers, and a black-holstered pistol hung from a black belt. The least credible feature was the hat, a black vinyl, peaked, and visored job variously described as being the headgear of an American high school drum major and as resembling a West German traffic policeman's cap.

Many folks couldn't decide if they were witnessing an operetta or shades of the Queen's Guard. The uniforms were designed by a Washington tailor, Jimmie Muscatello, whose store advertises "Pants cuffed free while you wait."

It was reported, by way of explaining the innovation, that President Nixon had been impressed by the uniforms of European palace guards and thought we might do well to emulate that aspect of the monarchy here at home. After becoming the laughingstock of the world, the White House guards scrapped their hats. Official explanation: The hats were too tight. Evidently Jimmie Muscatello is great on cuffs, but not too tough on hats.

Presidents have varied in their description of the job. Teddy Roosevelt, the man who called the office a "bully pulpit," later gave a more thoughtful version:

I declined to adopt the view that what was imperatively necessary for the nation could not be done by the President unless he could find some specific authorization to do it. My belief was that it was not only his right but his duty to do anything that the needs of the nation demanded unless such action was forbidden by the Constitution or by the law.

Andrew Jackson saw his primary responsibility to the people and to protect them from Congress:

The President is the direct representative of the American people; he possesses original executive powers, and absorbs in himself all executive functions and responsibilities; and it is his special duty to protect the liberties and rights of the people and the integrity of the Constitution against the Senate, or the House of Representatives, or both together.

Also cognizant of his responsibility to the people, Franklin Roosevelt cautioned that the President must be careful never to become a bore. John Kennedy was aware of the awesome decision-making responsibilities of the President, and he wrote: "In the end, he is alone. There stands the decision—and there stands the President." Harry Truman voiced the same sentiment by the plaque on his desk which read, "The buck stops here." And with his famous eloquence, Warren G. Harding summed up the role of the President: "My God, this is a hell of a job!"

Clinton Rossiter, Tom Wicker, and, I presume, others have parceled the contemporary role and duties of the President as: Leader of the West, Head of State, Chief Executive, Chief Diplomat, Chief Legislator, Chief Appropriator, Chief Economist, Party Leader, and Chief Opinion-Maker. So the modern President is commander in chief of a lot more than the Army and Navy.

As mentioned earlier, the President has assumed a role in foreign relations which makes a mockery of the Constitutional provisions placing such matters in the hands of the Senate. Since basic involvement in the Southeast Asia entanglements began under the Truman administration, it is appropriate that Harry S. Truman gave public acknowledgment of the President's usurpation of Senatorial powers. Speaking to a group of Jewish War Veterans in 1948, Harry Truman announced: "I make American foreign policy."

As Leader of the West (or commander of the non-Communist world arsenal) and Chief Diplomat, the President must travel abroad and confer at home. Scarcely a week passes that the President does not confer with the head of some government or an emissary. Of course, every time the President leaves the country, I get worried. Especially if he takes his wife with him. I just figure he might know something. Like after the first moon landing, President Nixon left the country and didn't come back until he found out the astronauts weren't contaminated.

As Chief Appropriator and Chief Economist, the President is the top man in financial matters, though one of the checks Congress is supposed to have is the power to withhold money from an overambitious President. Commenting on that reality today, Tom Wicker has written:

Congress retains the so-called "power of the purse," but it is a sadly diminished power. The President, through his legislative programs, his executive management, his idea of the national necessities, in effect has the power to say whether the budget shall be $90 billion or $70 billion; Congress retains the power, basically, to say whether it shall be $90 billion or $88.5 billion.

So the President's role is both traditional and greatly expanded. He lights the White House tree every Christmas and ignites rice crops in Vietnam. He presides over state dinners in the White House and decides whether to use his moral influence forcefully to wipe out hunger in America. He authorizes the sending of American boys to Vietnam and he pins medals on them when and if they come back. It's all part of being Chief of State and seeing that "the laws are faithfully executed."

The Vice President

Our first Vice President, John Adams, verbalized the sentiment usually applied to the importance of the office. Said Adams, longing for some kind of participatory power, "I am very apprehensive that a desperate anti-federal party will provoke all Europe by their insolence. But my country in its wisdom contrived for me the most insignificant office that ever the invention of man contrived or his imagination conceived."

Other Vice Presidents have been equally pessimistic in describing their job. Teddy Roosevelt, who was the number-two man for a brief period, said: "The Vice President is really only a fifth wheel to the coach." Franklin Roosevelt's first Vice President, John Nance Garner, said: "The office is itself entirely unimportant." Thomas Marshall, Woodrow Wilson's Vice President, used to tell a little story to get his point across: "There were once two brothers. One ran away to sea. The other was elected Vice President and neither was heard of again."

Marshall also described himself as "a man in a cataleptic fit," who "is conscious of all that goes on but has no part in it." Noting that it was appropriate for the Vice President to be a member of the Smithsonian Institution, Marshall said he had "opportunity to compare his fossilized life with the fossils of all ages."

During the debate over the 12th Amendment to the Constitution, Roger Griswold said that from that time on the Vice President would be "selected without any decisive view of his qualifications" and the office would be "carried into the market to be exchanged for the votes of some large states for President." Griswold proved to be a true prophet, and the Vice Presidency is, more than anything else, a ticket-balancing office.

It is hard to consider the Vice Presidential office without thinking first and foremost of the 39th Vice President, Spiro T. Agnew. Agnew has removed the office from the ranks of obscurity and elevated it to that of the President's "right-hand mouth" (to quote Bob Hope). Far from the days of oblivion expressed by Thomas Marshall, Spiro Agnew has been heard from again and again and again.

In July 1971, Vice President Agnew took a world tour, part of which took him to Africa. After conferring with some of the African leaders, Agnew described them as "dedicated, enlightened, dynamic and extremely apt for the task that faces them." Then the Vice President went on to say that American black leaders ought to learn to act more like African black leaders: "The quality of this [African] leadership is in distinct contrast with many of those in the United States who have arrogated unto themselves the position of black leaders, those who spend their time in querulous complaint and constant recrimination against the rest of society."

Whom had Agnew been talking to? Jomo Kenyatta, former head of the Mau Maus! I wish American black leaders would take Agnew up on his suggestion. I'd love to see Roy Wilkins, head of the NAACP, walk into Agnew's office leading two black panthers—real ones, live and wild. And then see Dr. Ralph Abernathy, head of SCLC, walk into the office right behind him carrying a burning spear.

While Agnew was in Kenya, President Kenyatta made the Vice President a "blood brother" in the Kikuyu tribe. When I read that, I couldn't understand why Agnew would go all the way to Africa just to get cut by some black cats. He could have taken the shuttle from Washington to New York, then walked up to Harlem, and he would have achieved the same result. Of course, there wouldn't be any ritual or anything like that.

The one thing that must be said, in all fairness, about Vice President Agnew is that he is consistent. Agnew talks about everybody. During the campaign of 1968 he talked about "Polacks" and "Japs." I wouldn't be surprised to see Agnew get on television and call Nixon a *honkie*.

But Agnew worries me, especially when President Nixon leaves the country. Agnew then becomes the number-one boy in charge. And he just reminds me of the type of cat who would make a crank call to the Russians on the hot line. I can hear him now: "Hello, Kosygin, how's your momma?"

In spite of anything that is said about the insignificance of the office, the Vice President is just one last gasp of breath away from being Chief of State. Presidential expiration led to the elevation into the highest office of the land of John Tyler (1841), Millard Fillmore (1850), Andrew Johnson (1865), Chester A. Arthur (1881), Theodore Roosevelt (1901), Calvin Coolidge (1923), Harry S. Truman (1945), and Lyndon B. Johnson (1963). Four such elevations were the result of political assassinations. Then there were men who served as Vice President and were later elected to the Presidency without first being placed in office by the death of a President: John Adams, Thomas Jefferson, Martin Van Buren, and Richard M. Nixon.

There have been thirty-seven years in the country's history when there was no Vice President, and it didn't mean much. The Senate managed to meet, conduct its business, and adjourn without any real difficulty. The major importance of the Vice President is the "what if something happened to the President" factor. Which should give Presidential aspirants a clue to the best life-insurance policy they can have. I tried to convince President Lyndon Johnson that if he was really smart, he would have picked me as his Vice Presidential runningmate in 1964. That way, he would never have to worry about someone being crazy enough to assassinate him. It begins to look like President Nixon adopted my idea.

The Supreme Court

Before the Nixon Administration, back in the days when Earl Warren was Chief Justice, I never referred to the nine judges on the highest bench in the land as "The Supreme Court." They rendered so many decisions for the benefit of black folks that I used to call them "our alternate sponsors." And it was as it should be. The cats wearing the white sheets took our rights away from us, it's only natural that the cats in the black robes should give them back.

The United States Supreme Court is the court of last resort in the country and has become the guardian of the Constitution. The original jurisdiction of the Supreme Court as outlined in the Constitution is quite limited—basically, all cases where a state is a party, or controversies involving diplomatic or consular representatives of foreign states accredited to the United States.

Congress has no power or control over the original jurisdiction of the Supreme Court. But according to the Constitution, it is also a court of appeals, having jurisdiction as to both law and fact, *with such exceptions and under such regulations as the Congress shall make.* In practice, whether the Supreme Court hears a case being appealed depends upon the Court's willingness to do so.

Early in its career the Supreme Court decided that it had the power to pass upon the constitutionality of acts of Congress. Oddly, the test case involved the Supreme Court itself. The case of *Marbury* v. *Madison,* which was decided in 1803, ruled that Congress did not have the Constitutional right to increase the original jurisdiction as outlined by the Constitution, an increase provided by the 1789 Judiciary Act. Since that time the Supreme Court has ruled upon the constitutionality of not only acts of Congress, but also laws enacted by state legislatures and city councils, as well as the actions of executive, administrative, and judicial authorities.

Although Supreme Court decisions are always sure to anger a segment of the United States population, the major drawback boils down once again to money. It costs a lot of money to take a case through the route necessary to get it heard by the Supreme Court. Carrying such an appeal costs in the neighborhood of $25,000. Only the very wealthy can effect such an appeal. Rich corporations, for example, can hire legal staffs, consultants, researchers, and even entire law firms. They are then able to exercise their right to get a hearing from the Supreme Court.

As I have advocated before, the Supreme Court can never truly be the court of last resort until all Americans, rich and poor alike, have the opportunity to have their cases heard. Legislation should be enacted immediately to provide the opportunity for lawyers and legal researchers to take any case on file and bring it up to the Supreme Court, and if a reversal of the original decision results, government funds should be used to pay such lawyers and legal researchers. Since the Constitution provides that the Supreme Court is a court of appeals "under such regulations as Congress shall make," a good regulation for Congress to start with would be the availability of the Supreme Court to all citizens.

The Constitution's institutions hold great promise, if they would only function as the Constitution says they should. The Founding Fathers kept the Constitution simple and to the point. They purposely left the basic outline open-ended, allowing for changing times, creative growth, and the infusion of the ideas of statesmen then unborn. They had a lot of faith in what this new country would become. Unfortunately, their descendants did not merit that faith and trust.

1

True or false: *"Old Glory* is a name used to refer to chairmen of Congressional standing committees"?

2

Millard Fillmore once said, "May God save the country; for it is evident the people will not." What do you think he meant? What does his statement mean to you?

3

True or false: "Congressional standing committees are so named because so many legislative bills are left standing in them"?

Lesson Eleven
Now That Voting
Has Caught Up with
the Draft

On Monday, July 5, 1971, President Richard M. Nixon conducted a ceremony in the East Room of the White House which officially certified the 26th Amendment to the Constitution. The amendment lowered to eighteen the minimum voting age in all United States elections. The amendment was certified as valid by General Services Administrator Robert L. Kunzig, who stood over a mahogany desk thought to have been used by Thomas Jefferson during the Second Continental Congress in Philadelphia.

President Nixon remarked that Jefferson also stood over the desk when writing because of his arthritis. In a less painful vein, the President observed that he felt it was particularly appropriate that the amendment should be certified on the 195th birthday of the United States (the July Fourth holiday was celebrated that Monday). The certification was a mere technicality, however, as the Ohio state legislature had ratified the amendment five days earlier, becoming the 38th state to ratify and giving the necessary three-fourths majority to make the amendment official.

The following Saturday, July 10, 1971, more than two hundred women of varying ages, ethnic backgrounds, and political persuasions gathered in Washington, D.C., to inaugurate the National Women's Political Caucus. The aim of the Caucus was to put more women in positions of real political power, ultimately working toward a goal of seeing half of all elective and appointive jobs in government filled by women. Betty Friedan, founder of the National Organization for Women (NOW), said that by the bicentennial celebration in 1976 "it will not be a joke that a woman might run for President."

Be that as it may, for the time being it seemed to be quite a joke to the President and his appointees. The next day the *New York Times* reported, President Nixon, Presidential adviser Henry Kissinger, and Secretary of State William Rogers were talking about the Women's Caucus in the presence of photographers and reporters. Mr. Kissinger happened to mention that writer Gloria Steinem had been in attendance. "Who's that?" the President asked. "That's Henry's old girl friend," Mr. Rogers replied.

Then Mr. Rogers spoke of a newspaper photograph which pictured Gloria Steinem, Betty Friedan, Representative Bella Abzug (New York City), and Representative Shirley Chisholm (Brooklyn).

"What did it look like?" the President inquired.

"Like a burlesque," the Secretary of State answered.

"What's wrong with that?" wondered the President of the United States.

Of course, President Nixon's innocence was understandable. For him politics and burlesque have always gone hand in hand.

Validation at Last

In spite of the lighthearted attitude of President Nixon and his cronies, the decade of the '70s should be the period when both the 19th and the 26th amendments to the Constitution are truly validated. The 19th Amendment, ratified in 1920, provided that no person could be kept from voting because of sex—which, although it applies to both sexes, had the effect of giving the vote to women for the first time. But even though women have had voting rights for five decades, the '70s represent a turning point in that women are consciously beginning to organize as a voting bloc and are *voting as women* rather than as women who can vote.

There is a big difference between the two. Women who can vote merely add to the total number of voters in the United States. Women voting as women create a strong voting bloc for real social change. If women had begun immediately after the 19th Amendment was ratified to rally as a voting bloc, uniting under the banner of their common womanhood, the deplorable political situation in America today, where women are so sparsely represented in elective and appointive offices, would probably not exist. There is one woman in the Senate. There are thirteen women in the House of Representatives. As Representative Bella Abzug of Manhattan (New York City) has said, if the Congress were truly a house of *representatives* the membership would be half women, eleven percent black, younger, and would contain more working people, teachers, artists, and so on. Mrs. Abzug also suggested that many laws and programs would be different with such representation in Congress.

Certainly five decades of women voting on the basis of their womanhood would have produced a female Presidential candidate, or at least a Vice Presidential candidate, by this time, as well as more members of Congress and Supreme Court appointments. Yet, as Betty Friedan suggested, it will take the concentrated work of the decade of the '70s to remove that thought from the joke category in the minds of many. The time is long overdue for a woman to run for the Presidency. Anyone who honestly recognizes the tremendous problems confronting the United States today, and admits that they are all the result of male leadership, must agree that women should have their chance to steer the country in a new direction.

So it is very important that the National Women's Political Caucus organize to run a woman for the office of President. Even if it is an independent third-party movement, where the chances of winning the election are minimal the first time around, the effort is still necessary to implant the idea of a woman President both in the minds of women themselves and in the minds of the male population. A woman candidate for President would have the same kind of mind-expanding, uplifting, and rallying effect upon women that independent black candidates for President had upon the black community. The nation must get used to the idea it is quite possible for a woman to occupy the White House (just as it is possible for a black person to become President).

Women do represent a powerful voting potential in the United States. In 1968 there were about 62 million women of voting age. About 45 million were registered to vote (or 74 percent). In 1970 there were about 70 million women aged 18 and older. Thus women represent a voting potential close to the total number of votes cast in 1968 for all three major candidates for President. A slight increase of 1 percent in registration over the 1968 registration for women would produce at least 52.5 million women voters, more than all of the votes cast in 1968 for Nixon and Wallace, or for Humphrey and Wallace.

Of course, as the Women's Caucus gains momentum, the established political order will be trying to downgrade the statistics. It is a strange thing about reporting total numbers of persons involved in political activity in America. The total goes down in direct proportion to the degree to which a group of people represent dignity and justice and trying to change the system. When a large crowd gathers somewhere in the United States to march against the system, the crowd count reported in the newspapers goes down. But when the astronauts get back from the moon and decide to go on a tour of American cities, the newspapers announce in advance what the crowd count of folks coming out to cheer will be.

Now that voting has caught up with the draft, giving the vote to all 18-year-olds, the papers have already begun to downgrade their total numbers. (Voting had already caught up with the draft before the 26th Amendment in Georgia and Kentucky. In Alaska the minimum voting age was 19, and in Hawaii it was 20.) We read in the newspapers that from 11 to 12 million new potential voters have resulted from the 26th Amendment.

I certainly hope the youth of the United States do not let the newspapers tell them how strong they are. If they do, they will never realize their true strength. Based on the most conservative possible evaluation of the projected population estimates of the Census Bureau, the total of new young potential voters in 1972 would be 18.6 to 19 million. More probably the total new voting potential would be from 20 to 25 million, or double the figure usually cited in the press. Which is about the way it usually works. To get a figure close to the truth of the total number of persons attending a human-rights or peace demonstration, you must double the figure reported in the press.

I also hope, now that young people have their voting

rights, they will relax at the beginning and have some fun. First of all, young people should band together and get themselves their own party. They should pick a catchy name —like the Doo Wa Diddie Party. Now, that would really shake up the establishment in America. Everybody would be asking "Who are the Doo Wa Diddies?" and "What do the Doo Wa Diddies want?" And the way young people would know that they had really arrived in the eyes of the establishment is when they heard older folks saying, "The Doo Wa Diddies are definitely Communist-inspired."

Then young people should use their new voting strength to shock the older established order into change. The first item on the agenda for the Doo Wa Diddie Party should be to vote back Prohibition. Can you imagine the reaction of the older folks? If that happened, we have yet to see a real Whiskey Rebellion in this country!

But the Doo Wa Diddies would have tremendous leverage if they brought back Prohibition. They could say to the older folks, "If you end the war in Southeast Asia, we'll give you your booze back." You'd be surprised how quickly the American boys would be called back home. President Nixon would probably have Air Force One shuttling back and forth to pick up soldiers.

On a more serious note, if youth rally around their number-one common denominator, we can expect to see some real change in the political life of the United States. The number-one thing young people in America—indeed, young people around the world—have going for them is their sense of honesty, morality, and ethics. Young people refuse to accept the lies and rationalizations of the established order. They will be looking for candidates who are honest, candidates who have a moral vision, candidates who are concerned more with solving social problems than they are with merely winning an election.

We are confronting a new situation today where statesmanship can enter into political life in the United States. Heretofore we have been governed primarily by politicians rather than statesmen. But the young voters will be looking for a new moral force rather than a winning candidate. Because of this, a candidate will not have to win an election to be recognized as a leader. The attitude of young people throughout the country today is "You don't have to win an election to be my hero." Make a survey of the men and women young people look up to and you will find that their credentials for admiration have not been winning elections.

Such an attitude among the new young voters will place a double burden on would-be candidates for public office. It will challenge them to stretch their moral vision and commitment to the outer limits. And it will demand that they do not desert their following just because a particular election is lost.

So new young voters should begin immediately to vote and organize along the lines of their strongest common denominator, which is a moral instinct. In so doing, their numbers will be added to increasing numbers of minority-group voters. Youth committed to identifying with the downtrodden, the forgotten, and the outcast in our society can greatly increase the voting strength of the quarter-million Indian Americans eighteen and over living on the reservations. Or the five million Spanish Americans in the United States who are eighteen or older. Or the half-million to a million Oriental Americans of voting age. Or the twelve million black Americans now qualified to vote.

When such a fusion of morality and numbers occurs, the 19th and the 26th amendments will be truly validated, certified, and celebrated.

The Black Model

As the new young beneficiaries of the 26th Amendment are preparing to exercise their new right, they would be wise to look to the experiences of black folks in America and their struggle to vote, both for positive and negative clues. Especially the young black voters should look to their own history so that they can avoid the hangups and stumbling blocks which hindered older black folks.

Officially black folks were given the right to vote by the 15th Amendment to the Constitution in 1870. The amendment was designed to enfranchise all black folks, but particularly in the South, where most blacks lived. But by 1876 Northern politicians were agreeing with their Southern colleagues to look the other way, and from that time to the early and mid-1960s few Southern blacks could exercise their Constitutional right.

Such discouraging devices as literacy tests (which required a Ph.D. to pass) and poll taxes were used against would-be black voters. And blacks who were allowed to register to vote had very little choice anyway, because they were barred from voting in primary elections. So white Democrats ruled the elective process in the South. There were some black Republicans who disagreed, but their voices were of little consequence.

In the North, blacks found themselves enjoying more of a right to *elect* but still very little right to *select*. Candidates

216

for primaries were usually hand-picked by machine politicians, and party leadership was always in the hands of white folks and blacks who served their interests.

For a long time black folks held an allegiance to the party of Abraham Lincoln, the Republican Party. But with the coming of the New Deal and Franklin Roosevelt the allegiance of black voters switched to the Democratic Party. In 1932 Franklin Roosevelt's first bid for the Presidency against Herbert Hoover, the black vote was still tied to the party of Lincoln. The urban areas of Detroit, Cleveland, Philadelphia, and so on found blacks casting their ballots for Hoover. In Cincinnati's heavily black Ward 16 Roosevelt got less than 29 percent of the vote. In Chicago Roosevelt received 59 percent of the white vote but only 23 percent of the black vote.

But by 1934 the picture had changed. Robert Vann, publisher of the Pittsburgh *Courier,* had told black voters: "My friends, go turn Lincoln's picture to the wall. That debt has been paid in full." Roosevelt's appointments had put more blacks in important positions than ever before, although there was not a single piece of civil-rights legislation passed during Roosevelt's four terms in office. The First Lady, Eleanor Roosevelt, had projected an image in sympathy with black aspiration. And New Deal programs had provided survival for many black folks in the form of relief.

Thus, in the 1936 election, when Roosevelt was going after his second term, Cincinnati's Ward 16 gave him over 65 percent of the vote. Every black ward in Cleveland went for Roosevelt. Blacks in Chicago more than doubled their vote for Roosevelt of four years before. In Pittsburgh, in the black Third Ward, Roosevelt was a winner 10–1. And by

1938 a *Fortune* magazine poll said that 84.7 percent of blacks interviewed considered themselves pro-Roosevelt. Black voters had turned Lincoln's picture to the wall—and replaced it with Roosevelt's.

But whether Lincoln or Roosevelt or Kennedy or anyone else was the hero, the result was the same—namely, being locked into a party allegiance. That is the mistake young voters, especially young black voters, must avoid. Before young folks ever get themselves trapped into supporting what they might feel to be the better of two traditional parties, which really means the lesser of two evils, they should band together and run their own independent candidate. Some people would say that such an effort is wasting valuable votes. Quite to the contrary, it would finally be the beginning of developing what has been needed in this country for more than a century—the establishment of a political ethic that might possibly save America.

One great benefit for black folks of switching to the Democratic party, as well as a by-product of the pattern of housing segregation in New York City which produced the ghetto of Harlem, was the bringing to the Halls of Congress of Congressman Adam Clayton Powell, Jr., Democratic Congressman from Harlem. Congressman Powell gave a lift to the political aspirations of black folks, as well as a vocal expression at the highest level of government of the secret thoughts and opinions of all blacks.

Adam Clayton Powell, Jr., went to Congress in 1945. Right away he found out that Congressional status didn't have much meaning in the nation's capital—not if you were black. He couldn't rent a room in downtown Washington. He couldn't go to a movie which starred his first wife, Hazel

Scott. He was not authorized to use such Congressional facilities as dining rooms, steam baths, showers, and barber shops. Powell used them anyway and insisted that his staff do the same.

But Congressman Powell rose to become the chairman of the House Committee on Education and Labor, which, according to the *Congressional Record,* processed more important pieces of legislation than any other committee. Powell sponsored legislation for federal aid to education, for a minimum wage scale, for greater benefits to the hard-core unemployed. He had a hand in the development and passage of such bills as the Anti-Poverty Bill, the Manpower Development and Training Act, the Vocational Aid Act, and many others.

Beyond his solid accomplishments in pushing vital legislation, Congressman Powell spoke out on the floor of Congress, in interviews, in articles and speeches, always telling white folks what they needed to hear rather than what they wanted to hear. The more Congressman Powell spoke out, the more he was loved in the black community. And the more he was disliked, resented, and rebuffed by his white colleagues. They finally got together and voted Congressman Powell out of the House, imposing a double standard upon him that they themselves were not following. Congressman Powell was later reinstated. In 1970 he lost his bid for reelection and was replaced by black Congressman Charles Rangel.

The combination of men like Adam Clayton Powell, Jr., the civil-rights movement of the 1960s, the voting-rights act of 1965, and the new black pride that swept through the black community in America produced a voting strength and an organizational momentum which have gotten results. And those results should encourage young voters in their own organizational efforts.

Especially in the South, the rise in black voters between 1960 and 1968 was remarkable. The Southern Regional Council's Voter Education Project reported that in 1960 there were 1,463,333 black voters and in 1968 there were 3,112,000. The U.S. Census Bureau places the 1970 total at 3,565,000.

A look at the percentage increase by state in the South between 1960 and 1968 indicates how thoroughly black voting rights had been denied: Alabama up 314 percent; Arkansas up 79 percent; Florida up 59 percent; Georgia up 91 percent; Louisiana up 92 percent; Mississippi up 1,041 percent; North Carolina up 45 percent; South Carolina up 220 percent; Tennessee up 23 percent; Texas up 138 percent; and Virginia up 155 percent.

What has been the result? In 1962 there were four blacks in the House of Representatives. Today there are 13 Congressmen and one Senator. In 1962 there were 52 blacks in state legislatures in the United States. Today there are 198. There are now 81 black mayors and 1,567 blacks elected to other state or local offices—about half of them in the South.

So now that voting has caught up with the draft, perhaps the combination of new young voters, women, blacks, Puerto Ricans, Mexican Americans, Indians, Orientals, and all others who have been so long denied representation can help this country to catch up with the realities of the 1970s. One way, of course, would be by voting an end to the draft, and then going on to replace armed forces with moral forces.

1

Make a list of as many women as you can find who have been the top government official in their countries. Why do you think a woman has never been a candidate for President of the United States? Why do you think a black man or woman has never been a candidate for President of the United States (on the Democratic or Republican ticket)?

2

In terms of this chapter, do you see a difference between an amendment being ratified and an amendment being validated?

3

Keep a record of the crowd count reported in the newspapers in stories covering peace rallies, civil-rights and human-rights demonstrations, and similar gatherings urging governmental change. Then try to find someone who attended the gathering reported and ask how many people were there. Are the figures the same? Why or why not?

Lesson Twelve
Techniques
of Persuasion

When it comes to persuading the electorate, there is currently nothing more important to a candidate than a wife, kids, and the right kind of animals. Dogs are great assets to candidates, and the feeling seems to be engendered that if a dog loves the candidate, he can't be all that bad.

If it can be said that Richard Nixon's road to the White House began with his first election to the Vice President's office, then it can also be asserted that a dog saved his political life. In 1952 young Richard Nixon was the Republican Vice Presidential nominee. Early in the fall the candidate was questioned about an $18,235 trust fund he maintained. The opposition accused him of taking money under the table and questioned such conduct on the part of a Senator, especially a Senator representing the national party ticket.

Nixon appeared on national radio and television to defend himself—indeed, to fight for his political life. The broadcast was aired from Los Angeles, September 23, 1952. Affecting his best folksy manner, he explained that he was not a wealthy man. That already established common ground with most of his listeners. He said he had accepted money from supporters for the necessary expenses his office entailed. He said he had never granted any special favors as a result, nor had the money been used secretly.

Nixon gave a breakdown of his personal assets. He said he had $10,000 in government bonds when he left the service; he received $1,600 from estates in his law practice; he inherited about $4,500; his family lived modestly in one mortgaged house in Washington, D.C., and another one in California; he had no stocks or bonds; he had life insurance on himself but not on his wife, Pat, or the children; and they owned a 1950 Oldsmobile. Nixon listed his debts: a $20,000 mortgage on the Washington house and a $10,000 mortgage on the California home; $4,500 to a bank in Washington; $3,500 to parents; and $500 on a loan from his life insurance.

The Vice Presidential nominee said that some Senators put their wives on the payroll, but he could never do that. "My wife's sitting over here," Nixon said proudly. "She's a wonderful stenographer. She used to teach stenography and she used to teach shorthand in high school. That was when I met her. I can tell you folks that she's worked many hours at night and many hours on Saturdays and Sundays in my office and she's done a fine job. And I'm proud to say tonight that in the six years I've been in the House and Senate of the United States, Pat Nixon has never been on the government payroll."

Of course, Pat had to pay a price for her husband's honesty. Said Nixon, "Pat doesn't have a mink coat. But she does have a respectable Republican cloth coat. And I always tell her that she'd look good in anything."

Then in one brilliant, sentimental stroke, Candidate Nixon got the *wife,* the *kids,* and a *dog* into the story all at the same time. Just to show he wasn't hiding a thing, not one little thing, from the public, Nixon told a little story about his personal life.

"One other thing I probably should tell you, because if I don't they'll probably be saying this about me too. We did get something—a gift—after the election." (Suspense.) "A man down in Texas heard *Pat* on the radio mention the fact that our *two youngsters* would like to have a dog. And, believe it or not, the day before we left on this campaign trip we got a message from the Union Station in Baltimore saying they had a package for us. We went down to get it. You know what it was?

"It was a *little cocker spaniel dog* in a crate that he sent all the way from Texas. Black-and-white-spotted. And our little girl Tricia—the six-year-old—named it Checkers. And you know, the kids love the dog, and I just want to say this right now, that, regardless of what they say about it, we're gonna keep it."

Nixon kept Checkers and the Vice Presidential nomination. The black-and-white-spotted cocker spaniel removed whatever spots had blotted the Nixon image.

Another President who used a dog to garner public support and sympathy was Franklin Delano Roosevelt. His dog Fala became as popular a White House figure as Dr. Henry Kissinger is today. And probably a plot to kidnap Fala would have produced more public outrage than the alleged plot to abduct Kissinger. During the 1944 Presidential campaign, when Roosevelt was going after his fourth term in the White House, the candidate spoke before the Teamsters' Union and issued a devastating attack upon the Republicans, answering their libels against "my little dog Fala."

So it's nice to have a dog around the house when you are seeking public office. Dogs not only breed affection, but they can breed and be promiscuous in other ways without danger of producing a public scandal. Dogs are a rare political asset: close friends, liked by almost everybody, unassailable in the public eye, and never able to get the candidate caught in a compromising situation. However, the candidate can bring disgrace upon himself by abusing the dog, as Lyndon

B. Johnson found out when he picked up his beagles by the ears in full view of newspaper reporters. Johnson claimed the dogs liked it, but the public was not convinced.

Cats, on the other hand, do not seem to be a political asset in this country, though they are the favorite pets of kings and queens. And it is understandable, since cats do not evoke the same sentiment in the minds of the American public that dogs do. Dogs are loyal, obedient, and faithful. They are much like Boy Scouts in that respect. But although a person may be "playful as a kitten," anyone being particularly vicious or slanderous is "catty," and many a politician has been described as "ornery as a polecat."

Kids, and the weddings of kids, are helpful in projecting the image of the all-American family. President Nixon has had two such weddings since his election to the Presidency: one preceding the inauguration and the other a White House wedding—the wedding of the little girl who named Checkers to Edward Cox.

I happened to be playing a club date at the Cellar Door in Washington, D.C., the day of that wedding. I told my audience that night I was sitting in my hotel minding my own business when the Secret Service came by my room. I said, "What do you want?" And the agents told me, "We just don't want you around the White House during the wedding." So I innocently asked, "What wedding?" "You know what wedding. The President's daughter." And I told them I really wasn't interested in that wedding. It would be different if she was marrying a Black Panther. Or planning to spend her honeymoon in Harlem.

And it is true that a White House wedding doesn't have the same impact on the black community that it has on the white community. While I was in Washington a newspaper reporter asked me, "Mr. Gregory, what is the feeling in the black community about the Tricia Nixon wedding?" And I told him, "Well, I wouldn't want to say the black community is exactly apathetic. But I would say the black community is about as excited about that wedding as we would be if Sears, Roebuck announced a sale on suntan lotion."

That wives are a political asset is demonstrated by the fact that we have only had one bachelor President in the history of America, James Buchanan. Adlai Stevenson would have been the perfect candidate except for the fact that he was divorced. And First Ladies attain fame which often rivals that of their husbands—for example, Martha Washington, Dolley Madison, and Eleanor Roosevelt.

The Women's Liberation and ecology movements will probably alter accepted traditions drastically before this decade is over. A candidate who would crowd the White House with kids could be seen as an anti-environmentalist. The current rhetoric of those concerned about the population explosion is that no couple should have more than 2.5 kids. I'm still trying to figure out what the half a kid is. The U.S. Constitution orginally defined black folks as "three fifths" of a man. But a half a kid is something else. Anyway, those concerned with the crowded environment would certainly see a large White House family as setting a bad example.

And the Women's Liberation movement may upgrade considerably the role of the First Lady, as well as create the new category of the First Man. (It would really be wild if the first woman President had a husband named Adam.)

So the day may not be too far off when we will see the

President walking the White House grounds with her dog beside her, trailed by an entourage of Secret Service men and women, on her way to a state dinner where the guests will be received by the Galloping Gourmet.

1

Using this lesson as a guide, write an essay entitled "Man's Best Friend."

2

Does the Biblical phrase "and a little child shall lead them" suggest any contemporary political activity in the United States? Give examples.

Lesson Thirteen
Studying War
No More

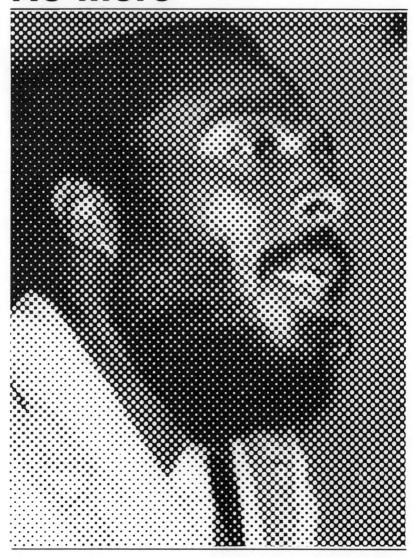

An instructive starting point for the study of war is to see just where the United States stands in comparison with other warring nations. A recent study (May 1971) directed by Dr. J. David Singer of the University of Michigan provided a chart rating the "performances in international war" of nations during the period between 1816 and 1965. The rating categories are "All Wars" and "Interstate Wars."

Interstate wars involve only wars between sovereign states, and all wars include imperial and colonial wars. Civil wars were not included in the study unless they became internationalized. The United States involvement in Vietnam is not included because the research team had a hard time finding a category for it. It began as a colonial war against the French (1945 to 1954), then evolved into a civil war until 1961, when the United States stepped in and pushed it up into the "interstate" category. It would be premature to include the Vietnam war in the chart anyway, as there is no category provided for a tie.

So, looking at the standings of the International War League, we see the United States is bombing a perfect 1.000, even though it has had its share of "errors" and "guns batted in."

The United States, as you can see, does not have as many victories as some other nations, but, after all, the United States is new to the league of wars and seems to be doing its best to escalate the season. The war chart is instructive on some levels and deceptive on others. For example, looking at the poor war record of the Papal States as compared with the perfect score of Israel, it is easy to understand why the Pope freed the Jews of the Crucifixion a couple of years ago.

Nation	All Wars	Interstate Wars	Nation	All Wars	Interstate Wars
England	16–2	6–0	Ethiopia	1–1	1–1
Russia	13–2	8–2	Guatemala	1–1	1–1
France	14–4	9–2	Two Sicilies	1–1	1–1
Italy			Württemberg	1–1	1–1
(Sardinia)	8–3	8–2	Argentina	1–1	0–1
UNITED STATES	5–0	4–0	China	3–4	2–4
Brazil	3–0	2–0	Bulgaria	1–3	1–3
Japan	5–2	5–2	India	1–2	0–2
Yugoslavia			Mexico	1–2	0–2
(Serbia)	4–1	4–0	Peru	1–2	1–1
Rumania	4–1	4–1	Salvador	1–2	1–2
Austria-			Ecuador	0–1	0–1
Hungary	5–3	3–3	Hanover	0–1	0–1
Belgium	2–0	2–0	Hesse		
Chile	2–0	2–0	Electoral	0–1	0–1
Germany			Hesse		
(Prussia)	4–2	4–2	Grand Ducal	0–1	0–1
Greece	4–2	4–2	Iraq	0–1	0–1
Holland	3–1	1–0	Jordan	0–1	0–1
Israel	2–0	2–0	Lebanon	0–1	0–1
Mongolia	2–0	2–0	Mecklenburg-		
Spain	5–4	2–3	Schwerin	0–1	0–1
Australia	1–0	1–0	Persia	0–1	0–1
Canada	1–0	1–0	Saxony	0–1	0–1
Colombia	1–0	1–0	Syria	0–1	0–1
Czechoslovakia	1–0	1–0	Bolivia	0–2	0–2
New Zealand	1–0	1–0	Denmark	0–2	0–2
Nicaragua	1–0	1–0	Finland	0–2	0–2
Norway	1–0	1–0	Honduras	0–2	0–2
Pakistan	1–0	1–0	Morocco	0–2	0–2
Paraguay	1–0	1–0	Papal States	0–2	0–2
Portugal	1–0	1–0	U.A.R.		
Poland	1–0	1–0	(Egypt)	0–2	0–2
(South Africa)	1–0	1–0	Hungary	0–3	0–3
Baden	1–1	1–1	Turkey	5–11	4–6
Bavaria	1–1	1–1			

On the other hand, it would be very risky to make future war plans simply on the basis of China's win-and-loss record.

But the International War League standing does not reflect other important war information. It does not reflect changes in policy, for instance. The United States Constitution clearly gives the war-making power to Congress, as well as the basic responsibility for determining foreign policy. Congress has the *sole* power to engage the country in war, a power *indisputably* not given to the President. Through a strange reversal of the mandates of the Constitution, the President has assumed—indeed, usurped—absolute power in foreign policy. Today, involving the United States in war is decided by the President and the Pentagon.

It all began with the National Security Act of 1947, which created the National Military Establishment, coordinating the Departments of the Navy (established in 1789), the Army (established in 1789), and the Air Force (established in 1947) under the Secretary of Defense, who had Cabinet status. The 1949 National Security Act renamed the National Military Establishment the Department of Defense. The offices, staff, files, etc., of the Defense Department are housed in the Pentagon. And from this structure emanates the practice of United States involvement in undeclared wars, beginning with the 1950 undeclared Korean conflict and moving up to the present undeclared war in Vietnam.

Nestled comfortably on the Virginia side of the Potomac River, the Pentagon covers 34 acres of land and has 204 acres of lawns and terraces. The location of the Pentagon on the Virginia side is symbolic. From there the Pentagon can overlook the city of Washington proper and the Capitol building, which it rules and commands. And the Pentagon is located near the Arlington Memorial Cemetery, whose graves it has been primarily responsible for filling.

The world's largest office building, the Pentagon is 5 stories high and consists of 5 rings of buildings connected by 10 corridors, with a 5-acre pentagonal court in the center. Each of the outermost sides of the building is 921 feet long and the perimeter is seven eighths of a mile. The total length of corridors is 17.5 miles. The Pentagon is twice as large as the Merchandise Mart in Chicago, and has 3 times the floor space of the Empire State Building in New York City. The Pentagon building was completed January 15, 1943, at a cost of about $83 million.

The Pentagon's 30,000 employees arrive daily from Washington and its suburbs over some 30 miles of access highways (and bridges), park about 10,000 cars in 3 parking lots, then climb 150 stairs or ride 19 escalators (escalation is big in the Pentagon!) to reach offices that occupy 3,707,397 square feet. While at work, they tell time by 4,200 clocks, drink from 685 water fountains, utilize 280 rest rooms, consume 30,000 cups of coffee, 6,000 pints of milk, and 5,000 soft drinks prepared or served by a restaurant staff of 600 persons and dispensed in 2 restaurants, 6 cafeterias, 9 beverage bars, and an outdoor snack bar. They make 200,000 telephone calls daily over 87,000 phones connected by 100,000 miles of cable, and receive 129,620 items of mail daily through the Defense Post Office in the building. Many facilities for daily use, such as a bank, a drugstore, medical and dental clinics, a ticket agency, are also located in the Pentagon. Imposing structures house imposing responsibilities.

There is little doubt that the Pentagon, along with the

CIA (Central Intelligence Agency), really controls the United States. That is why I sometimes feel so sorry for the President when he is given all the blame for involving this country in further war actions. The President is merely under orders from the Pentagon. When hundreds of thousands of citizens massed in Washington, D.C., in 1969, to protest United States continuing involvement in Vietnam, President Nixon acknowledged the demonstration, but said that "under no circumstances whatsoever will I be affected by it." He was merely saying that he himself was under orders.

When President Nixon sent troops into Cambodia in April 1970, it was *clear* he was only acting under orders. I'm sure he received a phone call from one of those 87,000 Pentagon phones saying, "We're going to Cambodia in the morning, do you want to announce it tonight?" And so President Nixon went on national television and did just that. And the final proof of the matter is the fact that when the American troops got into Cambodia, all the Vietcong were gone. Which means the Vietcong knew about the Cambodian invasion forty-eight hours before President Nixon.

So President Nixon's appearance on television was to try to explain to the American people why he was doing what he'd said he was not going to do the *last* time he was on television. Which was an appearance to explain the time before *that!*

President Nixon said, in effect, trying to rationalize the Cambodian invasion: "My fellow Americans, I know there has been a lot of criticism about my authorizing sending our troops into Cambodia. But I felt it was necessary to protect our troops in Vietnam. It is true that when we got to Cambodia, we did not find any Vietcong. Not even a Vietcong baby. But what the press has been very reluctant to tell you, and what must be told to the nation, is that we did find and confiscate many thousand pounds of *rice*."

Now, I'm sure that made Uncle Ben happy. But certainly nobody else in America could be enthusiastic over finding rice in *Asia!* My five-year-old daughter could find rice in Asia. I could see some cause for elation and satisfaction if our troops got over into Cambodia and found barbecued ribs, or a few thousand acres of watermelon.

President Nixon's national television explanation of the Cambodian invasion is like the Russians suddenly deciding to invade the United States, and when they got here, we were all gone. Premier Kosygin would get on television and say: "My fellow Russians, I'm sure you want an explanation of why we invaded the United States. I felt it was necessary to protect our troops in Cuba. And, although it is true that we did not find any Americans, not even a Navajo baby, I am happy to report that we did find and confiscate forty thousand tons of Colonel Sanders' Kentucky Fried Chicken."

So any demand seriously aimed at getting the United States to study war no more must first deal directly with the source. That observation discourages many would-be peace demonstrators because they see the Pentagon as a monolithic, immovable structure which does not have ears to pick up citizen protest. In February 1971 we found that the Pentagon *does* hear. Now we know that it is possible to lodge protests which will force the Pentagon to call a halt to killing.

It seems that there was a 15-acre section of pines in the 50,000-acre Milan (Tennessee) Army Ammunition Plant which over the past few years had become the favored roost of millions of blackbirds. Their presence was bothersome to the hog and dairy farmers in the area, to say nothing of Army personnel. Cows seem to have an aversion to eating food that the birds have "messed in," or so the farmers reported. Other farmers in the area reported that their field crops had been destroyed by the birds.

The ever resourceful Department of the Interior, in the person of Mr. Paul LeFebvre, came up with an ingenious plan to kill off the birds, a plan worthy of any chemical-warfare strategy employed in Indochina. A World War II B-17 bomber would be brought in to spray some two thousand gallons of a special solution over the pine roost. The solution would neutralize the birds' body oils so that in freezing weather they would quickly freeze to death. The Chamber of Commerce and the city board of Milan approved the plan, and everyone sat back to await a freezing cold spell.

But the national news media got wind of the idea before the birds did; stories appeared all over the country, and network camera crews converged upon Milan. Storms of protest began to roll in, primarily, it seemed, from East Coast sources. The Department of the Interior strategy was referred back into the Army chain of command, where it could be forgotten until the birds migrated back up North.

Unfortunately, it is much more difficult to get a Pentagon hearing when people are being killed. During the period of the blackbird furor in Tennessee, Pentagon operations abroad were going full scale. While the protests were being lodged to save the lives of blackbirds and starlings, the death rate of American soldiers killed in Indochina reached a three-month high. The Laotian operation was responsible for the sharp rise in deaths, even though the Pentagon reported that only one of fifty-one soldiers killed was actually inside Laos. Some nine thousand American soldiers operating in the northwest corner of South Vietnam to back up South Vietnamese troops crossing the border of Laos came under strong North Vietnamese attack.

In a macabre way the Pentagon decision at home was consistent with its rhetoric abroad. The Pentagon defined an *invasion* in the Laotian operation as an action involving ground combat troops. An attack by air was not considered an invasion (see Lesson Five). So, clearly, the birds in Tennessee were not invading, since their attack came by air. Perhaps a rampaging horde of wild boars or grasshoppers launching their attack on the ground would have been dealt with summarily.

The Milan, Tennessee, incident is just one more reminder that war is for the birds, but it might suggest a clue to halting the study of war. Some seventy percent of the American people have expressed the opinion that they would like to see the war in Vietnam stopped. Perhaps the peace movement could learn from the Tennessee experience and lobby for legislation to draft household pets, including the feathered varieties—parakeets, parrots, myna birds, and canaries—sending them to Vietnam, or any other war, to face certain death. Storms of protest would surely ensue. And maybe the Pentagon would listen. There seems to be an emotional attachment to domesticated members of the animal kingdom which does not carry over as strongly when *human* lives are concerned. Pet protesters might shut down the war machine forever.

"Inhumane" is a word which seems basically to be

reserved for humans' relationships to animals. Being in-humane means "not expressing those feelings of kindness and benevolence which are to man's credit." But war is placed in a different category, and is not seen to be *inhuman,* because that would mean "unlike what is normally human," and, unfortunately, war seems to be a totally human past-time.

Yes, But Can He Fight?

America's military obsession being what it is, the most promising candidate seems to be the man who has proven himself on the battlefield. Of course, that tradition begins immediately with George Washington, the great military hero of the Revolutionary War. Then there was General Andy Jackson, Indian clobberer and idol of the West in the War of 1812. William Henry Harrison was also a War of 1812 vet, commanding the forces in the Northwest. But his real fame came from beating the Shawnee Indians in a formidable battle at Tippecanoe on the Wabash River in 1811. Thus the campaign title "Old Tippecanoe."

Zachary Taylor was another Indian fighter in the North-west and Florida, and his forty years in the military gave him action in the War of 1812 and the Mexican War. His troops gave him a nickname guaranteed to sway votes, "Old Rough and Ready." Taylor was succeeded by another Mexi-can War veteran, a brigadier general named Franklin Pierce. The Civil War brought another brigadier general to the White House, the man who gave the Union its first major victory at Forts Henry and Donelson, Ulysses Simp-son Grant. At Fort Donelson, General Grant had said, "No terms other than an unconditional and immediate surrender can be accepted." Once more a vote-winning nickname was born, "Unconditional Surrender Grant."

Rutherford B. Hayes was wounded four times in the Civil War and rose to the rank of major general. While he was still on the battlefield, he was nominated to the House of Representatives, which, if the age requirements for Congressmen could be lowered, might give us a clue to troop withdrawal today. A well-organized voting effort could bring back more than five hundred soldiers to occupy their Congressional seats!

James Garfield also served in the Civil War, rose to the rank of major general, and retired from the Army when he was elected to the House of Representatives. Garfield's successor, Chester A. Arthur, was inspector general of New York troops in the Civil War and quartermaster of New York State, in which capacity he helped to organize the New York militia. (Arthur's successor, Grover Cleveland, couldn't serve in the Civil War because he had to support his mother and sisters. But he evidently realized how that might affect his political future, because he borrowed money to hire a conscription substitute.)

Brigadier General Benjamin Harrison served with distinction on the Civil War battlefields, as did William McKinley, though he only rose to the rank of major. Teddy Roosevelt overcame frail health and became famous during the Spanish-American War by organizing the volunteer cavalry regiment "The Rough Riders." The Teddy Bear is also named after him, so he was not as "rough" perhaps as he would seem.

Harry S. Truman saw action in France during World War I, was discharged as a major, and later became a colonel in the reserves. His successor was a military hero of the stature of Washington and Grant and the other connoisseurs of combat, General Dwight D. Eisenhower. Brother Ike went the whole military route, beginning at West Point. He rose to become U.S. commander of the European Theater of Operations during World War II. He then became a five-star general and chief of staff of the U.S. army.

John F. Kennedy served as a PT-boat commander during World War II, with the saving of a life to his credit during action against the Japanese off the Solomon Islands. Kennedy's successor, Lyndon B. Johnson, was already in Congress when Pearl Harbor was attacked, and was the first member of Congress to go into uniform. He was decorated for gallantry and rose to the rank of lieutenant commander. And Richard M. Nixon also served as a naval officer in World War II.

Not only for the Presidency, but combat scars can be invaluable in seeking lesser offices. Former Pennsylvania Governor Raymond P. Shafer commanded a PT boat in the South Pacific, completed eighty missions, and received a decoration for removing seventeen paratroopers from Corregidor in a rubber raft under sniper fire. Obviously the pot-shots usually directed at a Governor are minor in comparison. John H. Chafee, former Governor of Rhode Island and later Secretary of the Navy, was part of the first landing at bloody Guadalcanal. Senator Philip A. Hart of Michigan was decorated many times, having been wounded in the D-Day invasion of Normandy in World War II. Senator Howard Cannon of Nevada was shot down behind enemy lines in Holland and spent forty-two days in hiding before making it back to American troops.

As might be expected, considering the Pearl Harbor attack, politicians from Hawaii hold the combat record. Senator Daniel K. Inouye and Congressman Spark Matsunaga both served in the famous 442nd Regiment Combat Team, composed entirely of Nisei volunteers. Senator Inouye was leading a platoon sent to destroy three machine-gun nests in the Po Valley in World War II. He was shot in the stomach and the legs, and a grenade shattered his arm, but he continued to direct the attack. He lost an arm in combat and came out of World War II as a captain. Representative Matsunaga was wounded two times in battle, serving in North Africa and Europe, and he also came out of World War II as a captain. The 442nd Regiment, by the way, has been called the most decorated unit in history.

The moral of the promising military backgrounds of so many successful candidates is that the absence of war removes one of the most proven campaign assets a candidate can have. Without a combat record, candidates would be forced to rely upon other virtues—maybe even morality, ethics, and statesmanship.

In May 1971 thousands of young people gathered in their nation's capital to protest the war in Vietnam again. The Washington police, under the direction of the Department of Justice, set an all-time arrest record in the United States, making 7,200 arrests in a single day. And whatever else you might say about the Washington, D.C., police, you have to admit they are efficient. Do you realize how efficient a police force has to be to make seven thousand arrests in a single day and nab only peace demonstrators? In the entire massive round-up they did not slip and get one dope pusher, one prostitute, one pimp, one syndicate hoodlum, one purse snatcher, one Senator or staff member guilty of misappropriating funds—only folks who were lodging a protest against the continuation of killing. Now, that's efficiency!

The explanation, of course, is simple. The law-enforcement establishment in this country has determined what a "criminal" looks like, especially a "criminal" walking around the nation's capital. Such a person has long hair and a beard, wears strange clothes, sandals, beads, and is usually young. Whoever bombed the Capitol building in March (see Lesson Fifteen) probably knew how the police identified criminals. No doubt he had on a Brooks Brothers suit, was clean-shaven with a fresh crew-cut. And he was probably carrying the bomb in a red-white-and-blue box, with a picture of Jesus on one side of the box and a picture of Spiro Agnew on the other. Such a person could easily walk right past the Capitol police and say to the officer on duty, "How's the family?"

The young peace demonstrators had announced in advance that their strategy was to "shut down government operations" by blocking bridges so that motorists couldn't get in to work, and by sitting in front of government office buildings to discourage employees from entering. And again President Nixon reminded us of who really calls the shots in this country when he said, "Policy in this country is not made by protests." Tom Jefferson could have been surprised at that! In other words, those people most vitally affected by certain governmental actions really have no say.

If you check the arrest cards of the seven thousand persons arrested, you will find that they were 99.9 percent young folks of draft age. So civil disobedience was not an extreme tactic for them. They were simply sitting in front of cars on a bridge in Washington, D.C., so that they wouldn't have to sit in front of bullets on the battlefields of Southeast Asia. Sitting on the bridge is the quite obvious moral choice, especially when the intended goal is that no one need ever lie on a battlefield again.

If the draft laws were amended so that Americans could be drafted up to the age of seventy-five, there would be a whole lot of older folks sitting on bridges in Washington, D.C., along with the youth. If such a law were passed, I'm sure it would be a great shock to a lot of vocal right-wing grandfathers in this country. I can just see some kid walking up to his grandfather holding the morning paper and saying, "Grandpa, remember how you're always saying you'd like to get your arthritic hands on some of those Commies? With that bill that was passed yesterday, it looks like you might get your wish."

And such a law would make good sense. I think it is reasonable that if we must continue to fight wars, they ought to be fought by those people who really want to fight them. Since it seems to be the top half of the generation gap that is the most enthusiastic about going to war, why not send the Old Folks Brigade to Vietnam—with John Wayne leading them?

But the draft age being what it is at the present time, the burden of demonstrating for the cause of peace naturally falls upon the young people in America. And so many older people join their government in condemning the activities of the youth, without recognizing the debt all Americans owe them. The May Day demonstrations in Washington, D.C., were a perfect example. Washington motorists and other Washington residents were upset that their daily routine of life had been disturbed by the youthful protesters. As the tear gas used to disperse nonviolent demonstrators floated through open windows and into stores and restaurants, Washington residents became more and more angry.

An enlightened reaction of Washington residents would be one of welcome and gratitude. I am sure that if thirty thousand German youth had demonstrated in the streets of Berlin during the early '30's, saying they would shut down the Nazi government, some Berlin residents would have been angered because of the inconvenience caused. But if that kind of protest had been lodged, it would not have been necessary for the United States and Russia and the Allies to shut down Berlin with bombs later. And if America's military obsession ever leads to a world reaction against her, Washington residents have much to lose. The Pentagon would certainly be a priority target.

So, in May 1971 the government response to protesting the Pentagon was what it always is when the protest involves the taking of human life. The government offered elaborate rationalizations, of course, like saying the important governmental procedures cannot be halted. Yet long filibusters halting action on crucial legislation is part of standard Senate practice.

And the Senators who are so proficient in the art of filibuster are also profiteering from the spoils of war. Samuel F. Yette, in his excellent book *The Choice: The Issue of Black Survival in America,* writes of the actions of Senators and

Congressmen representing the "Rice Cup States" and exposes the economic realities of America's military adventures in Southeast Asia. Says Yette:

When the Decisive Decade—the 1960's—began, the United States was not a leader among the world's rice growers, exporters, or consumers. At the close of the decade, the United States still was not a big rice consumer, nor even a major rice grower. But, as an exporter, the United States was number one, despite a "Green Revolution" that dramatically increased rice yields in the Philippines, India, Pakistan, and South Vietnam—all customers for U.S. rice. As the decade closed, the United States still produced less than 1 percent of the world's rice but was, incredibly, the world's leading rice exporter, consuming only 35 percent of its rice produced, selling the other 65 percent abroad to a hundred countries, but mainly to South Korea and South Vietnam.

The bulk of commercial rice grown in the United States is produced in Arkansas, Louisiana, Texas, California, and Mississippi. The Congressmen from these states, and their Congressional partners from neighboring states, control virtually every key committee in both the Senate and the House of Representatives. For example, no bill can reach the floor of the Senate for debate without the approval of the Senate Judiciary Committee. That committee is controlled by Senator James Eastland of Mississippi, who, in turn, is backed up by Senator John McClellan of Arkansas. Senator McClellan also controls the Government Operations Committee, which keeps an eye on all bureaucratic operations (and also holds hearings about riots and civil disorders).

Thus, Sam Yette points out, "the Rice Cup sentiment controls 10 of the 16 standing committees of the Senate" and "the Rice Cup states command 7 of 11 of the most important House committees." So perhaps the discovery of rice in Cambodia really excited the Deep South Congressmen, who saw its existence as a threat to their rice empire. And certainly the continuing practice of crop defoliation in Vietnam comes into clearer focus when one understands the vested United States rice interest.

So this lesson ends with a warning: If America's tragic involvement in Southeast Asia does not lead to a studying of war no more, we can be sure that any further involvements will eventually self-destruct.

1

What is a pentagon? What is The Pentagon? How many sides and angles does each kind of pentagon have?

2

James Madison once said, "I believe there are more instances of abridgment of the freedom of the people by gradual and silent encroachments of those in power than by violent and sudden usurpations." Do you agree or disagree? Why?

3

True or false: "The United States Constitution clearly gives the Senate top responsibility in determining foreign policy, and Congress the sole power to declare war"?

4

True or false: "Presidents always respect the wishes of the Constitution"?

Lesson Fourteen
A Turnip
in Every Plot

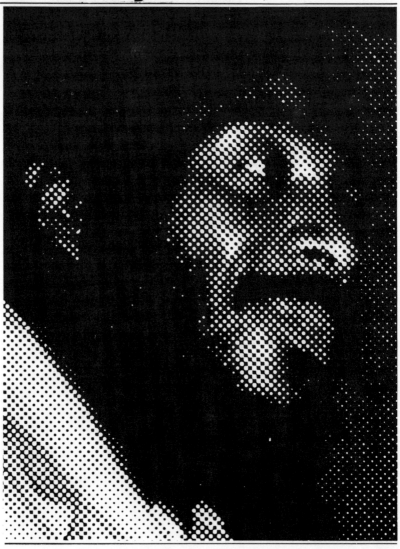

At the very beginning of the twentieth century, during the Presidential campaign of 1900, incumbent Republican President William McKinley defeated his Democratic opponent, William Jennings Bryan, with a cry of "a full dinner pail for four more years." Voters with the wisdom to vote correctly during that campaign were to receive the reward of "a chicken in every pot." During the campaign of 1928 Herbert Hoover picked up and expanded Republican food-consciousness in his Presidential race against the Democratic Governor of New York, Alfred E. Smith, saying that the promise of prosperity had moved from "the full dinner pail to the full garage." So Hoover ran on a campaign slogan which was to be a mockery of the actual turn of events during his administration: *"two* chickens in every pot and a car in every garage."

Thus, food-consciousness has a history among the American electorate, and I personally feel that food will once again be the major issue beginning with the 1972 national elections and increasing in intensity of concern throughout the '70s. Not that one, two, or even three chickens in every pot will be revived once again as a campaign slogan. With the eighteen-year-old vote now in effect, some folks feel the new battle cry is more likely to be "some *pot* in every chicken." Of course, such a campaign would be the supreme example of *"grass* roots" politics.

On the initial and immediate level, the food-consciousness issue will express itself with a concern for the rise in food prices. After that initial reaction, the food issue will expand to include growing concern over the availability of food, the purity of food, and proper eating habits. While older voters will readily identify with the food-price issue, the new young voters will carry food-consciousness into the broader areas of concern.

The price of food today is truly a cause for concern. Food prices are so high, it's really cheaper to eat money. Just take a dollar bill and spread some mayonnaise on it and you've got a better spread than the money will buy in food. Every time I go to the supermarket, I'm amazed to see little old ladies fighting at the vegetable counter. The same little old ladies who never argued over the price of steak are now fighting over the price of cabbage. And it's quite understandable. From those prices, you'd think the cabbage was cooked—with a side order of ham hocks! Looking at the prices in the supermarket these days is like looking at a menu in a restaurant.

Of course, most folks can't understand why I go to the supermarket when it's well known that I've pledged not to eat solid food again until the war is over in Vietnam. It's true I haven't eaten solid food since April 24, 1971. But I still go to the supermarket for the same reason most folks go to the museum. It's so nostalgic to look and remember "the good old days."

And I frequently accompany my wife when she is buying food for the family. It was on one of those trips that I really became aware of the outrageous price of food. We came to the checkout counter, and when our purchases were added up, the bill came to $83. The man at the counter said, "What do you want me to put this stuff in, Mr. Gregory?" I told him, "Never mind, I'll just put it in my pocket."

Caution: Eating May Be Hazardous to Your Health

More critical than the *price* of food is the *quality* of food sold to the American consumer with governmental approval.

Most foods sold in American supermarkets should bear a warning similar to that found on packs of cigarettes. An honest wording would be: "WARNING: The Surgeon General Has Determined *Not* to Admit That Eating This Product Is Dangerous to Your Health." And since "a chicken in every pot" has traditionally been a favorite campaign food slogan, let's look at the fowl facts of chicken consumption in America today.

Early in 1970 a group of scientists forming the permanent advisory committee to the Department of Agriculture (USDA) offered a recommendation seemingly designed to bring about the promise of a chicken in *every* pot. It seems that federal chicken inspectors, according to the panel, had been rejecting too many chicken carcasses, declaring them unfit for consumption. Of the 176 million frying chickens slaughtered under federal inspection in November 1969, inspectors condemned 2 million because of signs of cancer virus (leukosis). Inspectors rejected any carcass that showed signs of lesions or tumors traditionally accepted as obvious signs of the presence of the cancer virus.

So the government panel suggested revising the standards to eliminate such mass rejection of virus-ridden chickens. The experts felt that lesions and tumors were not reliable indicators of the presence of virus in a chicken's system. So their recommendation was that chickens bearing cancer virus be allowed on the market as long as the birds didn't "look too repugnant." The panel admitted that birds whose internal organs showed signs of leukosis should be condemned, but other birds could be placed on the market with no threat to human health.

The government experts realized that a tumor-ridden chicken sitting in the meat counter of a supermarket might pose certain problems for the average shopper. So as a practical measure, the experts admitted, such awful-looking birds should be kept out of the meat counters for "aesthetic" reasons. But, they insisted, there is no reason to waste all that "good" food. The solution? Whenever a tumorous portion of a chicken carcass is found, simply cut away that ugly portion—tumor and all—and use it in products like hot dogs, and then sell the remaining portions of the bird as cut-up chicken.

Not all experts agreed with the findings and recommendations of the government panel. For example, Dr. J. Spencer Monroe, a professor at New York University, had been doing some experiments as far back as 1963. He injected leukosis virus into some monkeys and found that the monkeys developed tumors as a result. Without getting into any hassles about evolution, it is not too much to suspect that the same thing might happen to human beings; at least, that was Dr. Monroe's suspicion. But human priorities being what they are in the United States today, I would venture a guess that more Americans would harbor feelings of hostility toward Dr. Monroe for what he did to those poor little chimps than would worry about eating chickens.

About a year and a half after the permanent advisory committee's recommendations to USDA, the consumers' champion Ralph Nader and his Raiders released the findings of a two-year study, part of which dealt with chicken consumption. Nader's findings should make interesting reading at your next picnic—especially if the menu includes both chicken and hot dogs. Nader found that as much as fifty percent of USDA-inspected poultry is contaminated with salmonella, a germ that causes stomach ailments. He cited evidence that meat and poultry inspectors who were a little bit too conscientious in their duties were fired or transferred for angering food producers. Meat packers bribe inspectors with free meat, overtime pay, or even mistresses.

"Poor sanitation in poultry plants," the Nader report suggested, "careless handling of processed food, and exposure of meat to filthy equipment in some meat plants may increase the incidence of food-borne disease in this country." And the Nader report further accused the USDA of "unlawfully" failing to enforce the 1967 wholesome-meat act and insisted that it intends to use the act as justification "for dismantling the federal inspection system and turning it over to the states."

Unfortunately, a decision to stop eating chicken, or to stop eating meat, for that matter, is no solution to the contaminated-food problem. Most of the food Americans consume has been tampered with, added to, and downright spoiled. William Longgood, in his book *The Poisons in Your Food,* wrote:

Virtually every bite of food you eat has been treated with some chemical somewhere along the line: dyes, bleaches, emulsifiers, antiosidants, preservatives, flavor enhancers, buffers, noxious sprays, acidifiers, alkalizers, deodorants, moisteners, drying agents, gases, extenders, thickeners, disinfectants, defoliants, fungicides, neutralizers, artificial sweeteners, anticaking and antifoaming agents, conditioners, curers, hydrolizers, hydrogenators, maturers, fortifiers, and many others.

Both the number of food additives and their poisonous effect upon the human body are known to the Food and Drug Administration, yet the government takes action only in very few and isolated cases.

The artficial sweetener cyclamate was banned from the public marketplace as of August 1971. The so-called "uninvited additive," the chemical pesticide DDT, was restricted to "essential uses" in June 1970. But even after the cyclamate ban was imposed, voices in high government places began to try to allay the fears of the consuming public, creating the impression that the food-additive problem was really not all that bad. One such voice was Dr. J. M. Coon of Philadelphia, vice-chairman of the White House Conference on Food, Nutrition and Health, a panel set up to work on food safety.

Dr. Coon maintained: "There is unwarranted fear about food additives. The furor about cyclamate reflects this." Dr. Coon insisted that there is no evidence that a single human being ever got cancer from artificial sweeteners. The whole furor arose over some sick rats. So Dr. Coon suggested that all Americans relax until it was discovered whether or not diabetics currently using cyclamates develop bladder cancers over the next twenty years.

Those who want to take Dr. Coon's advice might contemplate, while they are relaxing, the fact that there are some six hundred food additives which have yet to be reviewed by the Food and Drug Administration to determine their safe usage. And the FDA says it lacks the necessary funds to conduct such a review. But a mid-1969 confidential report made by a panel of FDA officials admitted that between two and ten million Americans become ill each year from eating contaminated food. And the Department of Agriculture studies (which would have to be conservative) indicate that the average American takes in about three pounds of food additives annually.

Dr. P. R. Peacock, of the Royal Cancer Hospital in Glasgow, Scotland, spoke of the effects of food additives on humans and animals. His conclusion as to the danger involved was totally the opposite of Dr. Coon's suggestion. Said Dr. Peacock:

Human beings are walking colonies of cells, which, in the course of thousands of years of evolution, have learned how to metabolize or adapt to many natural substances with which they have come into contact. Today, chemists have produced hundreds of substances that never existed before, and it may take thousands more years of evolution to learn how our bodies will react to these new synthetic substances. We cannot consider the laboratory animals on which we do our tests as little men, and give certificates of harmlessness for men to substances tested on animals. . . . It is entirely possible that a substance judged harmless by any of our tests on laboratory animals may produce cancer in man. . . . There would appear to be no justification, from the purely scientific point of view, for the needless addition of artificial substances to foods that are intended for human beings to eat.

Any shopper who gives some thought to the food in the frozen-food counter should be aware of food additives. Take frozen French-fried potatoes as an example. If you have ever peeled a fresh potato, you will know that the potato turns brown wherever you touch it in the process of peeling. Yet the potatoes you see in the frozen-food counter are peeled, sliced, and whiter than Nixon's Cabinet. Have you ever wondered why? Because the potatoes are treated and bleached to give them the snow-white color. The whiter-than-whiteness may be appealing to the eye, but the stomach and the body system are less aesthetically inclined.

Frozen orange juice is another example. It is obvious that additives are placed in frozen orange juice in the interests of preservation. How many times have you read in the newspaper that citrus farmers in California or Florida feared that an unexpected drop in temperature would ruin their crop of oranges? Heating pots are placed strategically in the orchards in case of such emergencies, and when the temperature drops to freezing, the pots are lighted in an effort to save the crops. If that's what freezing does to oranges, doesn't frozen orange juice seem rather suspect to you?

Rather than looking to animals in the laboratory for an indication of what foods are safe for human consumption, people should watch animals in their natural state for clues to a proper diet. Dr. Alvenia Fulton of Chicago, Illinois, one of the country's most brilliant nutritionists and my personal adviser during my many extended fasts, wisely admonishes advocates of the traditional American diet to observe the eating habits of wild animals. Says Dr. Fulton: "Wild animals are never fat or overweight. They have no heart ailments, indigestion, high blood pressure, or artery trouble, constipation, piles, etc. They have no colds or fevers in epidemic, mass scales that humanity has fought through the centuries. Animals adhere to a strict diet, even to fasting, as the Creator and Nature intended. You cannot force a sick animal to eat."

Imposing a human diet on animals results in some alarming and edifying consequences. And that, of course, is why so many household pets end up the chronic patients of veterinarians. For example, feed a dog only white bread for nine straight days and the dog will die. But before the dog dies, it will go stark, raving mad. That's the so-called "enriched" white bread most Americans feed their children, which the television commercials insist will help them through those crucial growing years and in which the flour has been chemically aged and bleached, most of the valuable nutrients having been removed (some twenty-five nutrients), before the dough is treated with chemical softeners and preservatives to make it appear fresh, and the starchy remains treated with three or four synthetic vitamins to replace the missing nutrients.

Or if you feed a young calf its own mother's milk after the milk has been pasteurized, the calf will die. Yet mothers of America lovingly feed their own children the "purified" product, not knowing its harmful effects. Traditional American dietary mythology holds that calcium is the vital ingredient in cow's milk and that it helps children to develop strong bones and teeth. It is really casein, rather than calcium, which builds the bone structure. The only catch is that the casein in cow's milk is intended to develop the bone structure of a calf. Thus the casein content is designed to develop a bone structure some three hundred times greater than that which would be provided by a child consuming his own mother's milk.

The excess casein taken into the body when a child drinks cow's milk turns into mucus. And it is the abundance of mucus in their bodies which causes most of the sicknesses from which children suffer—running noses, colds, and the like. Most children's sicknesses and deaths can be traced back to an excess of mucus in the body system.

America's dietary habits are so distorted that the foods which are considered choice are also the foods which flood the human system with excess mucus. A reorientation of dietary habits, learning to eat the proper foods, would have tremendous social ramifications, not the least of which would be population control.

For some strange reason, girl babies are better able to survive the abundance of mucus in the mother's system than boy babies. But Nature's way seems to be that more boy babies are born than girl babies. It has been said that Nature's ratio is three to one. Yet the female population of the United States is larger than the male population. The reason is that more boy babies die at birth or shortly thereafter than girl babies, because they are unable to survive the mucus in the mother's system.

If America's dietary habits were changed, so that less mucus-producing foods were taken into the body system, the natural result would be an increase in the number of boy babies surviving. That in itself would be a built-in birth-control system. A girl is limited biologically as to how many times she can become pregnant (a maximum of once every nine months), no matter how many boys she has sexual relations with. But a boy can impregnate an unlimited number of girls. Where there are more girls than boys, quite understandably there will be overpopulation because one boy can take care of a number of girls. But where there are more boys than girls, a natural limitation is imposed.

When nations go to war, it is interesting to note that there is an increase of boy babies on the home front. It has always been attributed to some quirk of nature making up for the young men killed on the battlefield. But the real answer is to be found in the diet of a nation at war. During war periods the major mucus-producing foods are rationed at home because they are being sent to the front lines—

sugar, meat, coffee, etc. Thus the mucus intake on the home front is decreased, and Nature's proper ratio of boy and girl births prevails. (An interesting research project would be to determine the ratio of boy and girl births among war babies fathered by soldiers overseas.)

One of the greatest dietary myths in the United States today is the protein myth. Most Americans believe that it is necessary to eat meat and drink milk to get the proper amount of protein. But there are so many other foods more natural and beneficial in this regard. One of the most perfect foods, rich as a source of minerals and proteins, is soybeans, and other soy products such as soy sauce. In health-food stores you will find soy products prepared to resemble popular meat dishes, for use by those who have a taste for meat and the wisdom not to eat it. It is the soy sauce rather than the rice in the Asian diet which provides proper nutrition. Adolf Hitler discovered that fact the hard way when he attempted to put his army on a rice diet, thinking if the Asians could survive on rice his soldiers could do the same; he nearly wiped out his own men. The nutritional value of rice was sadly lacking without the soy sauce.

Another feature of the protein myth is the assumption that a person must consume meat protein to provide the protein the body needs. A cow does not have to drink milk to produce milk. In like manner, humans do not have to eat meat protein to provide the protein necessary for muscle cells.

The famous American scientist Thomas Alva Edison shed a little more light than he is usually given credit for when he said: "The doctor in the care of the human frame is diet, and in the care and prevention of disease." Edison's words were echoed by Dr. Alexis Carrel of the Rockefeller Institute of Medical Research: "If the doctor of today does not become the dietician of tomorrow, the dieticians of today will become the doctors of tomorrow."

I have experienced personally over the past few years how a purity of diet and thought are interrelated. And when Americans become truly concerned with the purity of the food that enters their own personal systems, when they learn to eat properly, we can expect to see profound changes effected in the social and political system of this nation. The two systems are inseparable.

Fraud, Famine, and National Security

At the present moment, however, the political system is at odds with the personal body systems of individual Americans. Government agencies, government research, and governmental legislation regarding food are all controlled by those with vested interests in maintaining the current destructive American diet. Though the Food and Drug Administration knows the truth about the poisonous and death-dealing products being sold to the American consumer, the FDA remains silent because of strong pressure from food-production and agricultural lobbies.

For example, the FDA knows that more people die from cancer of the stomach and bladder as a result of drinking coffee than die from cancer of the lung from smoking cigarettes. But the coffee industry is strong enough to keep the FDA from informing the public and taking forceful action. Most recent word of the link between coffee drinking and cancer of the bladder came through an Associated Press dispatch from London, June 25, 1971. A group of

American scientists, working on the relationship between cigarette smoking and cancer, came accidentally upon the discovery about coffee and cancer of the bladder. Significantly, they reported their findings in the *British* medical magazine *The Lancet*. The unidentified scientists were from the Department of Epidemiology and Kresge Center for Environmental Health at the Harvard School of Public Health.

The FDA knows the truth about the relationship between cigarette smoking and cancer. The Surgeon General's report in the United States on smoking and cancer was really a compromise report. An earlier report in Russia indicated the truth of the matter. Russian scientists found that the use of tobacco definitely had an effect upon the sex glands.

But in America the report said that cigarette smoking caused lung cancer. The assumption was that there was a relationship between tobacco and cancer. The tobacco industry has always insisted that tobacco has no such effect, and their defense is correct. Tobacco itself is not the culprit, but rather the chemicals added to the tobacco and the cigarette paper. If you have ever been around someone who smokes a pipe, or who uses Bull Durham to roll his own cigarettes, you have no doubt noticed how the tobacco immediately stops burning when the smoker is not puffing. But a commercial cigarette continues to burn even while it is sitting in the ash tray. The commercial cigarette continues to burn because of chemical additives, which are also responsible for lung cancer. The cigarette industry knows this, but faster-burning cigarettes mean more cigarettes sold.

So the food industry in America is controlled by the same capitalistic forces of corporate dominance which are responsible for so many other forms of pollution in the national environment. Government agencies and legislators themselves are responsive to the pressures and influences such strong capitalistic forces exert. And legislators frequently have strong vested interests of their own. (For example, Senator James Eastland of Mississippi, member of the Senate Agriculture and Forestry Committee, represents Eastland Plantation, Inc., a farming corporation which receives large government subsidies, and Representative Charles M. Teague of California, a member of the House Committee on Agriculture, is part of the Sunkist family interest.)

Government research on food is usually handled by the breakfast-food industry, so you can readily see how "objective" such research findings would be. The breakfast-food industry has been deceiving the American public for years concerning the nutritional value of their products. On July 23, 1970, Robert B. Choate, Jr., a nutritional expert and former consultant to the Nixon administration, testified before a Senate investigating committee that forty of the top sixty breakfast cereals in the United States have little nutritional value, and that "the worst cereals are huckstered to children" on television. Wheaties, "Breakfast of Champions," was well down the list. And the government must have believed Mr. Choate. If Wheaties was really the "Breakfast of Champions," the American government would have fed some Wheaties to the South Vietnamese army and sent them back into Laos!

Not only are government agencies, legislation, and research lined up against the "eaters" of America, but the biggest threat to national security is found in food production and distribution in this country. The FBI, the CIA, and the military are all engaged in wiretapping and other forms of snooping, when they should be looking at where food is produced in the United States.

California has become the number-one food state in the nation. About forty-three percent of all the table food and seventy percent of all fruit are produced in the state of California. Truck farming, on the other hand, is concentrated on the East Coast. It is no accident that the truck-farming industry is concentrated where the nation's wealthiest citizens live. The super-rich are aware of the importance of food and want their fresh vegetables easily accessible on a daily basis.

But the food which is consumed by the masses of America, like frozen food, is primarily produced and distributed from California. When the nation's food supply became so predominantly concentrated in one state, the basic ingredient in national security was violated. Any nation or group committed to the destruction of the United States would find it ideal that the nation's food supply is so easily shut off.

The frozen-food industry being concentrated in California presents another problem for the consumer's own "internal" security. Frozen foods must be shipped from California to the rest of the country. Keeping frozen foods under high refrigeration during those long hauls is a very expensive matter, and I have been told the refrigeration is occasionally turned down as the foods move across the country on their way to local markets. By the time the food reaches the frozen-food counters in the supermarket, bearing the warning to the shopper "Do Not Refreeze After Thawing," it has already been refrozen.

Thus the "internal" security of the consumer is violated.

Ira I. Somers, research director of the National Canners Association, Washington, D.C., reported in an interview that storage temperature is very significant in vitamin retention in frozen foods. Zero degrees or lower results in "negligible vitamin loss over several months of storage." But at sixteen degrees Fahrenheit the Vitamin C loss after six months' storage of some vegetables is more than fifty percent. Additional Vitamin C loss occurs during the home heating process as the food is prepared. One can readily see the total lack of nutritional value of frozen foods by the time they come out of the family pot. Vitamin C would have to be added at home for any nutritional value at all.

Government officials interested in national security spend a lot of time watching Russia and so-called "Communist influences" in the United States. They would do well to look also to Russia for clues regarding the world food situation. National-security enthusiasts ought to realize that a cold war is not half as bad as a hunger war. And there is indication that Russia has some inside information regarding the future of world food.

Famines throughout the world occur according to definite cycles of Nature. In America we are taught to regard famine as a natural disaster. But really famine is Nature's way of pruning the earth. After a period of famine, crops grow better.

Certain clues from Russia indicate to me at least that the Russians have some high-ranking astronomers who have discovered the famine cycle in Nature and have convinced the Russian government to make necessary preparations. The Russians have diverted large sums of money from the space program to increasing their naval fleet. Such a fleet would be necessary for Russia to feed the world in the event of a serious famine crisis.

Another tip came when the Russians sent up their "space bungalow." Word began to filter back that experimentation was being conducted in growing cabbage. That should cause Americans to stop and think. Of all the things a nation can do in outer space, those Russian cats are farming! And, of course, it makes a lot more sense than spending millions of dollars to collect some rocks from the moon. As many times as I've been hit on the head with a rock, I just can't get excited when my country goes to the moon and all they have to show me when they get back is some rocks.

Russian scientists are also pioneers in the exploration of the sea as a source for food products. They maintain that the productive capacity of the sea (which covers seventy-one percent of the globe) is a thousand times greater than that of the earth's arable-land area. Thus, while the Russians are building up their merchant-marine fleet on top of the water, they are also probing the depths of the sea for foods to feed the world.

Back in the United States the "arable" land is fast disappearing, due to the abuse of the soil by the large farming enterprises. Government standards for measuring successful agricultural methods continue to emphasize quantity over quality in food production. As a result, as Dr. William A. Albrecht (Professor Emeritus and formerly Chairman of the Department of Soils at the University of Missouri College of Agriculture) has warned, the nation's soil fertility is sinking to dangerously low levels. Since the government criterion for measuring farming success is based on numbers of gallons of milk per cow, bushels of crops per acre, cattle shipped to market, etc., large farmers resort to all kinds of hyped-up tricks to excel by government standards. The soil is soaked in chemicals and hormone preparations. Pesticides poison away invading insects. Hybrid seeds are used and crops are juggled.

The result, according to Dr. Albrecht, is in no way an indication of soil fertility, but rather a stark example of the exploitation of the earth's nutrients. He has said: "We must soon face the dilemma of feeding ourselves on paved streets, because the rural community is about to be the dead victim of a parasitic, technical soil exploitation that has failed to appreciate the biological aspect of the soils in the creative business of feeding us all."

As Dr. Albrecht warns that we will have to look to the pavement as a food-growing space, William Longgood reminds us that there are still some backyard plots containing uncontaminated soil. Says Longgood: "Probably the most important protective measure anyone with a small amount of land can take is having his own garden. This assures many advantages: a constant supply of fresh products, economy, convenience and a pleasant and productive form of exercise. Many people, by using natural farming methods, are able to grow their own produce without the use of chemical fertilizers or sprays."

In contrast to this backyard hope, Longgood dramatically describes the current popular pattern of agricultural methods:

Our agriculture problem suggests a Gilbert and Sullivan operetta. We use chemicals to produce more food than we can use, sacrificing quality to quantity. Then the surplus must be stored at tremendous cost. To keep it from being devoured by insects it must be basted with powerful poisons; we seem to prefer eating poisoned dead insects to healthy live ones. Instead of consuming our "surplus" grains, butter, eggs and other protein products in health-promoting whole-wheat breads and other baked goods, we put chemicals into them that offer little or no nutrition. We remove the best part of the wheat, feed it to animals, and to what remains we add synthetic vitamins to make up for the removed nutrients; then we call this impoverished product "enriched." Finally, we spend millions of dollars on vitamins and drugs to make up for the nutritional deficiencies of our foods.

So there you have it in a nutshell. The food-production and agricultural industries, with the sanction, support, and approval of government, have created a situation where "a chicken in every pot" is the worst possible campaign promise. As a matter of fact, a smart candidate would accuse his opponent of trying to do just that—place a diseased, cancer-ridden chicken in everybody's home. And the best answer seems to be a return to backyard gardening. The candidate smart enough to place the "chicken stigma" on his opponent should then run on the slogan "A turnip in every pot."

During World War II a patriotic act for Americans was the cultivation of a Victory Garden, growing food at home so that the nation's regular food supply could be sent to the front line. The day is fast approaching when Victory Gardens will again be an American phenomenon because of the unpatriotic abuse of the nation's rural resources by government and the agricultural industry. Anyone who professes a "love of country" should certainly display an affection for that country's life-producing soil. And the first persons who become enlightened enough to bring back the Victory Garden concept will be the very folks who show their love of life and abhorrence of destruction today by displaying the V-sign of peace.

Many urban Americans, of course, do not have backyard plots for gardening. But even now it is quite possible to follow Dr. Albrecht's advice and "look to feeding ourselves on paved streets." The creation of backyard plots where there are only paved streets is possible through the application of hydroponics.

Hydroponics is the production of plants and crops without soils, using nutrients carried in water. It is a technology quite old in human history, having first been developed as a laboratory process in 1699 and still using the basic formulas developed by German scientists over a hundred years ago. In applying hydroponics to growing food, temperature, air supplies, moisture, light, and nutrients are controlled to produce the ideal product.

One growing example of hydroponics at work is the Magic Garden developed by Hydroculture, Inc., of Phoenix, Arizona. In the Magic Garden, a "closed system" greenhouse operation, tomato vines grow eight feet tall, producing fruit of superior size, appearance, flavor, and holding quality. And all without the use of death-dealing pesticides. Each mature tomato plant produces an average of 30 pounds of marketable fruit per year, in two growing cycles —three times that of field-grown plants (usually 8 to 10 pounds per plant per year). Thus, eight 26′ × 128′ greenhouses per acre of land can produce 240,000 pounds of tomatoes a year. It would take four to eight acres of land to produce an equivalent crop in the field. Plants in the Magic

Garden require only 1/29th the water required by field crops.

Tomatoes are not the only crops produced at the Magic Garden complex of greenhouses. Strawberries, chard, cucumbers, and melons have also been grown and marketed. And hydroponic processes have been used for some time by zoos in America and Europe to produce green-grass supplements for zoo animals.

Grocers and restaurateurs marvel at the quality and taste of foods produced by hydroponic processes. Developers of hydroponic methods talk enthusiastically about the possibility of converting vast wastelands into productive food-growing areas, with less than ten percent of the water consumption of conventional agricultural methods. They speak further of the time in the not-too-distant future when families can purchase units no larger than refrigerators for about $500 and grow all the lettuce, tomatoes, and other vegetables they need.

The potential of the application of hydroponic processes in urban areas staggers the imagination. Of course, the degenerate captains of the conventional food industry will fight such enlightened ways to deal with the problems of hunger and pure food in America. And they will be supported by their government lackeys. But both the prostitutes of profit and the destroyers of democracy will find themselves up against the rising food-consciousness of youth. As I travel to college campuses throughout the country, I am overwhelmed to see so many young people vitally concerned about the body, foods, and a proper diet. Health-food stores throughout the country are multiplying rapidly (in Los Angeles, for example, there were 96 health-food outlets by the second quarter of 1971, whereas there were only 74 in 1966). And I think it is more than coincidence that I have never seen a fat hippie!

So food will be an election issue for some time to come. When candidates begin to hear their traditional constituents grumbling about dinners and groceries in 1972, they will assume the real issue is the price of food and will turn their attention toward trying to manipulate the economy. But the young voters who will determine the social and political destiny of America are more concerned with the physical price one pays for eating bad food and are taking seriously the ancient wisdom of Hippocrates:

. . . it appears to me necessary to every physician to be skilled in nature, and to strive to know, if he would wish to perform his duties, what a man is in relation to the articles of food and drink, and to his other occupations, and what are the effects of each of them to everyone.

Whoever does not know what effect these things produce upon a man cannot know the consequences which result from them.

Whoever pays no attention to these things, or paying attention, does not comprehend them, how can he understand the diseases which befall a man? For, by every one of these things a man is affected and charged this way and that, and the whole of his life is subjected to them, whether in health, convalescence, or disease. Nothing else, then, can be more important or more necessary to know than these things.

Postscript

Every so often I find little indications that the government in the United States is more hip than people think. One of the best items to grow in your Victory Garden would be navy beans. Navy beans are rich in nutrients, and the best food to store up in case of famine or nuclear attack.

The House of Representatives Restaurant in the Capitol building in Washington, D.C., includes navy-bean soup on its menu every day. It had long been a favorite item on the House Restaurant menu when one hot and humid day in 1904, Representative Joseph G. Cannon of Illinois placed his order and found that navy-bean soup had been omitted from the menu because of the weather. Cannon, who was Speaker of the House, roared his disapproval: "Thunderation! I had my mouth set for bean soup. From now on, hot or cold, rain, snow, or shine, I want it on the menu every day." It has been on the menu every single day since Cannon's order.

So, courtesy of your government, I offer the recipe used in the Capitol kitchens. I personally, being a vegetarian, would amend the recipe to substitute olive oil for ham hocks.

> 2 lb. No. 1 white Michigan beans.
> Cover with cold water and soak overnight.
> Drain and recover with water.
> Add a smoked ham hock and *simmer slowly* for about
>   4 hours until beans are cooked tender.
> Then add salt and pepper to suit taste.
> Just before serving, bruise beans with large spoon
>   or ladle, enough to cloud.
> (Serves about six persons)

1

What did you have for breakfast this morning (if anything)? How do you feel? Give examples.

2

Using this lesson as a guide, write an essay interpreting the phrase "You are what you eat."

3

If an earthquake wipes out California, where will you get your food?

4

Delicious is to *nutritious* as:
- a. black is to white;
- b. bananas are to watermelon;
- c. gorgeous is to beautiful;
- d. death is to life;
- e. none of these.

Lesson Fifteen
Citizen
Surveillance

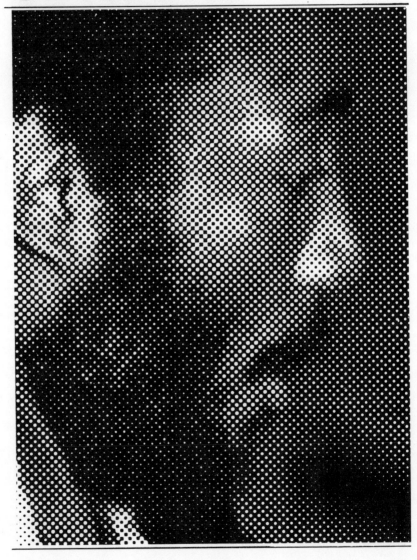

During the early months of 1971 most Americans were shocked and dismayed to learn of the extent to which the Pentagon and the Federal Bureau of Investigation have been snooping on the private citizens in this country. People began to see that Uncle Sam not only "wants you" but he watches you ever so closely. Hearings conducted by North Carolina Senator Sam J. Ervin's subcommittee on constitutional rights revealed the activities of former Army intelligence personnel as they spied on the citizenry. One witness, Professor Arthur R. Miller of the University of Michigan Law School, said America was fast moving toward a "dossier dictatorship." The subcommittee was told that the *average* American is the subject of from ten to twenty dossiers containing private information.

The snooping, bugging, and wiretapping activities of the FBI exploded onto the national scene in April 1971. On April 6 Representative Hale Boggs of Louisiana spoke on the floor of the House of Representatives comparing FBI Director J. Edgar Hoover to Hitler and Stalin and condemning the practice of keeping members of Congress under surveillance. Senator Edmund Muskie of Maine picked up the chorus the following week, condemning the FBI surveillance of speakers at the April 22, 1970, Earth Day rally in Washington, D.C., of which Senator Muskie was a part. He called such activity "intolerable in a free society" and "a dangerous threat to fundamental constitutional rights," suggesting that if an antipollution rally is considered suspect by the FBI, then no political activity in America is safe.

And the April 9 issue of *Life* magazine designated Hoover as the Emperor of the FBI, displaying a cover photo which clearly placed him in symbolic line with some of the more notorious emperors of the Roman Empire and a few pages of copy which indicated the problems of a man who had been too strong too long.

Personally, I was not as upset as most folks were to learn of the Army's spying activities. First of all, I had written of their activity in my last book, *No More Lies*. And then the headlines of the newspaper I happened to read were rather reassuring. I'm sure if I had read "Army Spying on Folks," I would have been upset. But my newspaper headline read, "Army *Intelligence* Spying on Civilians." I really couldn't get upset about that, because if you know anything about the Army, you know Army intelligence is a contradiction in terms!

I have been aware of the presence of Army intelligence agents since long before Senator Ervin's hearings. When I speak at colleges or at human-rights and peace rallies, I can spot them in the audience every time. When you see a person in the audience wearing a beard with the price tag still hanging from it, or a dog tag tangled up in his love beads, it is a dead giveaway. But the real clincher is to look down and notice a spit-shine on the sandals.

And I've long been aware of the fact that my telephone is tapped. I have so many bugs on my home phone that my wife and I put roach powder on it every night. I even have agents hiding in the bushes outside of my apartment building. People come by my house and say, "Look at Dick Gregory's bushes. They have feet." I tell them, "Yes, and my bushes change shifts every eight hours." One day, instead of watering my bushes, I'm going to go out and scald them.

I remember when the FBI agent came by in disguise to tap my telephone. He was so stupid that he knocked on my door. I said, "Who is it?" And he said, "Does Dick Gregory live here?" I said, "Yes, why?" And he answered, "I just didn't want to tap the wrong phone." Then when he did hook up the tap, he made the mistake of attaching it to my television antenna. When the agents back at the office tuned in, they thought they were listening to a conversation between Angela Davis and me, while they were really listening to a conversation between Flip Wilson and Moms Mabley.

I was on a television show not too long ago, and the interviewer asked me how I could be so sure my phone was tapped. And I told him it was my phone, so of course I knew. He said, "But you have to have definite proof." So I told him I really knew one night when I picked up the phone to call my cousin and he was already on the line. And my cousin doesn't even have a phone!

But the interviewer said that still wasn't enough proof to say my phone is definitely tapped. So I finally gave him irrefutable proof. I said, "Any time a black man in America can owe the telephone company twelve thousand dollars and they don't shut the phone off, you know that phone is tapped."

The reason I don't get too upset about my phone being tapped is that anyone who knows his phone is bugged can have a lot of fun with the buggers. I play little games with the tap. Sometimes I call up my wife and read the alphabet to her backward. I can just see all those Army and FBI computers trying to decode my message. One time I even put my youngest boy on the line who can't talk yet. When he started making those strange sounds, the guys on the tap thought I was sending messages in Swahili.

Of course, FBI citizen-watching becomes less than humorous when one considers the magnitude of the data collected. As far back as the mid-'60s, files on the arrest records of American cities alone occupied three floors of the FBI's huge records building—7,500 filing cabinets plus 5,000 more cabinets in the microfilm files. The index alone was a card file three blocks long. Today the files include more than 60 million arrest records on 19 million American citizens. Add to that the bulging files of raw intelligence data which include unevaluated hearsay, wiretap recordings, and informer reports on matters like the ideological and sexual peculiarities of thousands and thousands of plain, ordinary folks.

The Z Syndrome

Citizen-watching has become a big business for Army intelligence, the FBI, and the Central Intelligence Agency (CIA), and American citizens had better start doing some intelligent watching of their own before it is too late. A good beginning would be to watch the movie entitled simply Z. Though filmed in France and referring to the political situation in Greece, Z deals with topics increasingly familiar in America—government control, the attempt of concerned citizens to articulate a higher morality, and the resort to assassination as a sure way to silence both dissent and morality.

In the movie, the peace faction is the "enemy" of established government. Rallies and mass meetings are discouraged and frustrated by subtle officialities like denial of meeting permits and pressuring owners of meeting places to refuse rental privileges to the peace faction. After a mass meeting, the peace leader is struck down by a man in a truck.

An investigation is launched and unmistakable evidence points in the direction of assassination by government goons. Result: vindication of accused government officials, jailing or killing of all those wise to the governmental conspiracy (all under the umbrella of accidental death and due legal process), and, in the end, government by dictatorship.

All of the above should sound familiar to Americans, but some readers may still wonder what the movie Z has to do with America. For one thing, it deals with a very real situation in Greece. And America, whose governmental gut characteristic has never been an aversion to interfering in the affairs of other nations, stood silently by and watched Greek democracy fall. Then America's silence was broken when she officially recognized the newly established military dictatorship. That's the same America which is fighting in Vietnam supposedly to give democracy a chance.

Those who question how a military overthrow could occur so swiftly within the democracy of Greece will be pleased to know that thorough and careful surveillance of the private citizenry preceded it. Just as we are learning is happening in America today, files were created on everyone who might possibly oppose a military takeover, so that when the time came, opposition was easily identified and curtailed.

The Z syndrome runs deeper in America, and the Greece scenario could be a glimpse at America's not-too-distant future. Many Americans were shocked, horrified, and outraged when the late Malcolm X referred to the assassination of President John F. Kennedy as an example of "chickens coming home to roost." What passed for a flippant and callous disregard for the memory of the dead President was really a perceptive political comment. Malcolm X realized

the role of the CIA in the overthrow of foreign governments and the killing off of political leaders. He was merely
pointing out that an agency well schooled in the art of overthrowing governments is likely to apply that art one day to
our own government. The list of mysterious and convenient
deaths following the assassination of JFK bears a strong
resemblance to the movie *Z,* and should raise suspicions in
the minds of many concerning the role the CIA might have
played in the assassinations of JFK, Robert Kennedy, Malcolm X, and Martin Luther King, Jr.

The CIA, like the FBI, is capable of close and illegal surveillance, such as that mentioned in Supreme Court Justice
William O. Douglas' book *Points of Rebellion.* He mentions
the bugging and wiring of hotel rooms and the installation of
two-way mirrors right in the nation's capital, and I know
by experience of such practices. I have been followed and
watched, wired and bugged. But I also know of my deep
and abiding faith in the Constitution of the United States
and my commitment to humanity in general. If a man of my
ethical persuasion, moral standards, and honest orientation
can be considered a "security risk" by the CIA, I must conclude that the CIA is worried about its *own* security and
not that of the United States.

Consider some of the other people known to have been
under FBI, Army, and CIA surveillance. There's Bishop
C. Kilmer Myers, Episcopal Bishop in California, who began
his career in the priesthood by bringing hope and meaning
into the lives of hundreds of kids in the slums of New York
City. That activity is recorded in his beautiful book *Light
the Dark Streets.* Bishop Myers made the mistake of taking

the Prince of Peace whom he serves too seriously and participated in some demonstrations in 1969, so the Army has to keep an eye on him.

Then there's Dr. Benjamin Spock, who raised a whole generation of American kids. He's been under surveillance because he doesn't want to see those kids senselessly killed off.

Fathers Dan and Phil Berrigan became the prime targets of J. Edgar Hoover's wrath. Hoover claimed the two peace-loving and gentle priests huddled in jail and conceived a brilliant conspiracy to abduct President Nixon's number-one adviser, Dr. Henry Kissinger. If such a thing could happen, it seems to me the prison is what should be under surveillance. It would seem that prisons are the main threat to Presidential security, which, of course, is not far from the truth.

The late Whitney Young, Jr., who was director of the National Urban League at his untimely death in March 1971, was kept under watchful eye during his lifetime. The surveillance of Whitney Young must have posed rationale problems for the citizen-watchers. They always said they kept the Black Panthers under surveillance because the Panthers were trying to overthrow the government. What, then, could be the justification for spying on the man who for so long headed the number-one black organization trying to work within the system? The National Urban League has a proud history of job training, employment seeking, self-help and educational programs. Were the citizen-watchers trying to tell us that upgrading the disadvantaged is indeed overthrowing the government?

The list of good folks under surveillance could go on and on. But one thing is sure. As the dossiers multiply, the term "private citizenry" fades into oblivion.

Still, the CIA is generally regarded as a necessary presence to guard against "Communist influences." Such a point of view sells the CIA expertise short and gives so-called "Communist influences" more credit than is due them. The CIA is better trained, better equipped, and better prepared than any Communist-influenced group or individual in this country will ever be. So if a government takeover ever results in America, it will be the CIA's doing, not the Communists'.

Consider, for example, the awesome expertise that has been developed in the area of germ warfare. Only the CIA would possess the sophistication to use germ warfare and totally wipe out any particular group of people in this country and pass it off as an epidemic. Few people would question or suspect, just as few have really questioned the tragic assassinations in America.

The CIA has been very active infiltrating movements and institutions at home—the church, educational institutions, the news media, large foundations (which finance both movements and institutions), as well as the youth and peace movements. Such infiltration has to be for a reason, and it must run much deeper than a kind of political voyeurism.

Perhaps it would take a governmental overthrow by unsuspected forces within the government itself to make the majority of Americans realize what a precious commodity true democracy really is—much too precious to be mocked and ridiculed by the current infatuation with pseudopatriotism. It will be a sad day for many Americans when events force them to realize that men like Attorney Mark Lane and New Orleans District Attorney Jim Garrison, though voices crying in the wilderness of rejection, were really the true patriots of our land. Democracy lost will then be democracy appreciated, and perhaps the real incentive to make democracy work right once and for all.

We Bombed in Washington, D.C., and in Seattle and in Berkeley and in New York and in . . .

Watching the movie *Z* should lead concerned citizens to watch their newspapers a little more closely for clues about what is really going on in America. A concerned citizen watching the citizen-watchers would certainly pick up the *New York Times* mention in April 1971 of an FBI informant going into the office of Representative John Dowdy of Texas the year before with a tape recorder strapped to his back, thus giving a new definition to the concept of spinal support.

Writing in the February 28, 1971, issue of the *New York Times,* Grace Lichtenstein reported a meeting of a three-year-old organization in New York City called Computer People for Peace:

A bearded young man wearing a *dog tag* [italics mine] around his neck and faded dungarees argued that "force is the only solution."

"The only way to stop data banks is to destroy them," he said. "Go into an office, plant a bomb and that's it."

The mention of violence did not sit well with the rest of the audience. "Where are you from?" someone asked the young man. The youth did not answer. Officials of the group said later that they suspected the youth, whom they had not noticed at previous meetings, was an undercover agent.

Such a small newspaper item should raise the much larger question of who is really responsible for the bombings in this country which receive such great publicity and are always attributed to militants of the left-wing variety. As a case in point, let us consider the bombing of the United States Capitol building on March 1, 1971. A starting point for such consideration is to turn back the pages of history and remember the bombing of the German capitol building, the Reichstag. People who have learned to smell tricky governmental maneuvers in America were inclined to say, after the bombing of the Capitol building, *"Wieder der Reichstag!"*

On the evening of February 27, 1933, newly elected German Chancellor Adolf Hitler was relaxing at a family dinner in the home of Josef Goebbels. They were playing music on the gramophone and telling stories when Goebbels received a phone call from a Dr. Hanfstaengl: "The Reichstag is on fire!"

Hitler and Goebbels raced sixty miles an hour down the Charlottenberger Chausse to the burning capitol, which was described as looking like it was illuminated by searchlights with an occasional flame and swirl of smoke blurring the outline.

Hermann Goering was already there, sweating, huffing, and puffing excitedly, loudly proclaiming to Vice Chancellor von Papen and President von Hindenburg that "this is a Communist crime against the new government." The next day President von Hindenburg was persuaded to sign a decree, "for the Protection of the People and the State," suspending seven sections of the constitution which guaranteed individual and civil liberties. Thus Hitler was able to legally gag his opponents and throw the middle class and the peasantry into a frenzy of fear concerning the Communists and guarantee their vote in favor of National Socialism.

Though the true history of the Reichstag fire will never be fully known, there is no doubt that the Nazis themselves were responsible. At the Nuremburg trials Goering was quoted as having said: "The only one who really knows about the Reichstag is I, because I set it on fire!" Everyone in the know about the Reichstag died, most of them murdered by Hitler in succeeding months. But it was clearly a Nazi-planned arson serving Nazi political ends.

Thirty-eight years and two days later a bomb blast ripped through the United States Capitol building in Washington, D.C. President Nixon, aboard Air Force One on his way to make a speech in Iowa, issued a statement calling the bombing a "shocking act of violence which will outrage all Americans." Vice President Agnew said: "The bombing of the United States Capitol building early Monday morning was a calculated act of outrage which will be neither tolerated nor condoned by Americans who value our system and its institutions."

Other voices within government were also sure that it was a calculated act, but were further convinced that it had to be an *inside* job. The bomb went off in a lavatory so obscure as to be unknown to most people. Senator George D. Aiken and other Senators speculated that the bombing was the work of "a professional who had complete knowledge of the layout of the Capitol." Some Senators and Congressmen didn't even know where the lavatory was located.

The bombing was reported in *Chicago Today* as follows:

At about 1 A.M. Eastern Standard Time (midnight Chicago time), Mrs. Norma Fullerton, switchboard operator at the Capitol in Washington, received a phone call from an unknown man:

"The Capitol building will blow up in 30 minutes.

"Evacuate. You may have gotten other calls like this, but this one is for real. Evacuate the building immediately. This is in retaliation for the last decision which Nixon made."

Then the phone went dead. The bomb went off at 1:32 A.M., EST.

Newspaper headlines all over the country immediately captioned that the bombing was in response to the President's decision to get involved militarily in Laos. But the caller said the *last* decision that Nixon made. That wasn't Loas, but rather the suspension of the Davis-Bacon Act, which made construction workers feel they were unfairly singled out by the President and turned those former staunch supporters of the President and superpatriots of the nation into Nixon enemies.

When Air Force One landed in Iowa and the President deplaned to go to his speaking engagement, the motorcade was pelted with snowballs by protesting construction workers. The President chuckled and mumbled something about "everybody likes to throw snowballs." But snowballs are roughly the same size as eggs or hand grenades, so the pelting had more serious implications.

Then the Associated Press offices in Washington, D.C., reportedly received a letter dated Monday, March 1, 1971,

288

postmarked from Elizabeth, New Jersey, claiming credit for the "Weather Underground" for the bombing of the Capitol building.

Remembering the burning of the Reichstag, a concerned watching citizen is forced to ask whose ends are *really* served by stirring up American citizen anger and blame toward the radical left for such an "outrage." Who really knew where the obscure lavatory was? Since many Senators didn't even know, isn't it likely to be the very people who have been keeping extensive files on the Senators themselves? Anyone who can tap telephones and bug hotel rooms can certainly wire a toilet.

Citizens keeping their government under surveillance might also consider the case of the returned Vietnam war veteran Larry E. Ward, a black soldier who came back home to the ghetto of Seattle, Washington, with two Purple Hearts and an Army commendation medal. He came back March 27, 1970, after having successfully survived the gunfire of the so-called "enemy" in the jungles of Southeast Asia for fifteen months. May 15, 1970, Larry Ward lay dead in the street in his hometown, the victim of wounds inflicted by the Seattle police.

Los Angeles Times Reporter Richard T. Cooper unraveled a terrible tale which showed that Larry Ward was also the victim of the peculiar "planned, organized, maniacal madness" that pervades the American system. Larry Ward was allegedly lighting a bomb at the offices of Morris Hardcastle Real Estate in Seattle when he met his death. How he happened to be there is a sickening study in law and order.

A series of sixty bombings in Seattle over a two-year

period had placed the police under intense public and political pressure. The Seattle police and the FBI were working hand in hand when word came from a twenty-six-year-old convict named Alfred R. Burnett, in prison for robbery and parole violation. Burnett said he had information concerning who was doing the bombing in the Seattle ghetto (Central Area). Two months *before* Larry Ward was discharged from the Army, Burnett was released from prison on $5,000 bail.

Burnett began giving the police tips about expected bombings, and stakeouts were arranged, but none of the tips paid off. In a sworn statement to his family lawyer, Burnett tells how he made sure one tip would work.

Burnett began planting bombing ideas in the mind of Jimmy Davis, a former Black Panther and a friend of Larry Ward. The Hardcastle bombing was set up for the night of May 14, 1970, with a police stakeout carefully arranged by Burnett. Burnett had expected Jimmy Davis to be the bomber, but when the time came, Davis was nowhere to be found. So Burnett made an offer to Larry Ward, an offer which included a $75 payoff. (Larry Ward, incidentally, had not found work since his return home, though he had made several applications.)

So Larry Ward took his $75 and the sticks of dynamite and was driven by Burnett to the scene of the crime. He was unarmed. On the way to the site of the bombing, Burnett made an excuse to stop and he secretly made a phone call. Burnett told the police that the would-be bomber was Larry Ward instead of Jimmy Davis and that Ward was unarmed. Burnett also described the year, make, model, and color of the car he was driving.

The trap was set. When Larry Ward struck the match to light the dynamite, he ignited a volley of police fire from the stakeout. Supposedly the police did not fire until Ward started running away and refused to halt, but police experts testified that there were some bullet marks in the Hardcastle doorway.

Since the FBI and the Seattle police were working so closely together, one has to assume that the Bureau is involved in set-ups like that of Larry Ward. The FBI has grown so powerful and independent under the direction of J. Edgar Hoover that it can tap the phones, bug the hotel rooms, and otherwise watch the private actions of priests, nuns, ministers, lawyers, college professors, civil-rights workers, doctors, governmental officials, etc., without any curb on its activities. When such a network of surveillance grows to the magnitude it has, watchful citizens must realize that the time is very close when *no one* in America is safe. So citizens must begin to conduct their own surveillance of the FBI.

Citizen surveillance should lead to a demand for the definition of the legitimate role of the FBI. The FBI has become totally hung up on Director Hoover's obsession with his personal view of "internal security" at the expense of the real function of the Bureau. The FBI should be the number-one agency in the country which throws the fear of justice into the real outlaws and criminals in our society. By definition, the FBI should be the investigating agency involved in the apprehension of criminals rather than the self-appointed guardian of internal security.

A quick look at the FBI's Most Wanted Criminal list will indicate what has happened to its self-image. The list, by the way, has grown from ten to sixteen precisely because the Bureau is so hung up on "internal security." Half of the current list is comprised of young persons wanted for so-called left-wing radical political activity. Without them, the FBI would only have an Eight Most Wanted list.

Isn't it odd that on the entire list of sixteen there is not one dope pusher, not one dope smuggler, not one person involved in the illicit traffic of narcotics in any form? There is not one big syndicate hoodlum on the list. Any neutral outside observer would have to look at the FBI's Most Wanted list and conclude that narcotics are obviously not a problem in the United States. And of course the observer would be partially right. It doesn't seem to be a problem for the FBI. The Bureau is more concerned with the destruction of property than with the destruction of the life of a nine-year-old kid.

A vital part of citizen surveillance is to keep in close contact with the Government Printing Office in Washington, D.C. The United States government might be up to some terrifying activities, but one thing you have to say about the government is that it prints all of its dirt.

A more than sobering example followed the assassination of Dr. Martin Luther King, Jr., in April 1968. Rebellions of sorrow and outrage spread through the black ghettos of America. By most decent-thinking folks they were seen as understandable expressions of frustration and anger after the cruel extinction of the most respected black man in America. To the House Un-American Activities Committee (HUAC), however, the ghetto rebellions represented the organized actions of "black guerrilla-warfare fighters." A month after Dr. King's murder, HUAC Chairman Representative Edwin

E. Willis, Democrat of Louisiana, presented the committee's recommendations on how to handle the uppity black community to President Lyndon B. Johnson. The committee recommended:

Guerrilla warfare, as envisioned by its proponents at this stage, would have to have its base in the ghetto. This being the case, the ghetto would have to be sealed off from the rest of the city. Police, State troopers, and the National Guard could adequately handle this chore and, if they needed help, the Regular Army would be brought into service.

Once the ghetto is sealed off, and depending upon the violence being perpetrated by the guerrillas, the following actions could be taken by the authorities:

(1) A curfew would be imposed in the enclosed isolated area. No one would be allowed out of or into the area after sundown.

(2) During the night the authorities would not only patrol the boundary lines, but would also attempt to control the streets and, if necessary, send out foot patrols through the entire area. If the guerrillas attempted to either break out of the area or to engage the authorities in open combat they would be readily suppressed.

(3) During a guerrilla uprising most civil liberties would have to be suspended, search and seizure operations would be instituted during the daylight hours, and anyone found armed or without proper identification would immediately be arrested. Most of the people of the ghetto would not be involved in the guerrilla operation and, under conditions of police and military control, some would help in ferreting out the guerrillas. Their help would be invaluable.

(4) If the guerrillas were able to hold out for a period of time, then the population of the ghetto would be classified through an office for the "control and organization of the inhabitants." This office would distribute "census cards" which

would bear a photograph of the individual, the letter of the district in which he lives, his house and street number, and a letter designating his home city.

(5) The population within the ghetto would be exhorted to work with the authorities and to report both on guerrillas and any suspicious activity they might note. The police agencies would be in a position to make immediate arrests, without warrants, under suspension of guarantees usually provided by the Constitution.

(6) Acts of overt violence by the guerrillas would mean that they had declared a "state of war" within the country and, therefore, would forfeit their rights as in wartime. The McCarran Act provides for various detention centers to be operated throughout the country and these might well be utilized for the temporary imprisonment of warring guerrillas.

(7) The very nature of the guerrilla operation as presently envisioned by certain Communists and black nationalists would be impossible to sustain. According to the most knowledgeable guerrilla war experts in this country, the revolutionaries could be isolated and destroyed in a short period of time.

President Johnson did not put the HUAC recommendation into effect, suspending civil liberties and constitutional guarantees, as German President von Hindenburg had done after the burning of the Reichstag. But he could have under the Internal Security Act of 1950, the McCarran Act referred to in the HUAC recommendations. And any future President could do so with even less provocation than the uprisings in the wake of Dr. King's death. The Government Printing Office has other enlightening documents from HUAC and many other committees, so check them out.

A fitting close to this lesson is the thought embodied in

a poem by the East German poet Wolf Bierman entitled
"Morning Thought of General Ky":

> A government
> That fears
> Nothing else
> But the people
> Can hold out
> Precisely as long
> As the people
> Fear nothing
> Else but
> The government.

1

What are civil liberties? What is a private citizen? Cite examples, if you can think of any, of how the government might take liberty with the civil liberties of private citizens.

2

Make a chart of bombing incidents in the United States as they are reported in the newspapers and on radio and television. Include what public officials say about the bombings, who is blamed and/or arrested, and the results of any trials that occur. See how many names of accused bombers appear on the FBI most-wanted list.

3

Make a similar chart for narcotics crimes in the United States. How many persons arrested and convicted are narcotics users and how many are suppliers? How many names from this chart appear on the FBI most-wanted list?

Lesson Sixteen
Planetary
Politics

As strange as it may sound to some readers, a familiarity with astrology is important to an understanding of American politics. The Founding Fathers of these United States, especially Thomas Jefferson, were knowledgeable in the ways of the stars and planets, and that knowledge is reflected in the originally established traditions.

Of course, anyone familiar with black history is also quite aware of Thomas Jefferson's interest in science and astrology. One of the great scientific geniuses of the colonies in the 1700s was a black man by the name of Benjamin Banneker. Many black schools in this country today are named after Brother Ben.

Banneker was far in advance of his time in his studies of mathematics, astronomy, and medicine. He was also an inventor, and holds the distinction of having made the first clock in America while he was still a youth—a wooden clock which struck the hours.

Banneker also put out a series of almanacs which successfully predicted eclipses and contained valuable tidal information and astronomical observations, as well as medicinal formulas. Through his work Banneker gained the respect and admiration of then Secretary of State Jefferson, who sent one of Banneker's almanacs to Monsieur de Condorcet, Secretary of the Academy of Sciences in Paris. Jefferson also placed Banneker on the team of engineers working on the blueprints for the new nation's capital, Washington, D.C., and Banneker was the chief engineer responsible for the final layout of the city.

Thomas Jefferson's political theories and actions reflect his devotion to science as a way of life, which also included a profound interest in astronomy. Speaking of Jefferson and his interest in science, Joseph Charles has written:

Jefferson's interest in science was misunderstood by many in his own time, and its full implications still elude us. While specific achievements of his in mathematics, architecture, and invention are evidence of an amazing versatility, they are even more startling as evidence of unity and direction of purpose. His life-long concern with science was not primarily due to breadth of interest; it was rather the measure of his centrality and integration. Jefferson was not the jack-of-all-trades or the incessant dabbler he is so often pictured as being; he was, rather, an exponent of the application of reason and common sense to problems of every sort. . . . His two basic concerns, the advancement of learning and the practice of good government, were devoted to the same end, to benefit mankind. They do not show a dual purpose; the latter was simply an effort to apply, in the most difficult and important field of all, the conclusions which he drew from the former.

Thus Thomas Jefferson was well aware of planetary cycles, configurations, and influences. His writings make repeated references to a twenty-year cycle for "touching up" a revolution.

So it is no accident that July 4 was chosen as the birth date of our country. The date represents highly significant planetary configurations. From July 4 other significant dates in American tradition follow the astrological cycle of fours. Thus, national elections are held in November, the fourth month following July, and the original date for the inauguration of the President was March 4, the fourth month following November. Count four more months and you are back to the birthday of the United States.

It is curious that Jefferson's twenty-year cycle of change, if not revolution, has worked itself out since 1840, in that every President elected on the cycle has died in office.

The pattern began with William Henry Harrison, elected in 1840 and inaugurated March 4, 1841. He died of pneumonia a month later.

Abraham Lincoln, first elected in 1860, was assassinated the month following his second inauguration.

James A. Garfield, elected in 1880, was shot two days short of four months after his inauguration, and died September 19, 1881.

William McKinley, reelected in 1900, was shot September 6 of the following year and died September 14.

Warren G. Harding, elected in 1920, developed an illness in Seattle in the summer of 1923, while he was touring the West. Later, in San Francisco, doctors reported him suffering from pneumonia, though the earlier illness was the result of food poisoning. He died in San Francisco, August 2, 1923, of causes unknown, since no autopsy was performed. His death is usually attributed to coronary thrombosis.

Franklin D. Roosevelt, elected to his third term in 1940 and his fourth in 1944, died of a cerebral hemorrhage on April 12, 1945, at Warm Springs, Georgia.

John F. Kennedy, elected in 1960, was assassinated on November 22, 1963, in Dallas, Texas.

When I ran for President in 1968, I returned to the tradition of the four-month cycle. I ran as a "write-in" candidate, even though my name did appear on the ballot in some states. Though I lost in the number of total votes tabulated, I decided that I *was* the President of those voters who took the initiative in the 1968 election to write in my name. So on

March 4, 1969, my inauguration was held in Washington, D.C., as "Write-In President of the United States in Exile," complete with an inaugural address and two inaugural balls. So if the wishes of the Founding Fathers have any lasting influence in America, I am the true President inaugurated according to their design. Of course, the whole thrust of my Presidential candidacy was a return to the original ideal of democracy so clearly articulated in the Declaration of Independence and formalized in the Constitution of the United States. But knowing what I do about the twenty-year cycle, I will not be a candidate for President in 1980. That will be my year to run for Vice President!

Numerology seems also to have an influence on American political tradition. For example, the number of justices in the Supreme Court has become fixed in the American tradition as nine. Nine is indeed the appropriate number for a court designated as Supreme in the arbitration of government. Nine is the "supreme" number. It is the only number in calculation that, when multiplied by any other number, always reproduces itself. That is, 2 times 9 is 18, and 1 plus 8 again becomes the 9; or 3 times 9 is 27, and 2 plus 7 again becomes the 9; and so on with every number it is multiplied by.

The number nine has long been recognized for its mystical properties. On the ninth day the ancients buried their dead. On the ninth hour Jesus died on the cross. The Romans held a feast in memory of their dead every ninth year. In some Hebrew writings it is taught that God has nine times descended to this earth:

1st in the Garden of Eden,
2nd at the confusion of tongues at Babel,

3rd at the destruction of Sodom and Gomorrah,
4th to Moses at Horeb,
5th at Sinai when the Ten Commandments were given,
6th to Balaam,
7th to Elisha,
8th in the Tabernacle,
9th in the Temple at Jerusalem,
and it is taught that at the 10th coming this earth
will pass away and a new one will be created.

The Judiciary Act of 1789 originally fixed the number of Supreme Court justices at six. The original six members of the Supreme Court bench were reduced to five in 1801, returned to six in 1802, increased to seven in 1807, to nine in 1837, and to ten in 1863. In 1866 Congress reduced the number of justices to seven to prevent President Andrew Johnson from making any appointments. Since 1869, however, the number has become fixed at the supreme number, nine.

During the mid-1930s President Franklin Roosevelt devised a system to revise the Supreme Court membership. He had not had a chance to appoint a single justice during his first term in office. And the Supreme Court had held some of the items of New Deal legislation to be unconstitutional, such as the National Industrial Recovery Act and the Agricultural Adjustment Act. The Roosevelt plan would have increased the number of justices to a maximum of fifteen. Roosevelt's plan provoked a widespread furor of disapproval. Roosevelt was denounced as trying to pervert the Constitution and "pack" the Supreme Court. The Senate finally let the proposed bill die in committee. Thus the supreme number, nine, remained inviolate as it is today.

One cannot help wondering how much Franklin Roosevelt knew about astrology and numerology. He tried to throw off the supreme number, nine, and it didn't work. And he changed the inauguration date from March 4 to January 20. If that was an attempt to throw off the twenty-year cycle, again it didn't work, as both Roosevelt and Kennedy fell victims to it.

A comparison of the historical parallels between the lives of Presidents Abraham Lincoln and John F. Kennedy not only reveals some interesting items in numerology, but suggests that planetary configurations may have more of an influence in the doings of American politics and politicians than the voters.

Both Lincoln and Kennedy were in their thirties when they married. And they both married twenty-four-year-old brunettes who spoke French fluently. President Lincoln had a secretary in his employ named Kennedy. President Kennedy had a secretary named Lincoln.

A cousin of Abraham Lincoln became a United States Senator. Another Lincoln cousin was Mayor of Boston. And still another relative, one Levi Lincoln, a Harvard graduate, became the United States Attorney General. Robert Lincoln, the President's son, was Minister to London for four years.

John F. Kennedy's relatives held similar positions in government. Robert F. Kennedy, the President's brother and also a Harvard graduate, was the Attorney General of the United States and later became the junior Senator from New York. JFK's other brother, Edward Kennedy, is Senator from Massachusetts. President Kennedy's grandfather was

Mayor of Boston, and the father of the Kennedy brothers, Joseph P. Kennedy, was Ambassador to England.

Exactly a century divided the elections of Abraham Lincoln and John Kennedy to Congress. Lincoln was elected in 1847 and Kennedy in 1947. Both men competed for the Vice Presidential nomination—again a century apart. Lincoln competed in 1856 and Kennedy in 1956.

The Presidential campaigns of both Lincoln and Kennedy were marked by dramatic and decisive public debates, Lincoln debating Stephen A. Douglas and Kennedy debating Richard Nixon on television. Abraham Lincoln was elected to the Presidency in 1860 and John Kennedy was elected in 1960.

The tragic assassinations of Lincoln and Kennedy are strangely parallel. Both men were shot in the back of the head and in the presence of their wives. The wives of both men, incidentally, lost children while they were living in the White House. Both Lincoln and Kennedy died on a Friday.

There are also strange parallels in the lives of the alleged assassins of Lincoln and Kennedy. John Wilkes Booth, the alleged assassin of Abraham Lincoln, was born in 1839. Lee Harvey Oswald, the alleged assassin of John Kennedy, was born a century later in 1939. Both alleged assassins were themselves assassinated before they could be brought to trial.

Booth allegedly shot Lincoln in a theater and fled to a warehouse. Oswald allegedly shot Kennedy from a warehouse window and fled to a theater. The full names of both alleged assassins each have 15 letters.

Both Lincoln and Kennedy were succeeded in the Presidency by Southerners named Johnson. Both successors had served in the United States Senate. Andrew Johnson was born in 1808. Lyndon Johnson was born a century later in 1908. The names of the successors—Andrew Johnson and Lyndon Johnson—each have thirteen letters. Neither Andrew Johnson nor Lyndon Johnson succeeded himself for a second elected term.

When Andrew Johnson did not succeed himself in the election of 1868, the Republican candidate was a man named Ulysses Grant. When Lyndon Johnson chose not to succeed himself in the election of 1968, the Republican candidate turned out to be a man named Richard Nixon. Both names—Ulysses Grant and Richard Nixon—have the same number of letters.

In the election of 1868 Grant ran against a man named Horatio Seymour. In the election of 1968 Nixon ran against a man named Hubert Horatio Humphrey. Grant beat his Horatio in 1868 and Nixon did the same in 1968.

Thus there may be more to planetary politics than meets the eye. Today Presidents seem to be obsessed with reaching the moon and other planets. It might be to their advantage to understand the moon and other planets reaching us.

1

In December 1836, Martin Van Buren said, "The sun will shine on the Fourth of March." What did he mean?

2

What problems might there be in finding a Presidential candidate for the national election in 1980?

Lesson Seventeen
How to Evaluate
a Candidate

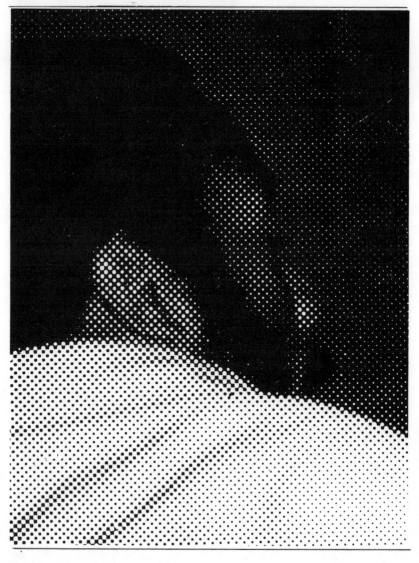

This final lesson raises the question of how to evaluate a candidate. There is one simple rule of thumb: Take all of the usual standards of evaluation and accepted qualifications and *reverse* them. Obviously the past standards of evaluating candidates have not worked. So it is high time for a totally opposite approach.

As we have seen in Lesson Thirteen, the military-combat record of a candidate has always been considered a campaign asset. Candidates proudly displayed their battle scars earned "in the service of their country." The time has now come for a new evaluation of battle scars. Candidates should be evaluated on the basis of their combat record in the struggle for human dignity. Whereas an arrest record was formerly seen as a political handicap, today's candidates should proudly display arrest records, convictions, and time served in jail as a result of civil disobedience and front-line demonstration on behalf of human rights.

Such candidates are the ones who are truly serving their country and their fellow human beings. Scars obtained on the battlefields of war are nothing more than wounds received protecting the system in America. Scars obtained in the front-line struggle for human dignity are wounds received proclaiming that *even* the American system shall not be allowed to oppress the downtrodden and deny men and women their essential humanity.

A complete reversal of the accepted concept of what constitutes a "criminal" provides another clue to evaluating a candidate. A person who has been arrested, convicted, and served time for participating in the struggle for human dignity is a *convict;* but he or she is not a *criminal.* Such persons are convicted because of their convictions. On the other hand, the majority of successful political candidates in the past are *criminals* who have never been *convicted*. They are the ones who are pulling shady deals, accepting payoffs, misappropriating funds, engaging in all kinds of high-level activities which mock the laws of the land. Back in 1967 when the late Senator Thomas Dodd of Connecticut was being investigated, the chairman of the Senate Finance Committee, Russell Long of Louisiana, said that half the members of the Senate Ethics Committee "couldn't stand the investigation Senator Dodd went through." He then expanded the statement to include "half the Senate." Though Senator Long later retracted his statement for obvious reasons, it is enough to call attention to where the yet-to-be-convicted criminals are to be found. And the hope of America, especially now that the voting age has been lowered to incorporate the voting ethics of today's youth, is that enough "convicts" will be elected to high public office so that the real criminals will then be convicted.

At least in modern times a candidate's educational background is given consideration as a qualification for holding public office. Most candidates for public office are high-school graduates. In the upper reaches of government, almost all members of Congress and Governors are college graduates, as would be the likely choice of the nominating convention of either of the two major political parties.

Thus candidates have a tendency to display their degrees. Reversing the accepted pattern, rather than looking to the degrees displayed by a candidate, look at the degree to which the candidate has been involved with the raw wounds of human suffering in America, the degree to which the candidate has been identified with the downtrodden and the heretofore unrepresented in our land. Candidates who display their degrees are merely indicating that they have been to school to try to learn how to make a living. Candidates who have a history of reaching out to the poor and oppressed have already demonstrated that they have learned how to live.

In the past, certain vocations have stood out as training grounds for public office. The legal profession heads the list. Almost 60 percent of American Presidents have been lawyers (22 out of 37), including the incumbent President. Sixty percent of the Congressmen currently in office are lawyers (67 percent of the Senate and 53 percent of the House). Lawyers know where to find campaign money, they are trained to think and talk on their feet, they are familiar with the social and political structures of the community, and they have learned to be actors and persuaders. Of course, in the latter respect they are no match for the actors who go into politics, like Governor Ronald Reagan and former Senator George Murphy of California.

Next in the vocational line for politicians are businessmen. They too are familiar with possible sources of campaign funding, and they have usually had some experience with selling the public. Further down the line come teachers, writers, publishers, and radio and television people.

Such favorite vocations of past politicians provide further clues for candidate evaluation. Rather than candidates who have represented their clients successfully, look for candidates who have truly defended the concept of justice for all men and women.

Rather than candidates who have been successful in business, look for those who have represented the consumer in America—those who, rather than trying to sell the public, have displayed a concern about what the public is sold. Rather than candidates whose businesses have added to the structures of corporate wealth, look for candidates who have helped to mobilize the business community to train the unemployed and unemployable; candidates who have been active in sensitizing the structures of the business community to the realities of human need.

Rather than candidates who have accommodated to the system's substitution of *indoctrination* for *education,* look for candidates who are teachers of a new way of life, a new way of looking at things, those who realize that true education is bringing out the essential wisdom and instincts which are acquired at birth.

Rather than candidates who have been vocationally engaged in writing or reporting, look for candidates who have put their bodies and their careers on the line to see that written laws are implemented; who, rather than reporting the great events of history, have been a part of history-in-the-making by tirelessly waging the battle for human dignity. There are those persons who "write" history by the lives they lead and the choices they make, and those who merely *record* that history after the drama has been played out. Look for candidates, then, who have proven themselves to be among the true "writers" of history.

At the present time, candidate evaluation is necessarily limited by the Constitution's age requirements for certain offices. Such age requirements handicap the effort to choose the best potential leadership and wisdom in the country. For example, those of us who advocate a woman in the White House are seriously handicapped by the age qualification. It is hard to find many women who will admit to being thirty-five years old!

So today, by Constitutional decree, we cannot have a President under the age of thirty-five, a Senator under the age of thirty, or a member of the House of Representatives under the age of twenty-five.

Since the 26th Amendment to the Constitution lowered the voting age from twenty-one to eighteen (in most states, though the eighteen-year-old vote has been allowed in the past in some places), thereby lopping off three years from *voter* qualification, the next logical step would be a 27th Amendment lopping off three years from *candidate* qualification. Such an amendment would help to initiate other reforms. Even if the seniority system was maintained in Congress, a Senator could have piled up thirteen years of seniority by the time he reached forty; and a Representative would have piled up eighteen years' seniority.

Let us end this lesson with an application of the new standards suggested for evaluating candidates. There are many persons in the country today who have demonstrated the political and organizational ability necessary to run the country in an intelligent and moral manner, as well as many others whose integrity and ethics stand out as obvious qualifications for offices of high public trust. Unfortunately, few such names will even be considered by the two major parties when the time comes to pick a Presidential candidate.

First of all, there are those who have held, or who are now holding, public office. Such persons would include Representatives William "Bill" Clay, Ronald Dellums, John Conyers, Shirley Chisholm, and Bella Abzug; state legislator Julian Bond; Mayors Carl Stokes, Richard Hatcher, Kenneth Gibson, and Charles Evers; and former Senator Wayne Morse.

Since the legal profession has been considered a training ground for the Presidency in the past, lawyers today who would be excellent Presidential timber include Alabama political reformer Orzell Billingsley; constitutional lawyer Leonard Boudin; civil-rights attorney William Kunstler; Jack Greenberg, who has long headed the NAACP legal-defense fund; crusading attorneys Mark Lane and F. Lee Bailey; and New Orleans District Attorney James Garrison. They have all defended the concept of justice for all men and women when civil liberties have been most threatened and denied.

Then there are those who have worked to infuse an appreciation for justice, decency, and equality of opportunity into the business community, as well as working to give the consumer a fair deal. Such names would include publishers Robert E. Johnson and Dr. Carlton Goodlet; the Reverend Dr. Leon Sullivan of Opportunities Industrialization Centers, Inc.; consumer advocate Ralph Nader; and Earle B. Dickerson, president of Supreme Life Insurance Company of America.

Others who have demonstrated their organizational ability and their devotion to the downtrodden include Alabama's National Democratic Party Chairman Dr. John L. Cashin; Chicago's William Berry; John Lewis, former head of the Studen Nonviolent Coordinating Committee; Dr. George Wiley of the National Welfare Rights Organization; Cairo's (Illinois) courageous Reverend Charles Koen; Operation Breadbasket's Reverend Jesse Jackson; and former directors

314

of the Congress of Racial Equality James Farmer and Floyd McKissick.

Writers and teachers who have shown themselves to be instructors in a new way of human living include Bob Johnson of *Jet* magazine; Lerone Bennet of *Ebony* magazine; Dr. Charles Hurst of Malcolm X University; Dr. Archie Hargraves of Shaw University; Dr. Benjamin Mays of Morehouse College; Dr. Kingman Brewster of Yale University; Alan Watts; and Studs Terkel.

Finally, there are those who have demonstrated the right kind of battle scars and who have adopted the high ideals of statesmanship as a way of life. Such a list would include Ossie Davis, Betty Shabazz, Fannie Lou Hamer, Coretta King, Huey P. Newton, the Reverend C. T. Vivian, the Reverend Chris Smith, A. Phillip Randolph, the Reverend Fred Shuttlesworth, Cesar Chavez, Jane Fonda, Dr. Ralph Abernathy, Roy Wilkins, Fathers James Groppi and Dan Berrigan, Justice Thurgood Marshall, and so many, many others.

The above list of persons most worthy of public office is in no way exhaustive, merely illustrative. And I am sure that illustrative list contains names unfamiliar to many students. If so, it is one more comment about the United States and its values. I seriously doubt that any student is unfamiliar with the names Al Capone, Jesse James, Bonnie and Clyde, and John Dillinger. There is something terribly wrong with a country when the most notorious criminals are household words, but the greatest living statesmen and -women are unknown.

1

Ralph Nader is:
   a. a citrus farmer who raises lemons;
   b. a film and television actor;
   c. chairman of the board of General Motors;
   d. none of the above.

2

Julian Bond is:
   a. a Georgia state legislator;
   b. too young to run for President by current Constitutional qualifications;
   c. a black man who would be an excellent Presidential candidate;
   d. all of the above;
   e. none of the above.

3

Is it possible for a person who has never served in the armed forces to have received combat scars?

Dick Gregory's
Do-It-Yourself Acceptance Speech

We stand tonight at the threshold of opportunity, ready as a party and as loyal Americans to carry the bride of promise over the threshold. As [*substitute* Democrats *or* Republicans] we realize that the vital issues confronting our country and our conscience are much greater than party labels and more important than partisan concerns. We have seen the terrible price that must be paid for giving partisanship a higher priority than patriotism under the leadership of the [*substitute* Democratic *or* Republican] Party.

But we also know that deep within the soul of every true American resides an instinct for freedom, for justice, for equality of opportunity, and for the inherent right of free men to determine their own destinies. From this moment on, let the word go forth and let us make it perfectly clear that it will be the untiring endeavor of the [*substitute* Democratic *or* Republican] Party to tap that reservoir of American conscience, so that our nation—indeed, the entire world and now even outer space—will be flooded with a tidal wave of honesty, justice, and freedom.

The task which faces us tonight is no easy endeavor. It requires nothing less than the total dedication and undivided determination of every man, woman, and child who loves liberty, who pursues justice, and who, as we know, is registered in the [*substitute* Democratic *or* Republican] Party.

You have bestowed upon me the great honor of leading this [*substitute* Democratic *or* Republican] crusade for freedom. It is an awesome responsibility, but one which no true American could refuse to willingly, and humbly, receive both as a duty and a challenge. I therefore accept your nomination.

Dick Gregory's
Literacy Test for Candidates

(If no candidates have sought your
opinion, you may wish to send this
to them. Please report any results
to your local paper.)

1

Clearly state five principles or solutions to basic problems which dif-
ferentiate you from the other candidates seeking the same office.

2

How many black friends do you have?
How many Puerto Rican or Mexican American?
How many Indian?
How many Chinese?
How many whose family income is below $4,000 a year?
Come to think of it, how many friends do you have?

3

On your campaign staff and in your office, how many black advisers
do you have?
How many Puerto Rican or Mexican American?
How many Indian?
How many Chinese?
How many formerly in the poverty ranks (assuming you are not
now paying poverty wages)?
How many women?
How many persons between the ages of 18 and 25?

4

What political promises have you made to obtain campaign funding?

5

Define statesman.

6

Define politician.

7

In 25 words or less, indicate the differences, if any, between the two.
To which category do you belong?

8

Do you believe the two-party system is a necessary component of
the American political process? If the answer is no, outline how you
would revise the current structure of two-party dominance.

9

List the newspapers and periodicals you read most frequently, and the titles of books, if any, you have read which have had the most influence on your social and political thought. (To be answered only by those candidates who have used their formal education as an indication of their qualification for office.)

Glossary

---

appointment
When an elected public official places someone in a government job. In the case of President Nixon filling vacancies in the Supreme Court, it is the fulfillment of the old adage, "If at first you don't succeed, try, try again."

ballot
From the Italian word *ballotta* or *balla* meaning "ball." A ballot is what the voter uses to register his vote, which in places like Chicago means "having a ball."

black
A Supreme Court Justice, Hugo Lafayette Black. Not to be confused with Justice Thurgood Marshall, who happens to be black.

bureau
Two meanings: (1) a chest of drawers; (2) a government office or subdivision. It has come to mean a government office where matters vital to the health and welfare of Americans end up in closed drawers —e.g., the Bureau of Indian Affairs.

campaign
From the Medieval Latin *campania* meaning "level country." It has come to mean the actions political candidates take before elections to level the country.

candidate
From the Latin word *candidatus* meaning "clothed in white" and *candidus* meaning "white." Also from the English words *candid* meaning "frank" and *ate,* the past tense of *eat,* which means "to devour or consume." All meanings merge in contemporary usage so that a candidate, frankly, is someone white who runs for office in a system which devours and consumes the people and Earth's resources.

caucus
From the Greek word *kaukos* meaning "a drinking vessel." Also from *Caucasian* meaning "white folks." So a caucus is a group of white folks getting together with drinking vessels to decide on policies or candidates. Black Caucus, on the other hand, is a group of black elected officials getting together to decide what can be done about the actions of those white folks.

CIA
Central Intelligence Agency. A job-training program for spies and assassins. A rather complete listing of CIA personnel can be found in *Who's Who in the CIA* (Berlin: Julius Mader, 1968), available from Progress Books, 487 Adelaide Street West, Toronto 2B, Ontario, Canada.

citizen
The original meaning was "a free man," but has changed to "one who owes allegiance to a government." Many citizens prefer the original meaning.

civil rights
What black folks are given in the U.S. on the installment plan, as in civil-rights bills. Not to be confused with *human rights,* which are the dignity, stature, humanity, respect, and freedom belonging to all people by right of their birth.

community
A body of people having a common interest and a common bond living in the same place.

community control
A group of people with common bonds and interests seeking to guide and direct the forces which most vitally affect their lives and destinies; usually interpreted as a "Communist-inspired" strategy by which black people and other poor people are trying to overthrow the government.

constitution
The various media or instrumentalities through which the basic features of a governmental system are established. In the United States, the Constitution is a health chart left by the Founding Fathers which shows whether or not the body politic is in good health. If the national body is found to be in poor health, the Founding Fathers also left a prescription for the restoration of health called the Declaration of Independence.

control
To exercise directing, guiding, or restraining power over.

convention
A gathering of delegates from a political party for the purpose of selecting candidates and/or drafting a platform, usually held in Chicago, Illinois. Conventions are good for hotel and restaurant business. On the other hand, peace *demonstrators* are not considered good for business, so they are discouraged from attending conventions by peace *officers* using clubs, tear gas, and mace.

court
Two meanings: (1) a space, primarily quadrangular, used for playing various games; (2) a place where justice is administered. A court, then, is a place where games are played in the administration of justice.

crime
An act forbidden by law; also a gross violation of human law. There are two kinds of crimes: those committed by people who are caught and convicted, and those committed by people who are not. Which category a particular crime falls into is directly related to the wealth, power, and prestige of the criminal. The former category includes such crimes as purse snatching, mugging, armed robbery, and breaking and entering. The latter category includes war atrocities, embezzlement, most political actions, and budget appropriations.

crime in the streets
America's new way of saying "nigger."

democracy
From the Greek words *demos* meaning "the people" and *kratein* meaning "to rule." The original meaning is a government in which the people rule. In the United States it has come to mean a government in which the use of the slogan "Power to the People" constitutes grounds for governmental harassment, arrest, surveillance, and in some cases even murder.

Democratic
One of the two major political parties in the United States, which support the above new definition of democracy (see above).

elect
To choose between candidates offered on the ballot. Should not be confused with *select,* which means to have a choice in deter-

mining which candidates will be on the ballot. American voters are urged to exercise their right to elect, but are rarely given the opportunity to select.

FBI
Federal Bureau of Investigation; seen on national television on Sunday evenings on ABC. The Bureau was originally formed to provide a lifetime job for Director J. Edgar Hoover.

law
Rules of conduct enforced by a controlling authority.

order
Public quiet or conformity to law or decorum.

law and order
The controlling authority's means of keeping the public quiet. The procedure usually involves the use of federal troops, National Guard, or local police. Not to be confused with *justice*.

legislate
To make the laws used by the controlling authority to keep the public quiet.

legislator
One who makes the laws used by the controlling authority to keep the public quiet.

lobby
A group which tries to influence those who make the laws used by the controlling authority to keep the public quiet. Also a waiting room in government buildings where persons who are seeking laws for the benefit of all people are kept for long periods of time.

majority
More than half.

majority, silent
A term created by the Nixon administration to mean everyone except minorities and their supporters (who actually probably add up to a majority).

minority
Less than half.

minorities
The top half of the unemployment statistics and the bottom half of tables of income.

nepotism
The result of political candidates believing their own campaign rhetoric that American voters are "one big happy family."

party
Two meanings: (1) a social gathering; (2) in U.S. politics, an organized group of the electorate that attempts to control government by electing its candidates to office. In both kinds of parties, alcohol is a crucial ingredient in keeping the party moving along. In political parties, those who have drunk too much alcohol often make important decisions while under the influence, like selecting candidates, writing platforms, and so on.

patronage
The political recognition on the part of successful candidates that one good turn deserves many others.

peace
An idea which seems to have originated in Switzerland but has never caught hold in the United States. Supporters of this idea are frequently accused of being unpatriotic and trying to create civil disorder.

platform
Erected by a political party to provide the foundation for winning an election. Much like the scaffolding used to paint, clean, or erect a building, or to hang someone, platforms are immediately dismantled when the job is completed.

politician
A person skilled in the art of compromise. Usually an elected official who has compromised to get nominated, compromised to get elected, and compromised repeatedly to stay in office. When election time rolls around again, the process is recycled. In times of crisis a politician flexes his muscle to solve problems.

politics
The art of compromise.

power
Exerted energy and capacity for action. When followed by the word *structure,* it refers to a group which includes America's most wealthy and influential citizens. When prefixed by the word *black,* it creates terror in the minds of the power structure.

primary
An election to determine who will be a party candidate. In Presidential campaigns, primary elections are held in various states to determine which candidates the voters of the nation would like to see representing their particular party. Primaries are held before delegates go to party conventions and choose different candidates.

promise
Political promises are much like marriage vows. They are made at the beginning of the relationship between candidate and voter, but are quickly forgotten. When voters catch a candidate breaking political promises, they try to overlook it.

Republican
See definition of *Democratic.*

statesman
One who cannot compromise with what he knows to be right or make political deals which will allow a form of evil or injustice to be even temporarily victorious. Usually not an elected public official. In times of crisis, the statesman flexes his mind and not his muscle.

statesmanship
The art of uncompromising devotion to humanity, the alleviation of suffering, and the creation of a decent and peaceful environment throughout the world.

vote
A word familiar to party workers, frequently used to complete the phrase *get out the* . . .

war
A problem-solving technique which is extremely popular in the United States but has never caught hold in Switzerland. It is highly unsuccessful in providing permanent solutions to problems and tends to be reapplied by nations who use it over and over again. It is very expensive and time-consuming. In the past 150 years 144 nations

have spent 4,500 "nation months" in battle, and at least 30 million lives have been lost on battlefields. That, of course, does not include civilian lives.

white

Another Supreme Court Justice, Byron Raymond White. Also the racial designation of all Supreme Court Justices except Mr. Justice Marshall.

A Gregorian Poll

Over the years, I've always followed the results of the Harris Poll and the Gallup Poll very closely. But I've alway been bothered by the fact that I've never seen a Harris or a Gallup pollster! Now, if that is true of me, it must also be true of many readers. So if the pollsters have never come to you, here's your chance to go to them. Fill in the opinion poll below and mail it to either the Harris or the Gallup office. The addresses are:

The Gallup Organization, Inc.   The Harris Poll Office
      53 Bank   1 Rockefeller Plaza
   Princeton, New Jersey   New York, New York 10020

1

Do you feel Presidential and Vice Presidential candidates should be chosen by the direct primary method; that is, the voters themselves recording their preference, thereby abolishing the present convention system?
☐ Yes ☐ No ☐ No Opinion

2

Do you feel that the electoral-college system for electing a President and Vice President should be abolished and that the total popular vote in the nation should be decisive?
☐ Yes ☐ No ☐ No Opinion

3

How do you feel about the money spent on election campaigning?
☐ Much Too High ☐ Too High ☐ A Little Too High
☐ About Right ☐ Too Low

4

Do you think strong new legislation is needed to regulate campaign spending?
☐ Yes ☐ No ☐ No Opinion

5

Do you feel the present two-party system in the United States gives adequate expression to political differences of opinion?
☐ Yes ☐ No ☐ No Opinion

6

Do you feel that today's Congressional procedures truly reflect the original intention of the United States Constitution?

☐ Yes ☐ No ☐ No Opinion

7

Do you feel the seniority system for choosing Congressional committee chairmanships should be abolished?

☐ Yes ☐ No ☐ No Opinion

8

Do you feel the Constitution should be amended to lower the age qualification for President, Vice President, Senators, and Representatives?

☐ Yes ☐ No ☐ No Opinion

9

Rate in importance the issues facing the nation.

	Very Important	Important	Not So Important
a. The war in Vietnam			
b. Unemployment			
c. The economic condition of the country			
d. The "generation gap"			
e. "Crime in the streets"			
f. "Crime on Capitol Hill"			
g. Pollution and other ecological abuses			
h. Inability of different groups of Americans to communicate with each other			
i. Governmental surveillance on private citizens			
j. Other issues of your own choosing and their rating (list below)			

10

In the following list of names, check those names you think would make good Presidential timber. Add your names in the space provided at the end of the list:

☐ Dr. Ralph Abernathy
☐ Rep. Bella Abzug
☐ Lerone Bennett
☐ Fr. Daniel Berrigan
☐ William Berry
☐ Orzell Billingsley
☐ Julian Bond
☐ Leonard Boudin
☐ Dr. Kingman Brewster
☐ Dr. John L. Cashin
☐ Cesar Chavez
☐ Rep. Shirley Chisholm
☐ Rep. William Clay
☐ Rep. John Conyers
☐ Ossie Davis
☐ Rep. Ronald Dellums
☐ Earle B. Dickerson
☐ Charles Evers
☐ James Farmer
☐ Jane Fonda
☐ Kenneth Gibson
☐ Dr. Carlton Goodlet
☐ Jack Greenberg
☐ Fr. James Groppi
☐ Fannie Lou Hamer
☐ Dr. Archie Hargraves
☐ Richard Hatcher
☐ Dr. Charles Hurst
☐ Rev. Jesse Jackson

☐ Bob Johnson
☐ Robert E. Johnson
☐ Coretta King
☐ Rev. Charles Koen
☐ William Kunstler
☐ John Lewis
☐ Justice Thurgood Marshall
☐ Dr. Benjamin Mays
☐ Floyd McKissick
☐ Wayne Morse
☐ Ralph Nader
☐ Huey P. Newton
☐ A. Phillip Randolph
☐ Betty Shabazz
☐ Rev. Fred Shuttlesworth
☐ Rev. Chris Smith
☐ Carl Stokes
☐ Dr. Leon Sullivan
☐ Studs Terkel
☐ Rev. C. T. Vivian
☐ Alan Watts
☐ Dr. George Wiley
☐ Roy Wilkins
(list other names)

_____
_____
_____
_____
_____

Tear out and mail to the pollster of your choice.

Notes on Sources

To the Student: Bicentennial Breakthrough

Two books were particularly helpful in providing quotations of the Founding Fathers and others, as well as an understanding of the events of the 1700s. They are *The Idea of a Party System* by Richard Hofstadter (Berkeley, Los Angeles and London: University of California Press, 1970), and *The Growth of the American Republic,* Volume One, by Samuel Eliot Morison and Henry Steele Commager (New York: Oxford University Press, 1962).

The excerpt from Washington's Farewell Address was taken from *An American Primer,* edited by Daniel J. Boorstin (New York: The New American Library, Inc., 1968).

The wisdom of former Senator Wayne Morse appeared in an interview in the *Washington Daily News,* June 21, 1971.

Lesson One: That Long, Hot Summer—1787

Several books were helpful in providing background information for this lesson: *The Landmark History of the American People: From Plymouth to Appomattox* by Daniel J. Boorstin (New York: Random House, 1968); *Politics in America* by D. W. Brogan (New York and Evanston: Harper Torchbooks, 1969); *Essentials of American Government* by Ernst B. Schulz (Woodbury, N.Y.: Barron's Educational Series, 1969); *The United States Political System and How It Works* by David Cushman Coyle (New York: The New American Library, 1967); *The American Presidency* by Clinton Rossiter (New York: Harcourt, Brace & World, 1960).

D. W. Brogan's description of the interests represented at the Constitutional Convention is found on page 22 of his work cited above; the world governmental situation when the Constitution went into effect is found on page 1; James Wilson's assessment of the Constitution is found on pages 23–4; James Madison's quote from *The Federalist* is found on page 24; and Lord Acton's description of the Revolutionaries is found on pages 8–9.

Lesson Two: Parties Prevail

Norman Small's description of Alexander Hamilton's style of operation is found on page 37 of *The Origins of the American Party System* by Joseph Charles (New York: Harper Torchbooks, 1961). Sedgwick's and Madison's observations concerning George Washington's solemnity are found on pages 38 and 39 of the same work.

President Washington's embarrassing spectacles and Teddy Roosevelt's eating spectacle are found on pages 89 and 97 of *The American Presidency* by Clinton Rossiter (New York: Mentor Books, 1962).

Quotations from the *Pennsylvania Gazette* are found on page 18 of Joseph Charles, *op. cit.* Charles' evaluation of Alexander Hamilton is found on pages 30–1.

Richard Hofstadter's description of Jefferson's view of the Federalists is found on page 127 of *The Idea of a Party System, op. cit.*

General Stephen Van Rensselaer's dilemma is described by Joseph A. Loftus in his chapter on "Third Parties" in *The New York Times Election Handbook 1968* (New York: Signet Books, 1968).

The quotations of Thomas Hart Benton and Henry Cabot Lodge are taken from Senator Birch Bayh's speech on the Senate floor, *Congressional Record*, Vol. 117, No. 6 (January 28, 1971).

The description of the patron St. Tammany is found in a note on page 124 of D. W. Brogan's *Politics in America, op. cit.*

William L. Riordon's quotation of George Washington Plunkitt is found on pages 697–8 of *An American Primer*, edited by Daniel J. Boorstin, *op. cit.*

The two quotations from Mike Royko's *Boss: Richard J. Daley of Chicago* (New York: E. P. Dutton & Co., 1971) are found on pages 63 and 67.

The election-day description by Lloyd Wendt and Herman Kogan is found on pages 63–4 of *U.S. Politics Inside and Out,* a *U.S. News & World Report* book (New York: Collier Books, 1970). The Tully campaign and the Pendergast exposure are described in the same source.

Lesson Three: The Primary Objective

In preparing this lesson, the 1970 *U.S. News & World Report* book *U. S. Politics Inside and Out, op. cit.,* was invaluable. Also helpful was Daniel J. Boorstin's *The Landmark History of the American People, op. cit.*

Lesson Four: Politics on Parade
Four books were most helpful in the preparation of this lesson: *The New York Times Election Handbook 1968; Politics in America* by D. W. Brogan; *U.S. Politics Inside and Out;* and *The Landmark History of the American People* by Daniel J. Boorstin, all of them cited previously.

Mike Royko's description of Mayor Daley's gleeful gallery is found on pages 188–189 of *Boss, op. cit.*

Lesson Six: Promises, Promises
The combat records of Presidential and other candidates come from *The New York Times Encyclopedic Almanac 1971* and *U.S. Politics Inside and Out, op. cit.*

The whole section on patronage relied heavily on Martin and Susan Tolchin's *To the Victor . . .: Political Patronage from the Clubhouse to the White House* (New York: Random House, 1971). The quotation concerning the contemporary hazards of patronage is found on pages 10–12.

Mike Royko's description of Chicago machine politics is found on pages 63–64 of *Boss: Richard J. Daley of Chicago, op. cit.*

Lesson Seven: The High Cost of Conviction
Two books were particularly helpful in the preparation of this lesson: *U.S. Politics Inside and Out, op. cit.,* and *America, Inc.* by Morton Mintz and Jerry S. Cohen (New York: The Dial Press, 1971). The findings of the team of *Washington Post* reporters are found in the chapter "The Politician as Investment," and the 1956 Congressional study of campaign contributions is found on page 171.

Lesson Eight: Power to What People?
The quotation from *America, Inc., op. cit.,* is found on page 151. The excerpts from Senator Long's Senate speech are found on pages 158–9. The entire speech is found in the *Congressional Record,* April 4, 1967, pp. S4582–83.

The quotation from Robert Semple's article "Who Runs the Government?" is found on page 148 of *Playboy,* September 1971.

Douglass Cater's *Power in Washington* (New York: Vintage

Books, 1964) was helpful in understanding lobbying, especially the chapter entitled "The Subtle Art of Pressure."

Lesson Nine: Missing the Party

For information concerning Huey Long, I am indebted to T. Harry Williams' article "The Gentleman from Louisiana: Demagogue or Democrat?" in *Journal of Southern History,* Vol. 26, No. 1 (February 1960).

For information concerning the National Democratic Party of Alabama, I am indebted to the February 1971 issue of *Imani* (formerly *The Faith*), published by the Communications Workshop of the Black Allied Student Association at New York University, 566 LaGuardia Place, New York, New York 10012, Box 27.

Lesson Ten: The Constitution's Institutions

A number of books were helpful in the preparation of this lesson: *Essentials of American Government* by Ernst B. Schulz (Woodbury, N.Y.: Barron's Educational Series, 1969); *Politics in America* by D. W. Brogan, *op. cit.; U.S. Politics Inside and Out, op. cit.; The American Presidency* by Clinton Rossiter, *op. cit.;* and *The New York Times Election Handbook 1968, op. cit.,* especially Tom Wicker's chapter on "The President" and Alvin Shuster's chapter on "The Vice President."

The quotation by Clem Miller is found on page 128 of Douglass Cater's *Power in Washington, op. cit.*

The description of the White House guards' new costumes is from *The New York Times Encyclopedic Almanac 1971,* pages 48–9.

Thanks also to *Jet* magazine for its coverage of the Agnew trip to Africa! Anyone interested in seeing a picture of "Blood Brother" Agnew should consult the August 5, 1971, issue.

Lesson Eleven: Now That Voting Has Caught Up with the Draft

Once again the *U.S. News & World Report* book *U.S. Politics Inside and Out, op. cit.,* was helpful in the preparation of this lesson.

The information concerning the black vote and Franklin Roosevelt is found in William E. Leuchtenburg's *Franklin D. Roosevelt and the New Deal* (New York: Harper Torchbooks, 1963).

Lesson Thirteen: Studying War No More

The University of Michigan study of international wars was reported in the *New York Times,* May 6, 1971.

The description of the Pentagon is taken from *The 1970 World Almanac,* published for the *New York Daily News* (New York: Newspaper Enterprise Association, 1970), on page 637.

The quotation by Samuel F. Yette is found on page 130 of *The Choice: The Issue of Black Survival in America* (New York: G. P. Putnam's Sons, 1971).

Lesson Fourteen: A Turnip in Every Plot

Quotes by William Longgood are taken from his book *The Poisons in Your Food* (New York: Pyramid Books, 1969), pages 11, 208, and 217. Dr. Peacock's quote is found on page 108 of Longgood's book; quotes by Dr. Albrecht on pages 183–4; and the quote by Hippocrates is found on page 170.

The findings of Nader's Raiders are from Betty James' article in the *Washington (D.C.) Sunday Star,* July 18, 1971, reporting the release of the 400-page Nader study *Sowing the Wind: Pesticides, Meat and the Public Interest.*

The quote by Ira I. Somers is taken from an article entitled "Health Food Hassle," by Jeanne Lesem in the *Washington Post,* July 18, 1971.

For a more thorough description of Arizona's Magic Garden, see the August 1970 issue of *Arizona Highways,* pages 2–9, published by the Arizona Highway Department, 2039 West Lewis Avenue, Phoenix, Arizona 85009.

Lesson Fifteen: Citizen Surveillance

The story of the burning of the Reichstag is found in William L. Shirer's *The Rise and Fall of the Third Reich* (New York: Fawcett World Library, 1970), pages 267–72.

Richard T. Cooper's report of the shooting of Larry Ward was printed as a special from the *Los Angeles Times* in the *Chicago Sun-Times,* Sunday, May 30, 1971.

The phrase "planned, organized, maniacal madness" is borrowed from Patrick V. Murphy, Police Commissioner in New York City, the wording he used to describe the unprovoked killing of two Harlem policemen.

The House Un-American Activities recommendation concerning guerrilla warfare is found on pages 32–4 of Samuel F. Yette's *The Choice: The Issue of Black Survival in America, op. cit.*

Lesson Sixteen: Planetary Politics
Joseph Charles' quotation concerning Jefferson's interest in science is found in his book of essays, *The Origins of the American Party System, op. cit.*, pages 76–7.

For a more complete account of the relationship between Jefferson and Banneker, see my own *No More Lies: The Myth and the Reality of American History* (New York: Harper & Row, 1971).

About the Author

Dick Gregory is a humorist, historian, sociologist, and political analyst. As cochairman of the New Party, he was a write-in candidate for the Presidency in 1968. Politically active in the civil-rights movement and protests against the war in Vietnam, he has been arrested more than three dozen times. He has lectured extensively at three hundred colleges across the country. His most recent book is *No More Lies: The Myth and the Reality of American History.*